RED BLOOD, YELLOW SKIN: ENDLESS JOURNEY

LINDA L.T. BAER

Formerly Nguyen Thi Loan

RIVER GROVE
BOOKS

The names and identifying characteristics of persons referenced in this book have been changed to protect their privacy.

Published by River Grove Books
Austin, TX
www.rivergrovebooks.com

Copyright ©2017 Linda L.T. Baer

All rights reserved.

Thank you for purchasing an authorized edition of this book and for complying with copyright law. No part of this book may be reproduced, stored in a retrieval system, or transmitted by any means, electronic, mechanical, photocopying, recording, or otherwise, without written permission from the copyright holder.

Distributed by River Grove Books

Design and composition by Greenleaf Book Group
Cover design by Greenleaf Book Group

Cataloging-in-Publication data is available.

Print ISBN: 978-1-63299-147-8

eBook ISBN: 978-1-63299-148-5

First Edition

CONTENTS

	AUTHOR'S NOTE	v
	ACKNOWLEDGMENTS	vii
	INTRODUCTION	1
Chapter 1	WHITE HONEYMOON	3
Chapter 2	SAIGON TEARS	30
Chapter 3	DREAMLAND	39
Chapter 4	HEAVY LOAD	65
Chapter 5	LIFE ON EDGE	90
Chapter 6	HIGH EXPECTATIONS	121
Chapter 7	MIDDLE EAST TRAUMA	126
Chapter 8	CYPRESS KNEES	153
Chapter 9	WESTBOUND	167
Chapter 10	TWO-FACED COIN	174
Chapter 11	SOUTHERN CHARM	190
Chapter 12	CLOUDY SUMMER	206
Chapter 13	BOAT PEOPLE	223
Chapter 14	LONELY FROG	234
Chapter 15	LIFE HAPPENS	244
Chapter 16	LEGAL DILEMMA	258
Chapter 17	HURRICANE HUGO	267
Chapter 18	WELCOME HOME, DAUGHTER	285
Chapter 19	SALON HUMOR	305
Chapter 20	MOTHER'S DEPTH	314
Chapter 21	MY LIFE'S JOURNEY	321
	EPILOGUE	342
	ABOUT THE AUTHOR	350

AUTHOR'S NOTE

I wish to apologize in advance to those readers who might be offended by some of my remarks in this book.

It is not my intent to mock, judge, or insult anyone. I simply want to relate some of my own experiences, for their inherent humor and enlightenment, especially as they pertain to the differences in customs, cultures, and languages, that I have encountered during my worldwide travels.

It is my cherished wish that the world will accept the variances of differences in race, gender, religions, and status and then live in harmony and peace.

Thanks for reading this.

Sincerely,
Linda Baer

ACKNOWLEDGMENTS

THANKS TO DON Baer, my husband of fifty years, for loving and understanding me, for being patient through the peaceful and turbulent times, and for being my mentor. Thank you for helping me with my English. Besides helping me with my writing, you spent time to research the history for my book and then made all of the preparations for publication. I also thank you for allowing me to share your most painful experiences, as they related to your alcohol and drug addictions, which almost cost us our marriage. But without you, my life and my book would not exist. Honey, I owe you my all.

Thanks to all who supported me and helped spread the word to promote my last book, *Red Blood, Yellow Skin*, and thanks to Carol Furtwrangler for proofreading this book in its early stages.

INTRODUCTION

THE DAY BEFORE our wedding, I paid two strangers to be my uncles and verify my identity in court, but I had to pay under the table to have my marriage papers signed. That was my daily life in Vietnam. I learned to deal with corruption, bribes, and the black market, starting with the highest government officials and filtering all the way down to the beggars on the streets. It seemed like everyone wanted a life of luxuries, but they came with a high price. I am not proud to say that I was involved.

The war tore my country apart, and it ripped the fabric of our society. It took away our spirit, our dignity, and our self-respect. And that resulted in chaos, trauma, and tragedy. But through it all, I found humor and something worth living for.

The first part of my journey started when I was four and is related in my last book, *Red Blood, Yellow Skin: A Young Girl's Survival in War-Torn Vietnam*. It tells of the horrors, the pain, and the absurdity, along with the romance and humor, of growing up during wartime in North and South Vietnam.

The Endless Journey continues where *Red Blood, Yellow Skin* left off. In it, I relate my family's close scrape with death when we missed boarding the C-5 Air Force plane, which crashed soon after takeoff, killing 155 passengers, who, like us, were trying to evacuate Vietnam in April 1975.

Our travels took us from country to country, including three years in Iran, where I found their religion, customs, language, and food to be fascinating. That is where I learned to speak Farsi and cook Iranian food.

At the end of 1978, we left Iran abruptly, during violent antigovernment demonstrations, and just weeks before the revolution took place, which overthrew the Shah and established the new leader, the Ayatollah Khomeini.

The new regime later captured fifty-two Americans and held them hostage for 444 days; we were lucky to be out of there.

Our love of warm weather took us to the gulf coast of Florida, where we bought a large waterfront property on Lake Panasoffkee. We planned to develop a fancy campground with a private recreation park. But it was a big mistake; it cost us all of our savings, and we were forced to abandon our dream.

In frustration, Don and I bought a twenty-five-foot camper, loaded up our three children, who were five, six, and twelve, and traveled west. We ended up in California, where Don worked with the Veterans Administration. While the kids were at school, I went to Chaffey High School, earned my GED, and later attended college.

In 1980, our family moved to Charleston, South Carolina, where I went to cosmetology school. Two years after I received my license, I opened and operated Linda B. Hair, Nail, and Skin Care, where sophisticated and high-class clients gathered, shared their family secrets, and created endless hours of drama, chaos, and hilarity. I hope you will like this story as much as I loved sharing it.

Chapter 1

WHITE HONEYMOON

IN THE MIDDLE of a quiet night, loud and terrified screams startled me from a sound sleep. "Help! Help! Somebody, please help me!" a male voice yelled. I jumped out of bed, turned on the light, and ran out to see what was going on. What I saw was the police chief, wearing only underwear, pointing his gun at Don, my fiancé, who stood at the entrance of the outside kitchen, wearing only boxer shorts, with a giant crab hanging from his right big toe.

Confused and afraid, I glanced at the six or seven people, including my mother, who were already at the scene. I looked down at Don's foot and realized he had stepped on one of the huge black mud crabs I had stored in a bucket; it must have crawled out. I ran to help him and motioned for everybody to calm down.

It seemed everyone was on edge, especially the police chief. Perhaps the intense war outside had something to do with it. They moved out of my way, making a larger circle, and talked among themselves. The police chief put his gun away and ran to help me loosen the crab's claw from Don's toe.

I took the giant crab back to the holding bucket and noticed most of the crabs stored there had disappeared. As I looked around, I saw them crawling in all directions, so I warned everyone to be careful not to get pinched. Don limped to the bathroom to clean off the blood and bind his wound.

"Please, everyone," I exclaimed, "help me gather all these crabs and put them back in the bucket." As we gathered the crabs, I explained to my mother and the friends who were staying in my house to help me prepare for my wedding the next day. "I planned to make crab eggrolls for the party tomorrow. But after I untied them, I was too tired, so I put them in a bucket and covered them up with a lid; they must have helped each other push off the lid and crawl out."

Mother joked, "One of them decided to have a piece of Don's meat before he got theirs." We all roared with laughter. Don finished in the bathroom and helped me secure the bucket lid with a heavy piece of cement, and then we all went back to bed.

ON FRIDAY, SEPTEMBER 5, 1969, Don and I went to the civil court in Saigon to get our marriage certificate signed. We stood in front of a man who might have been a magistrate, a judge, or just some person of authority; I wasn't sure. We just wanted to be sworn in and have our marriage papers signed, but before he signed them, he asked for two witnesses who knew us well.

"I'm sorry, I didn't know we had to have witnesses," I said. "I'll go home and come back with two of my family members." He nodded his head to excuse us. Just as we were about to leave, he said, "And don't forget to bring a gift with you." At first, his demand confused me, but I soon realized what he meant. He wanted me to bring him money for signing the paper, which was normal for someone in his position. The high authorities were the ones who could give or take away our right to marry, our livelihood, or even our lives.

I knew the drill and came prepared with a roll of money in my purse—we called it *coffee money*.

"Don't worry," I said with a smile and pointed to my purse to assure him I had the money.

We went outside, and I told Don what the man wanted and what my plan was. Don seemed concerned, but I just smiled at him.

"Don't worry; I'll take care of it," I said. "Since I don't have any family here, I'll get somebody else to stand in for us." Don looked at me in confusion.

"How can you do that?" he asked.

"I'll show you," I said with a mischievous wink.

We walked out to the street, and I waved down a couple of pedicab drivers. "Where do you want to go?" one of them asked. I motioned for them to get off their cabs and come closer.

"I don't want to go anywhere," I whispered when they came within earshot.

"Then why did you stop us?" the first man queried.

"Do you want to be paid to act as our witnesses?" I asked.

"What do we have to do?" the second one asked.

"I want you to go with me into that office," I said, pointing to the building behind me, "and tell the man in there that you two are my uncles."

They both agreed to help me; then one asked, "How much will you pay us?"

"Well, it depends on how good you are at convincing the man at the desk."

"Oh, I think we will be very good at that. Right, Tam?" The first one said.

"You're right, Cong!" he replied.

"Do you two know each other?" I asked.

"Yes, we're friends," they both answered.

Don looked back and forth at me and at the two strangers, confused. He had no idea what my plan was or what I was talking to the men about. He kept interrupting me with questions, and I kept telling him I would explain later. I turned to make an offer to the pedicab drivers.

"No! It is too low," Tam said, and then he countered with a higher amount.

"Ah, ah, too much," I said as I shook my head. We bargained back and forth until we finally agreed on a price.

Both men seemed happy with my offer and were excited to pretend they were my uncles on my mother's side of the family. I gave them a quick history of my family and repeated their roles to them several times, to make sure they remembered. When I felt confident, we went into the office. While we were waiting for the magistrate to return, I explained to Don what we were about to do and told him what to say.

"Whenever the man questions you, just nod your head and say, 'I do.' It doesn't matter what he says; just say, 'I do,' unless I jump in and stop you." Don rolled his eyes and shook his head in amazement.

When the man came back to his desk, he asked us many questions, but my two temporary uncles were very convincing, and the official seemed to have no doubts, especially when he saw the roll of money I had in my hand. He read the vows to Don and me in Vietnamese, and I translated them to English for Don. Don did what I asked him to do; poor Don, he had no idea what he was getting himself into. The man signed our marriage papers and handed them to me with a smile. I took the marriage license and gave him a stack of money. He grabbed it and stuffed it into his pants pocket. I thanked him, and we all went on our way.

Our wedding in Saigon, 1969

THE NEXT MORNING was Saturday, September 6. My mother; my sister; the two maids, Ba and Tu; and our friends helped prepare food for our wedding. While mother made red sticky rice, which was one of our traditional wedding dishes, I helped kill and clean the crabs, and then we made the eggrolls. It took us a whole day to prepare food, but we had so much fun cooking.

Later, at five o'clock in the afternoon, I wore a light-pink traditional Vietnamese dress, and Don wore a light-brown suit and tie. Together, Don, my family and friends, and I took taxis and brought food to our wedding party on the rooftop of one of the nicest hotels in Saigon. When we walked into the well-decorated room, all the guests were cheering and the live band started playing. I looked around and saw so many guests and friends there. They all applauded and yelled when they saw us. A friend then announced our marriage and asked us to slow dance to the song "Unchained Melody." In the middle of the song, we stopped and asked our friends to join us. We exchanged partners often and had a lot of fun. We ate, drank, and danced until past midnight.

Me and Don

Ba, my sister, Tu, me, Eddie, and my mom

Later, I realized no one in my family showed up, except for my mother and sister. I guess they were too busy and didn't have time to attend my wedding. Or perhaps they lived too far away and couldn't afford the transportation. Some might have been unsure or embarrassed about our mixed marriage. I knew others felt that way, but I hoped it was not true for my family. I wouldn't have blamed them, nor would I have held a grudge, even if it were true; I just wished more people in our society had open minds and accepted us for who we were. I hoped we would be given a chance.

We had to postpone our honeymoon, because we couldn't afford it. Don worked for Lockheed in Saigon, and I was in the black-market business, selling foreign made goods in Saigon. We made ends meet and tried to save money for a vacation. We used Don's old Honda motorcycle for transportation and were often in accidents. One time, he was driving on the very busy Tran Hung Dao Street and was trying to avoid hitting a young student, who was about ten years old, carrying books, and walking across the street by himself. The boy walked right in front of us; Don had to weave back and forth to avoid him, and we crashed to the pavement. The Honda and both of us were spinning like tops. When I came to my senses, I saw my shoe in one place and my purse in another; a car almost ran over both of us, but we were okay, except for a few cuts and bruises.

Meanwhile, the war still blazed on around the country, and it was hard for those of us who were struggling to survive from day to day. But somehow, we managed to survive.

IN JANUARY OF 1970, five months after our wedding, Don surprised me with a two-week honeymoon to Japan. At twenty-two years old, I had never traveled to another country or been on an airplane. I didn't know what to expect, but I was excited.

We took a taxi to Tan Son Nhut airport and, after a long wait, boarded a large airplane; I didn't know what model it was. I thought our flight was exciting and so much fun. However, after we landed, I learned from Don that we almost didn't make it because of bad weather and turbulence. At one point, the airplane hit an air pocket and plunged over four thousand feet. I rose from my seat, but the seatbelt held me in place. I thought it was normal and was yelling and laughing from excitement. I looked at Don and saw him look at me with a smile. I thought he was having fun too, but he was just trying to hide his fear.

Being a gentleman, Don carried my two large suitcases, and I carried his two small ones. We found the information desk at the airport, and Don asked them about our travel agency's location. After the man at the desk gave us the information, we thanked him and dragged our heavy suitcases to the street, where a line of taxis waited.

Our driver loaded our luggage into the taxi, and we were on our way to the travel agency in Tokyo. Once there, we dragged our suitcases into the building and walked up to a long counter, where a line of four or five well-dressed men bowed to us. They were so polite, but we soon discovered none of them spoke English well. I heard Don ask for a romantic mountain cabin near the beach for our honeymoon, but I could tell by the expressions on their faces that they understood very little of what he was saying. One of them turned to me and started speaking in Japanese, but I just shook my head, smiled, and said nothing. They began talking louder and louder and were soon shouting at us. I believe they hoped that with their louder voices, we would understand them better. Poor people, it didn't matter how loud they spoke; we still couldn't understand them.

Meanwhile, I was so cold I began to shake like a leaf. Those men must have thought I was crazy. I was wearing a thin see-through mint-green silk tank top with dark-green shorts and a pair of brown sandals. The men all wore sweaters, under suits and ties, with scarves around their necks to keep them warm.

I glanced at Don and saw him drawing a picture of a mountain and a cabin, but he forgot to add the beach to it. I thought, *It's okay. We'll find the beach when we get there.* When Don finished, the men smiled and nodded their heads, indicating they understood. One man made a phone call—I guessed it was to make reservations for us—the other wrote down some information, and another called a taxi. Don picked up the reservation papers, nodded his head, and shook all of their hands. They bowed deeply while shaking Don's hand. When we started to leave, the two men behind the counter raced toward us, grabbed our suitcases, and took them outside; Don and I followed. They left the suitcases near the curbside, turned to us, and began bowing again. At first, Don and I just nodded our heads, but they didn't stop bowing. We looked at each other, feeling awkward, and bowed back. This seemed to satisfy the two men, because they finally walked away.

When our cab arrived, Don handed the driver the piece of paper the men at the travel agency had given us. After he read it, he bowed, put our luggage in the taxi, and drove us to a train station. He stopped in front of a ticket booth and motioned for us to get our tickets. After Don paid him, they bowed to each other, and he drove away. We bought two tickets, dragged our suitcases onto a train, and lunged into two empty seats.

I felt even colder now. My teeth were chattering, and I was shaking all over. I looked around at people on the train. They were all bundled up, from top to toes, with heavy coats, shoes, hats, and scarves.

"Where are we going?" I asked Don, after we sat down.

"I don't know," he said.

"If you don't know where we are going, then how do you expect us to get there?"

"Well," Don replied, "I'll show the papers to one of the passengers to see if they know where we should get off."

Don got up from his seat and showed our papers to one of the men standing nearby. He looked at the paper but spoke no English. He said something to me in Japanese, but I just smiled, shook my head, and told him in English that I didn't understand. He then turned to talk to another man, and the other man turned to another. A voice from the back yelled in broken English, "Go Minakami, train stop, you get out." Don bowed, thanked him, and sat back down. We took turns looking out for the Minakami sign.

I noticed the scenery was turning white, and the farther we went, the whiter it became.

"Don, why is everything white?" I asked.

"Oh, that's snow," he replied. "I hope there's no snow where we're going," he said with a worried expression. I was puzzled.

"What is snow?" I asked.

"It's like powdered ice, and it is very cold," he said, "and we are not prepared for the cold or the snowy weather."

I was used to the hot climate of Vietnam, so everything I packed was light and sexy. My suitcases were full of silk blouses, short skirts, bathing suits, sandals, and a few thin bell-bottom pants. Don's suitcases were full of summer clothes as well. He and I expected to be on an island, with a beautiful beach and sandbars.

I stopped asking questions and looked outside.

Meanwhile, all of the men and the women nearby were staring at me; people had been staring at me since I arrived at the airport. I could tell some of the men were talking about me as well. I thought that maybe it was because my stylish clothes were too revealing. Most of the other women wore kimonos and covered themselves up, unlike me in my skimpy garb. Although I felt the cold the second I stepped out of the airplane, I thought nothing more about it until I sat in the train. I was sure if I could see myself in the mirror, I would see that my lips were purple and my face had turned a ghostly pale-white from the cold.

We had been in the train for a while, but because of the excitement and distractions, I couldn't remember how far we had gone or how many times we had stopped or even how long we had been on the train. It could have been two or three hours or even five or six hours. But I didn't really care, because it was our honeymoon.

As the train slowed down, I saw a sign for Minakami, and I woke Don from his nap. We waited for the train to come to a complete stop, grabbed our suitcases, and bolted out of the door. I stepped on the icy cold ground—everything was covered in snow. I'd thought we were going to a hot sandy beach—neither of us were prepared for the cold.

It was difficult for me to walk in my sandals and drag my suitcases on the slippery surface. As we approached a line of waiting taxis, a driver came toward us, but he stopped for a few seconds to look me up and down before taking the luggage from my hands. Don showed him our reservations for the log cabin. He looked at the paper, then at me, and frowned a little. No! Actually, he frowned a lot. He said nothing; he just put our suitcases in the trunk and then motioned for us to get in the cab. It took us a long time to reach our destination at the base of a high mountain because of all the snow. After the driver stopped, he motioned for us to get out, and then he went back to the trunk. He took the suitcases out and laid them on the snow. Don tried to pay him but didn't know how much, so he just opened his wallet and showed the driver a stack of yen, as he did with the other taxi drivers, and motioned for him to take what we owed. He took the money, counted it, took what he needed, and put the rest back into Don's wallet. Before the driver returned to his cab, he pointed to the top of the mountain and motioned for us to go up there. He took one last look at me and shook his head before driving away.

I had never been so cold in my life. I knew then why people were staring at me. It wasn't because of my sexiness but because of my stupidness. I thought I was going to die from the cold and wanted to get back into the taxi, but it was too late; the taxi had already disappeared. We had no choice but to drag our suitcases and follow the trail upward to the mountaintop. The trail, however, was slippery and almost impossible for me to walk on. Now and then, we had to step aside to let people pass us. I noted they all wore heavy clothes, with gloves and hats to cover themselves from head to toe. Each one carried two pieces of long, narrow, flat wood. They all stared at me as they passed by.

"Who are those people, and why are they carrying wood up and down the mountain?" I asked Don.

"Those are skiers, and those are their skis," he said.

"What do they use the skis for?"

"To ski," he said.

"How do they ski?"

"They strap a ski to each of their shoes and slide downhill on the snow," he explained.

"That sounds like fun, but this is not a beach, Don," I said. "And I didn't dress for this kind of weather. I hope they have warmer clothes up there."

"I'm so sorry for putting you through this," Don said. "This is not what I had in mind for our honeymoon. I thought Japan was an island, and since it is not too far from Vietnam, I expected similar weather; I'm not prepared for this weather either. We both need warmer clothes."

We trudged over the slippery trail with our heavy suitcases behind us for a long time but still did not reach the top. I looked up through the snow-covered trees and could barely see a cabin above the misty clouds.

"I hope we can make it up there before sundown," I said.

"I hope so too," Don replied.

At first, I felt cold, very cold, but then I felt pain, like millions of needles poking me all over my body. Then the pain subsided, and I felt numb, as if I was in someone else's body, but I still shook like a leaf. Now and then, I had to stop walking for a few seconds to catch my breath. At one of those breaks, I looked down at my feet and realized I had lost one of my sandals and didn't even know it. I was too tired to mention it to Don and kept on walking barefoot in the snow.

Finally, we reached the cabin and found our way to the registration office. It was late in the evening, and a man at the desk assigned us to our room. We walked back outside in the cold and entered one of the cabins. I looked around and saw that the room was already full of skiers, who had retired to their bunk beds built along the walls.

There were five bunks on each wall, occupied by people of all ages and genders. There were two empty bunks near the door; I guessed those were ours.

"Don! Is this where we're going to stay for our honeymoon?" I asked.

"I don't think so; this has to be a big mistake," he said. "I asked for a romantic mountain cabin on the beach, not a ski lodge; this is not what

I had in mind." He frowned and shook his head. "I have to find the manager to get this straightened out."

"I hope you can, because I don't like it here," I said.

"Stay right where you are, and let me go back to the office." He looked unhappy and left in a hurry.

I stood in the middle of the room—a bunch of strangers watching my every move. I didn't look at them, though I could hear them whispering and giggling. I'm sure it was because of my one shoe and the way I was dressed. I felt embarrassed and uncomfortable, but I forced myself to stand still, with my eyes fixed on my suitcases to avoid looking back at them, and hoped that Don would hurry back soon.

The sun was going down behind the mountains, and Don was still gone. He may have been gone for ten or fifteen minutes, but it seemed like hours. I began to worry that something had happened to him and thought, *Oh no, he might have been kidnapped. After all, he is an American and this is Japan. They were at war before, and who knows, someone might still be holding a grudge.* I was cold, tired, hungry, and scared. This was not a good start to our honeymoon.

Finally, Don came back to the lodge with good news. "They now understand me," he said. "I'm so sorry I put you through all of this, but the worst is over. All we have to do now is go back down the way we came up and catch another taxi to take us to a small village below," he smiled.

I felt better, knowing I didn't have to spend my honeymoon on a bunk bed, in a ski lodge, sharing a room with fifteen other people gawking at me.

"Can you wait for a little while?" I asked. "I need to get my sandals and clothes from my suitcase. I don't think I can go back down the mountain in my bare feet."

"Oh? What happened to your other sandal?" he asked.

"I lost it on the way up here," I said.

"Again, I'm so sorry for putting you through this." He shook his head and smiled. "Of course you can get your sandals and change your clothes."

As thirty watchful eyes peered at us from all different directions, I opened my suitcase, looked for a pair of bell-bottom slacks, and took out a pair of sandals, along with two long-sleeved blouses. I put the single sandal back into my suitcase, hoping to find its mate on the way down.

I went outside and found the bathroom. I put the newer clothes on top of the ones I already had on, layer after layer. I felt like a stuffed scarecrow, and I was sure I looked like one too. It reminded me of when I was younger and had to do the same thing with my clothes, when we were fleeing from North to South Vietnam.

Don looked at me when I came back from the bathroom, and started laughing. "You are so cute," he said. "You look just as good fat as you do thin."

"Thanks a lot," I said with a smile. "Can you find someone to help us with our suitcases down the mountain?"

"I sure can," Don replied. We found a Japanese man who helped carry the two larger suitcases, while Don carried the two smaller ones. I still had problems with the slippery trail, even though I wasn't carrying anything. I tried to be careful but still fell several times.

"Going down is harder than going up," I told Don.

"Just be careful," Don warned me, but right after his words, he fell, and all three of us started laughing.

"I just hope we don't slide over a cliff," I said.

Not too far down, I found my lost sandal, half buried in the snow. I picked it up and carried it as I continued to slip and fall. Don and our helper were concerned, and they asked me to hold on to them, but that couldn't keep me from falling, so I sat down and slid on my behind, which was kind of fun.

When we finally reached the road, there was a taxi waiting for us.

"The ski lodge people must have called the taxi for us," I said.

"Yes, I asked them to," Don replied.

The driver got out and greeted us. Don and our helper sat our suitcases down near the taxi, and all four of us bowed to each other. Don pulled out some money from his wallet and handed it to our helper, but he wouldn't take it. He just smiled and bowed to us as we smiled and bowed back.

The taxi driver and our helper exchanged some Japanese words, and they bowed; then we all bowed at each other again. At one point, I was so confused and didn't know whom to bow to next, so I bowed to Don, and he bowed back to me.

I thought, *If we don't stop bowing to each other, we will never get out of here.* I wondered if bowing was a custom or if they were just competing to see who could bow the most. After a few more bows, our helper started back up the trail, and we climbed into the taxi.

The taxi took us to a small village below, not too far from the ski resort. He stopped at one of the largest hotels in the area, and after the driver took the suitcases out of the trunk, Don paid him; we bowed once more, and he drove away. We entered the hotel, dragging our heavy suitcases behind us.

A young man at the desk saw us and stood up. He bowed and said, "Hello and welcome." In English! Don explained to him what happened. As Don talked, I saw the young man nodding, but we both soon realized his English did not go beyond "hello" and "welcome." Don showed him our reservations, and he showed us to our room, where we exchanged a few bows before the young man exited to the corridor.

I looked around the simple room and saw a small television against the wall and a short rectangular table in one corner, with two small pillows underneath. On the opposite side, I saw an open closet with a shoe rack, but I didn't see a bed, just a large, thin mattress and two large pillows in the middle of the floor.

While Don organized the suitcases, I walked toward one of the walls, hoping I could find a bathroom. I stared at the strange-looking wall for a second and walked closer to investigate. I touched it and realized it was made of paper, a white, waxy paper! I gave it a little push, and it opened into another room; to my surprise, it looked just like ours. I slid the wall back into place and said, "Hey, Don! You won't believe it, but the wall is made of paper, and it's moveable."

"I heard they have paper walls in Japan because of the earthquakes," he said as he changed his clothes, "but I never saw one." He continued, "It's late; let's change into our pajamas and go to sleep. I'll check it out later. I'm so tired."

"Okay, honey," I replied. We hit the mattress as soon as we changed into our pajamas. We gave each other a kiss, and that was all I remembered.

We woke to a knock on the door the following morning. I jumped up and answered it. At first, I saw no one, but then I looked down and saw a female attendant, dressed in a kimono, kneeling on all fours. A tray containing a teapot and two cups was on the floor beside her. She said something in Japanese and bowed. I stepped aside and signaled for her to come in. She picked up the tray, walked timidly to a table, and set it down. She poured tea into the two cups, bowed again, returned to all fours, and crawled backward out the door, without once looking at me.

Me and our hotel attendant

Don climbed off the mattress and sampled the tea as I opened the curtains. What I saw was unbelievable. I thought, *This could not be on earth; I must have frozen to death last night, and now I'm in heaven.* Excited, I opened the sliding door and stepped out on the balcony.

"Hey, Don, come here!" I yelled. "Look, look!"

Don drinking tea in his kimono

Don put his tea down and ran toward me. We stepped outside, and from the balcony, we saw a deep, half-frozen white canyon, with a misty fog hanging over a stream. Farther up on my right, there was a beautiful waterfall glistening in the sunlight, with a red arching bridge built above it. Heavy snow covered its rails and let only partial red spots show through. I looked down on my left and saw white steam hovering over the slow-moving water. On the opposite side, I noticed a few small birds chasing each other on top of the white tree. Other than a few protruding grey rocks and some brown spots under the tree's branches, everything was white. I never dreamed of seeing anything on earth so magnificent. It was one of the most beautiful things I'd ever seen.

Don walked to me, gave me a kiss, and we held each other tight as we stood and drank in nature's art. Don bent down and whispered in my ear, "Happy honeymoon, baby."

I looked up into his tender eyes and made a vow, "Happy honeymoon to you too, babe! I love you with all my being, and I will continue to love you until the day I die, and that is forever."

"I love you even more. I promise you I will love you for eternity, and if possible, I will continue to love you after my death," he responded as tears pooled in his eyes.

"It's not possible for you to love me more," I smiled with tears running down my cheeks. "But I won't argue with you today, since it is our honeymoon. Thank you for bringing me here," I said.

"There is a rainbow after the storm after all," he said, smiling.

We loosened our grip a little and continued to watch the water flow, forgetting we were still in our pajamas.

"I love it out here," Don said, "but it is so cold. I can't take it anymore. I have to go inside."

"I'm cold too, baby," I said. "Let's both go inside." We held hands and walked through the door.

"We have to go to a store and buy warmer clothes and shoes if we want to go anywhere," I said.

"I think so too," Don agreed.

We opened our suitcases and found the warmest things we had.

"Before we change," Don said, "we have to find a bathroom."

"Where is our bathroom?" I asked Don. "I haven't seen one in here."

"I sure hope they have one indoors." Don smiled. "Otherwise, we will freeze our buns out there."

"I agree," I said, and we both laughed.

Still in our pajamas, we opened the door and stuck our heads out to look up and down the hallway. When we didn't see anybody, we tiptoed back and forth in the quiet corridor, trying to find a bathroom.

"This door has a man and a woman symbol with Japanese writing on it, and it looks different from the rest. Would you like to open it?" I asked.

"Yes, we should try," Don said and pushed it open; we discovered what looked to be a community bathroom. A tall white towel rack stood in one corner, near a large sunken hot tub. We walked a little farther and found toilets, sinks, and showers. "Where is everybody?" I asked.

"I don't know," Don said, shrugging his shoulders. "I was wondering that myself."

We went back to our room to get our toiletries and a change of clothes. When we returned, we used the bathroom and then grabbed a towel from the rack.

"I hope these are the right towels and the right bathroom for us to use," I said, and we both laughed.

"I hope so too," he said as we went into our own shower. We took a long, hot shower and changed into clean clothes.

"I feel better," I told Don.

He smiled and said, "Me too."

On the way out, I pointed to the large steaming hot tub.

"The tub looks good," I said. "We'll have to come back tonight and try it out."

"What a great idea; I can't wait." Don winked at me, with a mischievous smile.

"Okay then, we will do the tub when we get back from shopping and sightseeing," I said as we walked back to our room. We grabbed the things we needed and walked back out.

A young man intercepted us at the hallway; he bowed and asked, "Are you Mr. and Mrs. Baer?"

We both answered, "Yes, we are."

"My name is Hiro, and I am one of the hotel managers," he said. "I heard you are Americans and need a translator. I am studying English, and I would be happy to assist you."

We were so excited to meet him. It was a great relief. Finally! There was someone who understood and could help us. Hiro took us into his office, where he gave us a map and all of the information we needed, including what we should see and do and what to say to the taxi drivers. We thanked him, bowed to one another, and then we were off.

Don and I walked hand in hand through the ice-and-snow-covered street to look for a clothing store. I couldn't walk very well and had to cling to Don to keep from falling. Each time I slipped, Don caught me, and when it was his turn, I stabilized him before he fell. We laughed at each other and had a good time.

We entered a small clothing boutique run by a friendly Japanese lady, who greeted us with a bow and a smile. I tried on the only red coat hanging on the rack. It was a little large for me, but it was thick and warm; I had no choice but to buy it. I picked out a few sweaters, several pairs of socks, and a pair of white boots. Don bought the clothes he needed, and after paying for everything, we changed into them. The sales lady put our old clothes into a bag, and we walked out.

"There, I feel much better," I told Don. "Now I am ready to explore."

"Me too," he replied.

We stayed in the very small town of White Valley, near Minakami. It catered to skiers, and there was not a lot to do other than walk around and take pictures.

Beautiful surroundings and my new coat

Later, we got hungry, so we found a restaurant and walked in. Although it was small, there were quite a few people in it, and all of them seemed to be enjoying their meals. We found an empty table and sat down to wait. The restaurant looked very busy, but I saw just one server wearing a colorful kimono, and it seemed she was running the whole show all by herself. A few minutes later, she brought a large tray full of food and set it at one of the tables behind us. Don saw an opportunity and waved to her. She walked toward us, smiled, and gave us several small nods and bows.

Don asked her something in English, and she answered him in Japanese. Just as we expected, she didn't speak English and didn't understand a word he said. In desperation, she turned to the tables nearby and asked people for help, but no one in the whole restaurant spoke English. After talking with his hands for few seconds, Don looked behind us and pointed to the tray she had just served and motioned for her to bring us the same one.

She smiled, bowed, and walked away as fast as she could in her tight kimono. About thirty minutes later, she returned to our table with a tray full of food, along with half a dozen thin, long forks. She carefully set everything in front of us, bowed, and left.

Unfortunately, we didn't know what to do with a tray full of uncooked food. I looked closer at the food tray and saw a small pot full of oil sitting on top of a tiny flame burner in the middle. Surrounding it was a pile of peeled shrimp, bite-sized pieces of fish, a handful of dead baby octopi, several long pieces of eel or snake, and a mountain of assorted raw vegetables. Besides all of that, there were two small bowls, each with a small egg in it. I figured the eggs were raw too. I looked at Don, and he looked back at me; we smiled and made funny faces at each other. I knew he was just as confused as I was.

"What are we going to do with these?" I asked.

"I have no idea," he replied with a frown. "I just hope we don't have to eat everything raw."

"I don't think so," I said. "I'm sure the cooking burner is for cooking our food. But I need for the waitress to come back and show us what to do with everything, especially those eggs in the bowls."

We sat there, looking at our food, made faces, stuck out our tongues at each other, and grinned. I watched as the flame under the pot burned brighter, and the oil in the pot bubbled faster. I heard my empty stomach growling as my mouth began watering, but I couldn't do anything except stare at the food. When the waitress came back to our table, she looked at our untouched food and realized we were dumfounded. She smiled, rolled up her kimono sleeve, and showed us how to cook and eat our food.

First, she broke a raw egg into each of our bowls, added a little soy sauce, and stirred. Next, she took one of the forks, poked a piece of fish, lowered it into the boiling pot, and then, using another fork, pierced a vegetable and placed it into the boiling oil. She looked at us, smiled, gave us forks, and signaled for us to do it ourselves. We speared a couple of shrimp and an octopus and lowered them into the pot. We continued until all six of the forks were in the steaming-hot cooker. The oil in the pot was burning too hot, and it almost boiled over. She turned it down, and a few minutes later, she took the cooked food out and dropped it onto our plates. Then, with a regular fork, she picked up a piece of hot food and dipped it into the bowl of raw egg mix, which was there to cool off the food. Then she motioned for us to eat it. We did. It was delicious.

After the lesson, we began to cook for ourselves. I was a quick learner, and I was doing well for myself. Don, however, was a little confused and was having a hard time getting the food to stay on his skinny forks, especially the clammy octopus. He'd never cooked for himself before, but I gave him credit for trying.

Suddenly, I heard Don cry out loud, "Ouch! Ouch! Ouch!" Everyone in the restaurant stopped eating and looked at him. He had eaten his food directly from the hot fork without letting it cool! His lips and chin turned bright red, and he had an imprint of the fork on his face. He was embarrassed and in pain, so we paid our bill and left the restaurant as fast as we could. We found our way back to the hotel, still hungry.

The hotel manager greeted us at the entrance and asked, "How is everything?" I knew Don was in too much pain to talk, so I took over.

"Oh, everything is great!" I said as I winked and smiled at Don. "Don didn't do well at the restaurant though; he was very hungry and tried to eat his fork straight out of hot boiling oil." I laughed, but Don didn't. Hiro frowned and wondered why Don tried to eat his fork, so I explained about the hot cooking pot.

"Oh, I am sorry," Hiro said with a smile. Don couldn't smile, but his eyes told me he was going to make me pay for making fun of him. We found out from Hiro that what we ordered was called "fondue." I was sure it would have been a lot of fun to do if Don hadn't burned himself. I believed it would be a long time before Don would have any more fondue. We went back to our room, where I examined Don's burns.

"It looks bad," I said. "You have a long, narrow blister from your mouth down to your chin; I think the burn was not just from the hot fork but also from the hot dripping oil. I'm afraid it will be a while before you can kiss me," I joked.

"Thanks a lot," he responded. "That's all I need for our honeymoon—no kisses."

"Let's go out to our balcony and enjoy nature's beauty," I suggested. "You'll forget about your burns."

"I think that's a good idea," he said as he took my hand and led me outside through the sliding door.

We sat on the balcony floor, hand in hand, with our heads leaning toward each other. Silently, we watched the fading sun go down behind the snow-covered trees. I looked down at the misty white creek below, and it looked even more mysterious in the twilight. I believed there was no greater place of beauty, peace, and serenity on this earth. I thought, *If there is a heaven, this must be it.* We sat in peaceful silence until nature went to sleep.

I turned to Don and asked, "Hey, babe, do you feel like going to the hot tub we saw this morning?"

"Yes!" he exclaimed. "It would feel good after sitting on the cold balcony." Don stood up first and helped me to my feet, and we walked shoulder to shoulder through the door.

I found a skimpy bikini and put it on, while Don put on his swim trunks. I felt pain in my hips, and I looked down. I discovered I was black and blue with bruises on my hips, thighs, and legs.

"Hey, Don! Look at my bruised legs; I don't think I should go to the hot tub in my bikini." I pouted.

"Don't worry," he said, "it doesn't matter how your legs look; there's no one here to see them except me."

"I guess you're right," I said with a weak smile.

Don came closer to examine my legs. "Let me see how bad," he said. "Wow, your legs do look bad." He was showing concern at first, but then he started to laugh, with his hand covering his blisters. "Now your legs match my blistered lips," he said. "We're in great shape for our honeymoon."

"Well! Thanks a lot. I'm glad you think that it's funny." I frowned and then laughed.

"Besides, I hope nobody will ever see those legs but me anyway," he said and winked at me.

I grabbed his hand and dragged him out to the hallway toward the hot tub. It was very quiet.

"The hotel is almost empty," I remarked.

"It must be the wrong day or wrong season," Don replied.

"Who knows?" I said. "But now we have the whole place to ourselves."

The hot tub was very inviting; it was clear, bubbling, and steaming hot. I felt good to have our own private spa, and I began lowering myself into the sunken bath.

"It's hot! Be careful," I warned Don. "We need to go in slow and let our bodies get used to the heat." Don was holding on to my hand as he stepped down into the tub.

"Oh, wow! It is hot!" he exclaimed as he lowered himself deeper into the water.

We moved closer and sat down next to each other. We were talking, holding hands, and enjoying ourselves.

Just then, two middle-aged Japanese men appeared, with towels around their waists.

"I hope they don't come into the tub with us," I whispered to Don.

"I hope so too," he replied.

The two men bowed as soon as they saw us. We nodded slightly to them, because the water level in the spa was up to our neck. They came within a couple feet of the spa and pulled their towels off. To our shock, they were both naked! I stopped smiling and immediately looked away as they lowered themselves into the tub.

Don and I felt so awkward, but the men paid no attention to us. We wanted to leave, but we lingered, trying to act cool. I saw Don frown, so I signaled for him to stop by kicking him under the water. Lucky for me, one of them sat close to me, and each time I glanced down at the crystal-clear water, I saw his turtle's head popping up and down, as though it were alive and dancing with the bubbling waves. When our eyes met, the men smiled at me, and I couldn't help but smile back at them.

"I can't take any more of this," I finally whispered to Don.

"Me either!" Don said. "Are you ready to go?" he asked.

"I am more than ready," I replied, and we both stood up. We bowed to the men, and they nodded back. They couldn't bow, because the water was up to their chins, and if they bowed, they would drown. We helped each other climb out of the tub and went straight to the towel rack. I looked back at the two men and noticed they were staring at my black-and-blue legs. I whispered to Don, "I'm sure they looked at my bruised legs and think I had it rough last night." We both laughed.

"If they looked at my swollen lips," Don added, "they might think I did too." We laughed again.

"Hey, Don," I said, "you were wrong about nobody being here to see my bruised legs," I giggled.

"Yes, I was wrong," he said. "Now, let's hurry up and get out of here." We went to the shower, rinsed off, wrapped ourselves in a large towel, and giggled all the way back to our room. As soon as we closed the door behind us, we started laughing so hard that our backs and stomachs hurt. I saw Don hold his mouth while he was laughing and told him to be careful with his burns.

"I saw the guy's private part in the tub," I told Don, laughing. "It looked like a turtle's head, swaying back and forth, daring me to catch it," I exaggerated.

"I'm so glad it didn't crawl out and bite you!" he said. Poor Don, his burned lips really hurt him when he laughed, but it was too funny not to.

After changing into our pajamas, Don turned on the TV. The picture was in color! I had never seen a color TV before. Even though we didn't understand most of the programs, we watched them anyway. But we were tired and soon fell asleep.

The following morning, the attendant came back. After she served tea, she went to one of the walls, and to my surprise, she pushed it open. I looked through the open door and saw a bathroom. I watched her as she walked in and looked around for a few seconds, but the bath was in perfect shape, and she walked out. I didn't know it was a bathroom; I thought it opened into another hotel room, like the other wall.

Each morning, the hotel maid came to our room and performed the same ritual of serving us tea, cleaning the toilet, and then getting down on all fours and crawling out backwards. Each afternoon, a female host, who spoke no English, came to our room and dressed us. She took the kimonos from our closet and helped us put them on, then escorted us to a restaurant in one of the hotel's wings. She left us there long enough for us to eat and then came back to take us to a nightclub in another wing, for drinks and live entertainment.

Don and me in our kimonos with our geisha girl

Our host at the nightclub dressed in a fancy kimono and wore white makeup with very red lipstick. She was very friendly. We thought of her as our personal geisha girl, and we liked her very much.

Back in Tokyo city

I was often mistaken for a geisha girl, and many of the men flirted with me. Some even tried to touch me. Don was more than a little jealous because of the inappropriate attention I received.

While we were having dinner one night, several men were sitting at a table across from us. We noticed they were looking at and talking about me among themselves. After a few drinks, they began talking to me in Japanese. Of course, I didn't understand a word they said; still I gave them friendly smiles, but my smiles weren't enough for them. They must have thought I was being snobbish, because I didn't speak to them. They became angry and glared at me. Although I didn't understand Japanese, I could tell they were cursing at me.

"There it goes again," I said to Don. "I have to put an end to this misunderstanding." I took my papers out of my purse and walked toward them. I smiled as I approached their table and handed my ID card and passport to them. They read them and realized their mistake. They all stood up, bowed to me, and offered their hands. I believed they were apologizing, so I shook their hands and smiled. They also came to our table and shook Don's hand and ordered him a drink. From the expression on their faces, I could tell they were embarrassed.

After one week, we ran out of things to do and decided to go back to the big city. Tokyo was large and alive with people on the move. There were many tall buildings, packed tight with stores, restaurants, and all kinds of entertainment. The price of everything in the city was very high, far more than we had expected, and more than we could afford.

Within days, we almost ran out of money, had to give up our hotel, and went to Yokota Air Force Base, on the outskirts of Tokyo. Since Don was a retired officer, we were able to stay in the Officers' Quarters at a reasonable price. We dined on snacks and noodle soup most of the time; for entertainment, we walked up and down the streets, taking pictures and window-shopping. There were many nice restaurants, with mouth-watering entrees displayed in the windows, but we couldn't afford to go in.

While at the air force base, Don met a couple of his old friends and their wives. The six of us spent time together playing cards and listening to music. We also went to a bar and casino, where I played the slot machines.

On our last night in Japan, I was lucky and won enough money to buy all six of us dinner and drinks. We stayed out late that night with our friends and had a great time. Early the next morning, they took us to the airport, and we said farewell. We arrived back in Saigon later that evening.

Leaving our hotel in Japan to go back to Vietnam

Chapter 2

SAIGON TEARS

THE VIOLENCE OF the war raged on right outside our doorstep. There was no safe place for any of us. One day, a theater and a nightclub were blown up. The next day, a restaurant and a hotel were bombed. Even a street market was shattered by an explosion. I didn't feel safe at work or at home, and I didn't know when all the violence would end.

Don was working at Bien Hoa Air Base, and a mortar exploded right outside of his office. A piece of shrapnel flew right over his head and embedded in the wall behind him. Thank God Don was sitting down. If he had been standing or was a few inches taller, he would have been decapitated. He removed the five-inch piece of razor-sharp shrapnel from the wall and kept it as a souvenir.

My stepbrother, Den, was a major in the Vietnamese Rangers. Part of his leg was shattered during combat. He lost a lot of blood and needed transfusions. My family and I took turns visiting him at a distant hospital. Thanks to Don's job, we were able to purchase an old blue Datsun, which we used to take my family to and from the hospital to see him.

When I was on the road, the police often stopped me for little or no reason at all. Each time I was pulled over, they asked me for my driver's license and ID card, which I always had. For one reason or another, I always had to pay fines. It was not just the money; it was the nuisance as well. The fines I paid were not because I did something wrong but because I drove a car. They believed anyone driving a car had to have money; if people had money, they were sinners, and sinners had to pay fines. There was no exception; the police always looked for a reason to make me pay. They charged me for driving too fast or too slow, or my horn was too loud or didn't work, or the lights were too dim or too bright. I was surprised they didn't stop me for the car's ugly color; even I didn't like the pale blue.

If the police couldn't find a reason to charge me, they would ask, "Can you spare us some coffee money?" I got used to the drill and came prepared. Each time they stopped me, I handed them a roll of money, with the larger bills on the outside to make them think there was more, and then I kept moving. I always looked in my rearview mirror and smiled as I watched them count it.

I didn't blame the police. In many ways, I felt sorry for them. Some of them were very poor, with little income and large families to feed, just like many others, including myself; we all did what we could to feed our families.

After a while, Den's wound healed, and he was able to walk, but there was one drawback: The blood he received was tainted, and he developed hepatitis. One day, he said to me, "It's better to have hepatitis and be on my feet than not to have it and be six feet under." I agreed with him but wished the circumstances were different.

SINCE DON OFTEN used the Datsun for work, I bought myself a new Honda motorcycle and called it my two-wheeled car. I used it for all my transportation needs—going to my English classes and to church and for my black-market business. I strapped a large box on the back seat and packed it with everything I needed to carry. I loved my bike. Often, if I had time, I would go for a drive outside the city with Don or my friends. I loved feeling the fresh country air blowing on my face.

Every Sunday, Don and I took the motorcycle to church. Gas was cheaper, and it was easier for us to find a parking space. After church, we often went for a drive, usually to Bien Hoa or Thu Duc, about ten or fifteen miles outside of Saigon. The traffic was always bad, and sometimes it took us an hour to get there. I was a faster and better motorcycle driver than Don; I knew the road and was able to weave in and out of traffic without trouble. When we arrived at our destination, we often went to our favorite restaurant to have a bowl of pho, Don's favorite rare beef, or chicken noodle soup. Other times we just went to our familiar café to drink a special coffee processed by a catlike creature called an Asian palm civet.

The little civets love red coffee beans, but they can't digest them, so the whole bean comes out the other end. The poor people who worked on the coffee plantation collected the beans expelled by the civet, took them home, washed and roasted them, and brewed them for their coffee. Later, civet-processed coffee became popular and very expensive, and it's supposed to be the best coffee in the world, and only the rich can afford it.

Don and I weren't addicted to the civet poop; we just went there because everyone else did. It was the place for "people of high status" to go for their coffee. It was always very busy, and we had to wait a long time, and after we each had a cup, we returned home. Frankly, I couldn't tell the difference between the civet-processed coffee and the one I had in my own kitchen, which probably contained rat and cockroach poop. Of course, the FDA regulates the amount of poop and carcasses that remain in my coffee to protect me. It reminds me of what I heard about the American lobsters, which were once considered trash and were only eaten by poor people, until plantation owners discovered they tasted good. After that, the price of lobsters went sky high.

ONE SUNDAY, DON was taking me home from church, and while we were on a bridge about two blocks from our house, there was a loud and terrifying explosion just in front of us at the Truong Minh Giang market. The violent blast shocked Don so much that he almost crashed. After swerving back and forth, he was able to gain control and stop the bike. We stood in silence, watching people running around, screaming for help. I looked at Don and saw his lips harden to a straight line. He was shaking his head in disgust. Although we had no idea what caused the explosion, we blamed the war for what happened. All we could do was stand there, watching part of the market burn down.

MY BUSINESS WAS running smoothly. Through my friends with American husbands or boyfriends, I was able to buy whiskey, cigarettes, canned goods, and sometimes stereos and American currency. I took them home, separated them, and priced them one by one. I piled the merchandise into a large box, tied it on the back of my two-wheeled car, and took it to various well-known stores. I sold them for double or triple the cost, depending on how slick I was with my bargaining skills. That was how I made a living—thank God for the black market. By putting our money together, Don and I were able to purchase a few investment homes in Vung Tau and were able to help my family and my poor relatives in need.

My beloved uncle Ky borrowed a large amount of our money to change my cousin Bao's age on his birth documents to avoid the military draft. His other son already sacrificed his life to war, and my uncle did not want to see Bao die like his brother. The more money he paid to corrupt government workers, the younger his son became. Hopefully, by the time my cousin reached draft age, the war would be over. I lent him a large amount of money and hoped it would save his son's life.

Most people in Vietnam, including my own family, did not have their real ages and names on their ID cards or their birth documents; people could make up anything they wanted, as long as they had money to pay for it.

Besides being a black-market dealer, I also attended English class in Van Khoi School three times a week. I liked the school and hoped to improve my English before Don and I moved to the United States.

One Wednesday, after my class, I walked to the parking spot where I parked my bike, but it wasn't there. I looked around, but I couldn't find it. I ran to ask the guard about it, and he acted as if he didn't know what I was talking about. In desperation, I ran around asking everybody, but no one had seen it.

How can this be? I thought. My red Honda was the newest model and had many extra attachments. I paid extra money to the school for a parking space inside, behind a locked gate, which also had guards. I didn't understand how my Honda could disappear without a trace. The guard advised me to talk to the principal. The principal told me to talk to the supervisor. The supervisor told me to talk to the guard. After talking to the guard the second time, he advised me to call the police.

Two officers with bad attitudes arrived soon after. One man stood with his legs parted and his hands behind his back. He just stood there and stared at me, with a know-it-all kind of smile, while the other one questioned me as if I was the thief who stole the bike. Since there was no law to protect me and no point in me looking anymore, I went home crying.

AFTER HIS ELECTION, President Nixon vowed to end the Vietnam War. He promised President Thieu his plans would bring peace with honor, and I couldn't wait to see that happen. I thought if the war ended right away, it would save millions of Vietnamese lives and some of the 280,000 American soldiers who were still in our country. Don and I were anxious to see peace come to Vietnam, but after Nixon took office, the war still raged on.

In February of 1971, Don's contract with Lockheed ended. While we sat at the coffee table one morning, Don turned to me and said, "I'm getting so tired of this war, so tired of watching friends and innocent people die." Don sighed and continued, "I think it's about time for me to take you to America to meet my family. What do you think?" he asked.

"I think it's a good idea!" I replied. "I heard America is like heaven on earth. I heard it is clean, beautiful, and interesting, with sky-high buildings and all nice people, who don't lie, cheat, or steal."

Don looked at me with a smile. "They are all rich people and don't work and still get paid. And if someone has to work, they use machines and don't have to do hard labor like we do here in Vietnam." Don rolled his eyes.

I stopped to catch my breath and continued, "I heard America is the most perfect country on earth. I can't wait to go there." Don shrugged his shoulders, as if he only half agreed.

"Where did you hear all of that?" he asked.

"Everywhere I go. If the topic of America comes up, everyone says they want to go there; I think everyone in this world wants to go to America. And now, I will have a chance to see America for myself; I can't wait." I smiled and danced around Don.

"I'm so glad you're happy and want to go to my country with me." Don stopped me from dancing and hugged me.

It took weeks and a lot of money for us to prepare the legal papers and passports for my son Eddie and me. Eddie was five years old, but we had to change his age to three and a half, because the Vietnamese government officials told me they would not allow boys five years or older to leave the country. "They are potential soldiers," they said, and I had to pay a lot of money to have his birth certificate changed. I didn't know whether it was true or not. Maybe he just wanted to make more money from me. Normally it cost less for those who wanted to change their documents, but because Don was an American and most Vietnamese believed all Americans were rich, they thought we could afford to pay more. The rules were simple: if someone had money, they should pay extra for everything.

Even with the extra money I paid, it still took us a long time to get Eddie's birth certificate and our passports ready. While waiting for our papers, I spent a lot of time shopping for gifts and souvenirs for Don's family in America. Before we left, we sold our car to Chuck, a friend of Don's, and I sold most of our furniture. We kept some for my family. I gave my old clothes to the maids and packed the rest.

A few days before we left, my mother and Bay, my beloved thirteen-year-old brother, came to stay with us to say goodbye. It was sad to leave my family, but at the same time, I was excited to see America, the country I had heard so much about—the country made of diamonds and gold, where they ate food without having to cook, lived in tall buildings without having to walk up or down stairs, and walked through doors that opened and closed automatically. *I can't wait!* I thought.

Since Don had asked me to go with him, I couldn't sleep well, especially since my mother and my brother had come to stay with us. We cried our eyes out whenever we were together and talked about my departure.

The day Don and I prepared to leave, we all had a sad breakfast together, and then we carried our luggage to the front gate. While waiting for the taxi to take us to the airport, Mother began sobbing.

"This is it," she cried. "I will never see you again. I heard rumors that when Vietnamese girls go with their husbands to America, most of their American families are very prejudiced; they are not going to like the Vietnamese women, and if the husband gets tired of his wife, he will kick her out and bring home a new one. Sometimes they sell the old wife to another man. You'll never be able to come back to Vietnam!"

"No, Mother," I replied, "don't worry. Don and I will never, ever get divorced, but if we do, you know I'm smart and can take care of myself if something like that ever happens to me." I tried to convince her. "Besides, I don't think American people are as bad as you were told, so don't believe everything you hear." She cracked a weak smile and seemed relieved by what I said. I could tell from her swollen eyes that she had cried all night, just as I had. Even my five-year-old son and the two maids had red eyes.

"Where is my brother?" I asked Mother when I didn't see him.

"I just saw him a few minutes ago at the sink, washing his face," she answered in a sad voice.

I went back inside to look for him and found him lying on my bed, with his face in my pillow, sobbing. I sat next to him, stroked his hair, and let my tears stream down my face. A few seconds later, he pushed himself up from the pillow and hugged my neck. I could tell he had been crying all night too. I knew my mother would miss me, but I believed my brother would miss me even more. He was very close to me; I was like a second mother to him.

Whenever he found out I was coming home to visit my family, he always trapped wild birds, caught sand lizards, or dug mud crabs in the river behind the house, and then he cooked them and saved them for me. He knew what I liked to eat, wild and weird food. According to other family members, after he cooked the food, he hid it and would not let anyone touch it until I came home. I loved him so much and couldn't bear the pain of a long separation. But there was nothing I could do, except cry.

"Don't worry, my little brother," I said as I pulled him closer to my chest, "I will only be gone for a while."

"No! I think you will be gone forever," he sobbed.

"No! You are wrong. I could never leave you for good, and I promise you I will come back one way or another." I murmured through my tears, "Now let's go outside. I think the taxi is waiting."

I got up first, held out my hands, pulled him off the bed, and we walked outside.

Don and the driver loaded our belongings into the cab while the rest of us hugged and said farewell. The moment before I entered the taxi, Bay ran to me, threw himself at my feet, and hung on to my legs tightly. "Please, my dearest sister, please don't leave me," he sobbed. "I don't want you to go. Mother said when you go, you will never come back, and we will never see you again!" He held on to my legs even tighter and cried.

I bent down, pulled him up to his feet, hugged him, and let my tears soak his shirt.

"Don't worry, my little brother," I whispered. "You will see me again; I promise. I will come back for you one way or another; you have to believe me."

I let go of him and jumped into the waiting taxi as fast as I could. Without looking back, I urged the driver to hurry up and go, go, go.

Saying goodbye to my mother was hard, but saying goodbye to my brother was excruciating.

Me, Don, my brother Bay, and Eddie at Saigon Catholic Church, days before we left Vietnam in 1971

Chapter 3

DREAMLAND

IT WAS A long, rough flight to America, but I was so excited I could hardly sit still. As soon as I heard the tires hit the runway, I opened my seat belt, grabbed my purse, and left my seat. I walked toward the exit door amid hundreds of staring eyes. As soon as an airline attendant saw me, she signaled for me to sit down in an empty seat near her and told me to buckle up. I sat and waited near the door, positioning myself to be the first one to get off the plane. When I heard the engine turn off, the stewardess unbuckled her seatbelt, so I unbuckled mine. I stood up and went near the door. She had to ask me to move out of her way so she could open it. As soon as it opened, I bolted out.

I led a throng of fast-moving people through the corridor. When I looked back, I didn't see Don or Eddie. I moved aside to wait for them and let the other passengers walk past me. It seemed like an eternity before Don and Eddie caught up with me. I smiled as soon as I saw Don, but he frowned as he inched closer to me.

"Why didn't you wait?" he asked with irritation. "You aren't supposed to go in front of people. Since we were way in the back, we should have waited for people who were in front to go first and then followed them, not the other way around."

"I'm sorry. I didn't know," I mumbled. "In Vietnam, it's first come, first served. One has to have fast hands and quick feet. I thought I was doing the right thing, but I'll never do it again."

I had just stepped off the airplane into a new world, and I already had to learn a new rule.

We marched along with the group of passengers toward the luggage claim, where I saw my first American worker, with a long-handled dustpan and a broom, picking up trash from the floor.

"What!" I said to Don in shocked surprise. "I thought American people didn't have to do that!"

Don was a little surprised at my reaction. "Do what? What are you talking about?" he asked.

I pointed to the tall black man carrying a dustpan and broom. "Him!" I said with wrinkled brows. "Him."

"What about him, Linda?" Don asked.

"I thought all Americans used machines to do their work and didn't have to do manual labor themselves," I said in disbelief.

"You're wrong, honey," Don explained. "We have to work hard, just like other people in this world, if we want to eat. Where do you think our food comes from if we don't work?" he asked with a smile.

"I know we have to work in my country, but . . . but . . . but I thought, uh . . . uh . . ." I couldn't explain myself. "Never mind," I said as we continued walking. It was something else I learned about America in the first few minutes after my arrival.

We reached the luggage carousel, and I helped Don grab our luggage. He told me to stand guard while he looked for help. A few minutes later, Don came back with two men pushing two oblong carriers. They helped Don load the luggage onto the carriers, and then they pushed the heavy carts out to the street.

Eddie and me, fresh off the airplane

After they loaded our suitcases onto a waiting taxi van, Don tipped them and they left. We hopped into the back seat, and Don told the driver where to go. Five-year-old Eddie was tired and went right to sleep between us.

"Where are we going?" I asked Don.

"We're going to a hotel outside of Los Angeles," he said. "We'll stay there for a few days to visit my son Steve and give you guys a chance to get to know each other."

"Sounds good to me," I said. Steve was Don's thirteen-year-old son from a previous marriage, who lived in California with his mother.

As we made our way through the countryside to Los Angeles, I looked out the window and saw many small subdivisions and rundown homes along the country road. There were rows and rows of fruit trees and vegetable fields, along with cows, pigs, and farmers, who sat on their tractors plowing the dusty fields.

From a distance, it reminded me of Vietnam. I realized American workers were no different from those in my country. They raised animals, planted vegetables, and worked in the fields just the same way we did. It was nothing like I had imagined.

The van pulled up in front of a small motel, much smaller than I had expected. In fact, it was smaller than all of the hotels we had in Saigon.

Where are all the high-rise hotels and the robots—the heaven I always dreamed of? I thought. *Where are the Americans who walk on air and build homes above the clouds? This is the same old planet earth! What a disappointment.*

The next morning, Don rented a car and drove to his ex-wife's house to pick up Steve. She had hair rollers on her head and was wearing a housecoat. She spoke with Don in her yard for a few minutes, and after a little while, a redheaded teenager came out, hugged Don, and followed him to our car. We said hello to each other as he opened the back door and entered. Steve was a sweet but shy boy; we liked each other and got along well.

While we were in Los Angeles, we visited the zoo, SeaWorld, and

Disneyland. Those days were great, and we had a wonderful time together—maybe America was heavenly after all.

One week later, Don took Steve back to his mother and returned the rental car, and we flew to Ohio, where Don's family was waiting to see us.

"I'm excited for you to meet all five of my sisters," Don said, "and maybe my brother too."

"Wow! What a big family," I said with a smile.

Don's sisters—Gavis, Betty, Dee, Phyllis, and Karen—as I saw them in 1971.

Many hours later, we landed in Dayton, Ohio. There was a long line of people waiting for their loved ones, and five cheerful, slightly chubby women were waving and smiling at us.

"Those are my sisters," Don said and ran toward them. From far behind, I saw them hug, kiss, and talk to each other. When Eddie and I caught up with Don, he introduced us to his family. They each gave Eddie and me a light hug and said, "Welcome to America."

"Thank you," I said shyly. "You all look so healthy and white," I complimented them.

They immediately stopped smiling and looked at each other and back at me. The excitement had ended. I didn't understand why my comment caused them to react that way. Don and his sisters continued to talk and laugh with each other as they walked toward the parking lot.

I held Eddie's hand and followed behind them; I wondered if they liked me.

We followed them to their mother's house. When we arrived, I saw a woman, who was about sixty or sixty-five years old, preparing food in her kitchen. When she saw us, she ran to hug Don and welcome him home.

"This is my mom," he introduced me to her. "Mom, this is my wife, Linda, and that is Eddie." We smiled and hugged each other awkwardly.

"I am glad to finally meet you," she said as she let go of me.

"I am happy to meet you as well," I said politely. She patted Eddie's head and smiled.

"Let me get back to the kitchen," she said. "I'm cooking you guys an American meal today." She walked away, and Don and I went back outside to bring in the luggage. Then we went to the kitchen to help her with dinner.

While we helped her prepare the meal, one of Don's sisters let me know in a friendly way that my comments in the airport were insulting to them. She also said my constant bowing and calling them *ma'am* was getting on their nerves and made them feel old. I felt very bad for hurting their feelings and tried to explain.

"In my country," I said with a soft smile, "it is our custom to bow to those who are older to show respect, especially in family ranking, and that is why I bowed to all of you, because you are older and deserve my respect. When I said you were white and healthy, I didn't mean to insult you; I was complimenting you," I explained. "For instance, if you are overweight, it means you are wealthy and healthy looking. If you have light skin, you are beautiful. It means you're rich and don't have to work hard out in the fields like a pauper, whose skin turns dark from the sun; we consider them ugly. Having a tan and being skinny means you are poor and unattractive. Everyone in Vietnam would love to look like you." I ended with a big smile.

"Now we understand," another sister said.

During dinner, I made a suggestion: "From now on, since our customs, culture, and traditions are so different, we need to make clear to each other what we mean by what we say." They all agreed with my suggestion, and we had a happy meal. I loved Don's big family in Ohio, but Don told me there were more of them in Indiana; I couldn't wait to meet them all.

We stayed with Don's mother in Ohio in the house his father built many years earlier. Sadly, he had passed away before I had the chance to meet him. It was not large, but it was comfortable, with three small bedrooms and one small bath, located a couple of miles from Wright Patterson Air Force Base, in Fairborn, Ohio.

While living with Don's mother, I showed her my deepest respect, as a good daughter-in-law should, according to Vietnamese culture. To her, however, I was too polite, and she told me to cut out all of the bowing and the *yes ma'ams* because it was too much for her to handle. Meanwhile, she constantly showed me how to do things the American way. One day, I was washing a pile of dishes in the sink; she came in, grabbed the sponge from my hand, and said, "Let me show you how Americans do dishes." As she demonstrated, I saw no difference from the way I had been doing it, but I just smiled and said, "I see, thank you, Mom."

By the way she acted and the way she looked at me, I didn't think she liked me much, perhaps because of my race. She often mentioned Don's ex-wife to me and told me how much fun they used to have together. She also showed me the old pictures of Don and his ex-wife hugging and kissing; it made me feel very uncomfortable and jealous.

I wished her feelings for me were as tender as mine were for her. Regardless of how she felt about me, I loved her and respected her as if she were my own mother. Of course, I understood it was hard for her to accept me, because of where I came from and the differences in our culture, customs, and traditions. Nevertheless, I still loved her, because she was my mother-in-law, and in my heart, that would never change.

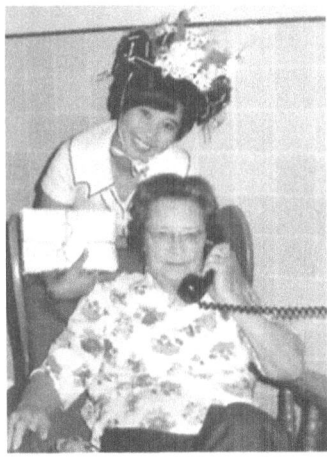

I won a prize for a self-created hat contest at Don's mom's church

AT TWENTY-THREE, I had to leave my homeland, move to a different country, learn their new rules, customs, and culture, and eat their strange food. I did not feel particularly loved by my new family, and it was not easy for me.

During those difficult times, I tried to make the best of my situation by being extra friendly and helpful, whether I felt like it or not. I always had a smile on my face. As the old saying goes, "Fake it till you make it." I did, and soon my smile was real.

I thanked my mother-in-law many times for giving birth to my husband and raising him to become a nice man. I also told her how much I appreciated her and her hard work raising him. My mother always taught me, "When you eat fruit, don't forget the person who planted the trees."

AFTER SEVERAL WEEKS in Ohio, Don came to me and gave me a big hug right before bedtime.

"Hey, baby, I want to take you around the United States to show you my whole county; what do you think?"

"Oh, that would be great," I said. "We've stayed here long enough, and I don't want to wear out our welcome."

"Well, we'll need a car, a boat, and a camper," he said.

"I know nothing about cars, boats, or campers or their cost," I said.

"Me neither," he replied. "I will check into it. It will probably take time for me to purchase all of them." We gave each other a kiss and went to bed.

Don spent a lot of time searching through the newspapers and talking to family, friends, and neighbors about what we needed. Within one week, he found a used 1968 white Plymouth Barracuda, an aluminum boat with a small outboard motor, and a large pop-up camper.

Before we set out on our journey, Don decided to take Eddie and me to Rocky Fork Lake, near Springfield, Ohio, some sixty miles away, to try out the boat. The morning of our fishing trip, Don strapped the boat on top of the car and put the motor and our fishing gear in the trunk. We had breakfast with his mother and headed for the lake. It took us almost two hours on a small country road to get there. Don didn't want to drive too fast because he was afraid the boat would fly away from the top of the car. He stopped at a tackle shop near the lake to buy supplies and bait, and then we drove to the boat dock. He pushed the boat into the water, tied it to a tree, and attached the motor. We helped each other unload our gear from the car to the boat. Eddie and I put on our life jackets and climbed aboard. I was so excited, because I loved to fish just as much as Don did, if not more.

The lake was huge, and Don didn't know which way to go. He looked around for a few seconds and turned right from where we started. He was following a small, winding canal into the wilderness, looking for a perfect fishing spot. A half hour later, he was still looking.

"Why can't we fish here?" I asked.

"Because I'm looking for a spot with a lot of trees hanging over the water, for bass fishing," he explained.

"Okay, but if you go too far, you might not find the way back," I joked.

"Don't worry!" He grinned. "I will find the way out of here." And he kept moving. A few minutes later, he announced, "I think this is a good place to fish," and he turned off the engine.

"We are in the middle of a jungle," I said. "It's so quiet I can hear my heart beat."

"Isn't it nice? We have the whole place to ourselves." Don grinned again.

"Where is everybody?" I asked. "Don't American people like to fish?"

"Yes! We do, but this is early April," he said, "and it's still too cold for fishing."

Don dropped anchor and helped Eddie with his rod and reel, explaining to him how to use it. Then he began rigging his own. I prepared mine, although I'd never used a rod and reel before. I learned by watching Don or asking him what to do.

By late evening, we had caught two full strings of fish, mostly crappie and bluegill, and a few small bass. I caught a good-sized flathead catfish, but Don told me to throw it back, because it wasn't good to eat.

We were preoccupied with our fishing and didn't pay much attention to the time or the weather, until I heard thunder. I looked up and saw the sky turning dark, with black thunderclouds rolling rapidly overhead.

"Hey, Don, we better get out of here!" I warned. "The sky looks bad, and I think we're going to be in trouble."

Don looked up and replied, "You're right. We better get out of here fast, before the storm hits us!"

Don and I reeled in our fishing lines and told Eddie to do the same. At first, Eddie didn't want to leave, but after explaining the dangers of the storm to him, he reeled in his line. Don pulled up the anchor, and I pulled up the two stringers of fish. But when Don tried to start the motor, it wouldn't start. He was worried at first, but then after a few more pulls, he began to panic.

"This stupid old motor doesn't want to start!" he yelled.

"What do you mean?" I asked. "I thought you just bought it."

"I couldn't afford a new motor, so I bought this stupid used one," he grumbled and kept on pulling.

"Oh no," I said. "How can we get out of here?"

"Don't worry," Don reassured me, "I'll get us out of here somehow." He opened the motor's top and nervously poked around at it a few times, closed it back, and tried it again, but the motor still didn't start. Minutes later, he took out a spark plug, blew on it, put it back, and pulled the rope again. That time it started, but by then it was too late. The heavy rain already poured down on us.

The rain blinded and confused Don, and he didn't know which way to go; he just kept moving, hoping he was going in the right direction.

A strong wind picked up, and heaven opened its doors to let more ice-cold water pour down on us. I took the flashlight, moved to the front of the boat, and turned it on; it was too dim. I was worried and tried to ask Don a question, but because of the wind, rain, and the boat's motor, he couldn't hear me. We were lost, but he didn't want to admit it. As the lightning and thunder grew worse, I became frightened. I grabbed Eddie and moved toward the back of the boat to sit near Don. I pulled him close to me and shielded him from the cold rain. By then, the boat had taken on a lot of water, but we didn't have anything in the boat to bail it out. I sat helplessly, watched the water level rise higher and higher, and hoped the boat wouldn't sink.

Suddenly, there was a loud, terrifying blast right over our heads, and we all screamed at once.

"I don't like the sound of that!" Don yelled. "If lightning hits the water near us, we will be electrocuted."

"Why?" I asked in a loud voice.

"Because the boat is taller than the surface of the water," he explained, "and the lightning will hit the tallest object first." I was terrified.

"I'm scared, Don! Can we get out of the boat right now?" I asked.

"I would love to," Don said. "But where?"

"Anywhere out of the water!" I said. "I just want to get away from the lightning."

Don tried to talk louder than the thunder. "When I was a kid and lived in Indiana, I was inside a house when it was hit by lightning, and I was almost killed." Just then, Eddie started to cry. I held him close to me and told him everything would be okay. He stopped crying and stuck his head close to my chest. I was so frightened that I almost cried myself.

A streak of light suddenly exploded, and a shattering boom hit right above us. Don was terrified and headed straight for a bush on the shore. He shouted for me to go to the front to grab hold of a branch so the boat wouldn't drift away. I did what I was told and held on to a branch hanging over the water and pulled the boat close to it. Don stopped the motor and jumped onto the shore. He tied the boat to a tree with a rope and then helped Eddie onto the bank. I jumped off into the darkness. I felt something wet and slippery under my feet; I just hoped it wasn't a giant snake, or worse.

We stayed right there, waiting for the storm to pass. But instead of getting better, it got worse. The heavy rain, thunder, and lightning in the dark unknown created a nerve-racking terror. Eddie cried nonstop. Don and I shielded him between us and tried to calm him down.

"Everything will be fine, son; there is nothing to be afraid of," Don said.

And I added, "The noise you hear is the sound of God playing his drum."

"I like to play drums too." Eddie said. I squeezed Don's hand to signal to him that Eddie would be fine.

And then, out of nowhere, lightning struck a tree near us; it shattered our eardrums and ignited a fire. We jumped from our seats and flew toward the boat. I climbed in with Eddie while Don untied the rope, pushed the boat away from shore, and climbed in.

He grabbed the boat motor's string, made one frantic jerk, and, thank God, it started. We got out of there as fast as the boat could take us. Don moved along the shoreline under the thunder and lightning until we saw an open swamp. He slowed down and shouted, "Do you think this would be a good place to stop?"

I shook my head and yelled back, "No! It's too wet." Don continued moving until we both saw a small, dim light up a hill. Excited, Don piloted the boat closer to the bank.

"I hope it's a recreation park's light," Don said.

"I hope so too. If it's a park, it will have a place for us to sit and wait until morning," I replied.

"Let's go up there and check it out," Don suggested.

Don steered the boat toward the shore, and once again, I grabbed hold of a limb hanging over the water and pulled the boat closer to land. I jumped off first, holding a rope to secure the boat. Don jumped out after me and took the rope from my hand to maneuver the boat. Instead of tying it to the tree, he pulled the whole boat up on the shore, with Eddie still in it. I helped Eddie out, and together, we trudged through the thick, wet mud, under the downpour, toward the light.

It was farther up the hill than we thought. Every now and then, Don and I had to pull each other out of the deep mud. "I hope the park has some cover to protect us from the rain," I said.

"I'm afraid not," Don replied. "It's not a park. I can see it's just a light on a pole in someone's backyard."

"Well, I hope they will let us in," I said. Eddie did not like what was going on, and he asked to go home.

"No, we can't go home yet," I said.

"Why?" he asked.

"Because we can't find our car," I told him.

We approached the back of a house, and Don knocked on the door. An elderly couple came to the door. They both frowned as they opened it. "What on earth?" the woman exclaimed, before we had a chance to say anything.

"What are you people doing here?" the man added as he stepped aside and motioned for us to come in.

"We're too muddy," I said. "I'm afraid we will mess up your house."

"Come in! This is the mudroom; you can't mess it up," the woman said with a smile.

The man cocked his head to one side, signaling for us to come in. Before we stepped farther, we gave them a quick explanation of what happened. They both felt sorry for us.

"You better come inside quick!" the man urged. "If my two Great Danes see you, they might not hurt the child, but they would tear you two apart."

I didn't wait for him to finish his words and crammed into the mudroom; I was afraid of big dogs.

The man continued, "They were trained to be guard dogs, but because of the thunderstorm, they must have hidden in the basement." He shook his head. "You people were lucky tonight."

"Thank you for opening your door," Don said. "We really appreciate your kindness."

"Yes, thanks to both of you so much," I added.

"You are welcome," they both said.

"Stay right where you are. I will be right back," the lady said, and she left the room for a few minutes while we took off our muddy shoes. She came back with three pairs of pajamas and handed them to us.

"Luckily, I have a grandson who's about your boy's size," she said. "But I think ours are too big for you two," she continued. "Anyway, they will keep you both warm."

"Thank you! Thank you!" Don and I repeated.

"After you guys are done with the shower, give me your wet clothes, and I will put them in the washer and dryer so you can wear them dry and clean in the morning." She smiled. Don and I listened and nodded our heads. "Now, all of you get washed off. There is the shower; go ahead and use it," she said and pointed her finger to the corner; they both walked away, leaving us alone in the mudroom.

We all showered and then changed into the pajamas she gave us. The clothes fit Don and Eddie, but mine were large enough to swallow me whole; we were so grateful to have them, though, and thanked God for our generous hosts.

After our shower, the lady led us to a guest room and told us to sleep well and she would take care of our dirty clothes. We thanked her again and jumped into a soft bed; I didn't remember much after that.

A knock on the door woke me. As my eyes opened, I smelled bacon and eggs cooking. "Yes," I answered as I bolted toward the door and opened it.

"It's breakfast time," she announced with a big smile.

"Thank you so very much," I said with an early morning grin.

"Don't mention it," she replied. "Just wake your husband and child and come to the dining table."

"Okay, I will, and thank you again," I replied as she walked away. I turned around and saw Don already sitting up with his feet on the floor and a sleepy smile. I looked at Eddie and saw him sitting up and rubbing his eyes, trying to get them opened.

We went to the bathroom and washed our faces before we joined them.

As soon as we stepped into the breakfast nook, we were startled, held our breath, and stepped back at once; two huge Great Danes charged toward us from under the table. They stopped in their tracks when the man shouted "No!" I was about to wet my pants—actually, the owner's pants.

Eddie was scared and started to cry, but the man put his finger up to his lips and signaled for Eddie to hush and waved to Eddie to come to him. Eddie obeyed and walked slowly toward the old man. While the man kept an eye on his dogs he instructed us to approach the table.

"You two, walk slowly to the table, but do not make eye contact with my dogs. They might still attack, if they feel challenged," he warned. "I will try to introduce you to them." The man stopped talking to us and started talking to the dogs while Don and I inched nearer the chairs and sat down. I glanced at the dogs nervously and saw that one of them was light brown and the other was darker; both were taller than Eddie and longer than me.

"Oh my God," I murmured. "They are so big! I have never seen dogs like that in my life. They look more like small cows than dogs." Don and I sat next to each other at the table and were still shaking. The owner turned to Eddie and saw that tears still damped his face.

"Oh, don't cry," the owner said. "You can pet them if you want, but I don't recommend your dad do so."

While we ate, we shared our stories. Don told them about his time in the military and how we met and married. In turn, the man told us about his military experiences in Korea and how he met and married his wife. I shared my experiences about being a new girl in a new country and the differences in culture, customs, rules, family life, and general misunderstandings; we all had a good laugh. After breakfast, we excused ourselves and told them we needed to go home.

"Thank you both for your kindness and generosity. We do appreciate it," Don said.

"Yes! Thanks so much for your hospitality," I said. "We hope someday we can return the favor."

After saying goodbye and changing into our clean clothes, we walked toward the lake. Instead of wading through the muddy swamp, we found a dryer path. Through the tall king grass, I could see our boat not far away.

"If we had only come a few yards farther last night, we wouldn't have to walk through the mud."

"I agree," Don said. "But remember, it was dark, and we couldn't even see our hands, much less a few yards ahead." He held his hand out to stop me from walking farther and said. "Stay where you are, and let me go through the mud to get our boat so you guys won't have to."

"Aww! You are so nice." I smiled. "Thanks for being so thoughtful." He grinned and walked away to my left; I glanced to my right and saw a familiar boat dock on the other side of the lake. I squinted my eyes, looked closer, and realized it was our boat dock. I saw our white barracuda at the landing and couldn't wait to tell Don.

Don maneuvered the boat back toward us, and when he was within earshot, I yelled, "Look! Look where we are!" I pointed to the other side of the lake. "We're so close to our car!"

His eyes followed my pointing finger, but he couldn't hear me over the sound of the motor. When he turned it off, I repeated myself. Don shook his head and said, "With our luck, I'm not surprised."

I helped Eddie onto the boat first and then jumped onboard. Don started the motor and pushed it away from the bank. Those two Great

Danes appeared from nowhere and charged towards us. They were barking and growling like crazy.

"Oh my God! I hope they don't jump into the water and swim after us," I said.

"I don't think they can swim," Don said. "The owners must have kept them inside until they heard our boat's motor running; they must have thought we were gone and let their dogs loose."

"Thank God we were in the boat and off the shore," I said.

I looked down at my feet and saw the fish we caught the previous day and wondered what to do with them.

"These fish have been dead for too long. I'm afraid they might be spoiled. Why don't we throw them away and catch fresh ones?" I suggested.

"Yep! I think you're right about the fish," Don agreed. "Let's stay a little longer to catch fresh fish."

I took the fish off the stringers and threw them one by one back into the lake. I looked at the floating dead fish and thought, *What a waste.*

Don steered the boat across the water and came within a few yards of the dock. He threw out the anchor, and we fished right in front of it; we didn't want to take another chance on getting lost. The fish weren't biting, so we decided to get out of the boat and fish along the bank. Hours later, we had caught another two stringers full of fresh fish and were ready to go home. After loading up our fishing gear and the boat, Don drove to a restaurant for dinner, and then we returned to his mother's house that evening.

As we walked into the door, we were surprised to see the house full of people, including Don's two big sisters. They were all sitting in the living room talking. When they saw us, they all jumped to their feet and ran toward us. At first, they all smiled and seemed relieved to see us, but then Don's mother looked upset.

"Where on earth have you been?" Gay, Don's oldest sister, asked.

"Why didn't you call us?" Don's mother scolded.

Before Don and I had the chance to answer, Phyllis, another sister, asked, "Where did you stay last night? We were worried sick about you three."

Don and I were confused. *What did we do wrong?* I thought to myself. *Why is everyone acting happy to see us and angry and upset at the same time? I just don't understand these American people.*

"You put us through a sleepless night last night," Gay grumbled. "We were all worried about you. We heard that the weather turned bad where you went fishing, and when you guys didn't come home, we called the police and reported you missing. They sent out a search team to look for you, but the weather was too bad, and they had to give up after midnight. They just called us and told us that they still couldn't find the boat with two people and a young child on board."

She stopped to catch her breath, and before she continued, I said, "The reason they didn't see three people on the boat was because we were fishing on the shoreline."

"We stayed up all last night," Gay said, "hoping and praying to hear some good news. Thank God you guys came home safe."

I realized we made a big mistake by not calling them or coming home earlier. I wished we had borrowed the phone and called them the night before, but we hadn't thought about it. We thanked them for their concern, apologized for our thoughtlessness, and went to the kitchen with our fish. Don waited for everyone to go home, wrapped all the stiff dead fish in newspapers, and put them in the refrigerator. We washed up and went to bed. The next morning, I helped Don clean and cook the fish. We invited those who were at the house the night before to come back and join us for the fish fry.

THE NEXT DAY, we set out on our journey. We packed our belongings in the Barracuda, strapped the aluminum boat on top, and hooked our pop-up camper to the trailer hitch. We said goodbye to Don's family, and he began backing out of the driveway.

"Where are we going?" I asked Don.

"I haven't decided yet," he replied. "I would like to take you to Canada, but I'm afraid it's still too cold up there. So I think I'll take you south to Florida, where it's warm and sunny," he said as he turned the wheel.

A couple of hours later, we passed Cincinnati and crossed the Ohio River. I saw a sign that said, "Welcome to Kentucky." Don turned to me, grinned, and said, "Welcome to Kentucky, baby!"

"Thanks," I replied. "Doesn't this state store all of America's gold?" I asked.

"Yes," he answered in surprise. "And how do you know that?"

"My brother Den told me," I said. "He was assigned to Fort Knox, Kentucky, while he was here for military training."

"That's right, I forgot," Don said.

Don drove us through the hills of Kentucky on Interstate 75. I looked at the countryside and thought to myself, *This is a large and beautiful country but nothing like the heaven that I dreamed about. This is the same planet Earth, just a different part of it. We are all alike, just humans, with red blood underneath all of our different colored skins. Americans all work, eat, sleep, and go to the bathroom the same way Vietnamese do. What a letdown.*

Don turned into a nice overlook rest stop along the freeway. We got out and stretched. "Where are we?" I asked.

"I'm not sure," Don smiled, "but I do know we are somewhere in the rolling hills of Kentucky."

Three Wanderers, 1971

A few minutes later, we got back in our car and continued into the mountain range. I saw a big sign that read, "Welcome to Tennessee."

Don again turned to me, smiled, and said, "Welcome to Tennessee, baby."

"Thanks," I said with a smile.

"We've passed two state signs. How about that?" Don said.

"Two states down," I said, smiling. "And forty-eight more to go."

"Yes, baby, and we'll get there sooner or later." He smiled. "Actually, we only have forty-six more to go. You forget we've been to California and Ohio?"

"Yep, I forgot." I smiled, looked out through the windshield, and watched the misty clouds hovering above the mountain range.

"Is that beautiful or what?" Don asked. "I love the mountains, especially the Smokey Mountains."

"I like the mountains too," I commented. "It reminds me of my childhood. I often went up in the mountains with a bunch of girls to collect wood for cooking. When the heat was too bad, we went to a little waterfall and waded in a small pool." I smiled as I remembered us chasing each other, naked, around a cool mountain pool. I continued, "Now that I don't have to do that anymore, the mountains seem more beautiful."

Don hesitated and then said, "How would you like to stay here for a while, before we go to Florida?"

"Sure, why not?" I replied. "It looks beautiful here."

"Will you help me keep an eye out for a campground sign?" Don asked.

"I sure will. I just hope we find a campground soon, because I like it here," I said.

A few miles down the road, I pointed to a sign; it read, "Douglas Lake Campground—Five Miles Ahead."

"That sounds perfect!" I exclaimed.

Don turned off the freeway and followed an unpaved road to the campground nestled right on a magnificent lake. He parked at the first building he turned into and told Eddie and me to stay in the car while he went inside to register. He came back and drove us to the campsite, just ten feet from the waterline—exactly what we both wanted. We couldn't wait to get out of the car and explore.

Before setting up our camper, we walked around the water's edge, enjoying our new temporary home. The lake was beautiful, and the air was fresh and full of the aroma of honeysuckle. I took a deep breath and inhaled the crisp, clean air into my lungs.

"I never want to leave this place," I said.

"I want to stay here forever myself," Don responded. "Let's stay here as long as we can, okay?"

"I don't see why not," I said. A few minutes later, we walked back to our camper.

Don prepared to set up our tiny home, and when he opened the camper, it looked much larger inside. It had two beds, one on each end, a small sitting area, and a kitchen with a little stove and a small refrigerator in the middle. Even though it didn't have a bathroom, it was still comfortable and cute.

I opened three cans of noodle soup, poured them into a cheap aluminum pan, warmed them up on a tiny stove, divided them into three plastic bowls, and served them for dinner.

The campfire warming us on a cold April night

It was my first dinner from a can, and I didn't know what to make of it, except I knew I didn't care for it; it tasted very different from the fresh foods I was used to. After dinner, Eddie went outside and chased lightning bugs; I cleaned dishes, and then Don helped me tidy the camper.

"I need to go pee," I said. "Do you know where the bathroom is?"

"Over there, honey," Don said as he pointed to a square cement building and added, "We need to get our toilet articles so we can take a shower and brush our teeth too."

"Okay, but I need to go really bad," I said with a painful look on my face. I grabbed my bathroom articles, ran toward a dull-grey cement block building, and let Don and Eddie run behind me. We split into two groups; Eddie went with Don to the men's side, while I entered the women's side. I pushed the old broken door open and saw a line of dirty, rusty sinks mounted on the wall. I looked to the opposite side and saw a few rectangular, rotted wood partitions, used to divide the toilets from the showers. I took a closer look at the rough cement floor and noticed it was covered with all kinds of dead insects. After using the toilet, I went over to the sink to wash my hands. I turned on the faucet, but it didn't work. I tried the second sink, but the faucet was loose from its base. The third one did not work either. Finally, I found one that did. While brushing my teeth, I fought with flying bugs, which constantly tried to land on my head. I grew tired of fighting them and returned to the camper without a shower. I kissed Don and Eddie goodnight, but instead of going to sleep, I just lay there, listening to the sounds of crickets and frogs until I dozed off into my dreamland.

The next morning, I made Spam sandwiches for breakfast, and then we drove off to sightsee. Later, we returned to our camper and had more canned food for lunch. We used the bathroom, and then we were on our way again. When we came back to our camper, we ate more canned food, took a quick shower, and before we went to bed, Don announced, "I'm going to get up early tomorrow morning to go fishing. Do you want to come with me?"

"I might," I replied, "but I have to see how Eddie feels first. If he's too tired, I'll stay home with him and rearrange our little nest."

"If you don't go, would you mind if I do?" Don asked. "I won't stay out long; I might even come back before sunrise."

I smiled and said, "Of course I don't mind. Just come back with lots of fish, because I'm already tired of eating canned food." We gave each other a good night kiss and went to sleep.

I woke up to a knock at the door. When I opened it, Don was outside with a huge, happy grin on his face. "Come out here to the boat," Don said. "I want to show you the fish I caught; it is big!" It was still dark inside the camper, and I had to turn the light on to find my sandals.

As we walked toward the lake, Don said, "I caught a carp, and it must weigh at least thirty pounds. We don't eat carp in this country, but I just wanted to show it to you before I throw it back." I didn't say anything because I didn't know what a carp was, until I looked in the boat and saw the fish.

"Oh my God!" I screamed. "It's huge! You better keep this fish, because if you throw it back," I threatened, "you'll have to jump in the water to get it out. People in this country might not eat carp, but in ours, it is a delicacy. I'll show you how to clean and cook it," I said with confidence.

Don was a little surprised, but he didn't argue with me. I helped him carry the giant carp to the picnic table. Once the fish was on the table, it looked even bigger. I realized, with some apprehension, that I had to kill it and cut it up.

"How are you going to clean it?" Don asked.

"Well! I'm hoping you will help me," I said.

"I'll help you clean it, but I've never cleaned a carp before," he said.

"I don't mind cleaning it myself, but we don't have a knife big enough, and I'm afraid I can't chop its head off with a butter knife," I explained.

"Well, do you want me to throw it back?" Don asked.

"Oh, no! I don't want to throw it away, I will use our kitchen knife and do my best," I said.

Don with his huge carp

Since I made such a big deal out of the fish, I had to figure out a way to clean it. I ran back to the camper, grabbed a four-inch knife, the sharpest thing we had, and returned to the picnic table. I saw Don holding on to the fish, trying to keep it from jumping off the table.

"Hey, Don," I asked, "do you know how to cut off the fish's head?"

"I'm sorry. I don't have the slightest idea—a small fish, yes, but not one this big!" Don said with a headshake and a frown.

"Oh well," I said, "let me try to cut him up, but you'll have to help me hold him down."

"I understand!" Don said.

I held the small knife in my right hand and tried to help Don move the fish around with my left. Together, we turned the heavy, slimy fish around and around and over and over, trying to look for the right place to cut. The more we turned him, the heavier he became.

My long fingernails were not helping any. If anything, it was much harder to hold the slimy fish. Although I am a good cook, I am not good at killing animals. In fact, I had never killed anything larger than a crab or a little grasshopper for food before. In Vietnam, the slaughterhouse and the vendors in the supermarkets prepared most of the meat we ate.

His eyes were still wide open and staring at me, and his mouth was moving as if he were trying to beg me for help. I couldn't stand to look into his eyes anymore, so I ran inside and grabbed a stack of newspapers to cover the fish's head. I told Don to hold the paper in place as I gathered all my nerve. With both hands on the tiny knife, I closed my eyes and jabbed it into the fish. The small knife, however, wouldn't penetrate its tough scales. But it must have felt the pain because it started to jump up and down as I continued to stab it.

"Oh my God, oh my God," I said to myself each time I stabbed the fish. *I am a murderer!* I thought. *But I can't stop now! I can't show Don my weakness or fear.*

It didn't matter how hard or how many times I stabbed the fish, its tough quarter-sized scales didn't let the flimsy little knife penetrate its flesh. Instead, the knife only acted as a tickler and made the fish jump even more. I stopped poking at it for a few seconds to catch my breath; I looked to Don for help, but he just stood there, holding the fish's head, looking helpless.

"Let me try it," Don said as he took the knife from me and started poking all over the fish. It jumped hard and almost jumped off the table. I watched Don for a few seconds but couldn't take it anymore. I held out my hand and said, "Give me back the knife, please!"

With the knife, I began removing its scales one at a time, starting at its tail, and it worked. I managed to remove a few scales and began to cut into its soft flesh. I pulled off bite-sized pieces of meat, one at a time, but each time I cut into a nerve, I felt its body jerk.

"Oh my God; you poor fish!" I said out loud. I wanted to stop, but I was too proud. So I continued to torture the fish by cutting meat from both sides of his tail. Eddie was up and watched the whole thing in horror. He made faces and let out a little noise each time I sank the knife into the fish.

When I thought I had enough meat for a meal, I told Don to put the remaining three-fourths of the fish in the garbage can, hoping it would die in peace. I took the meat inside to prepare our lunch. Within ten or fifteen minutes, the meat was cooked and lunch was on the table.

"This is the best sautéed fish I ever put in my mouth!" Don exclaimed. "It's beyond delicious! I'm so glad I didn't throw it back, and from now on I will keep everything I catch, even alligators, because I believe you can cook them too." We laughed.

"But the next time, you have to kill the victim yourself; I can't do that again," I said, smiling. Although the fish tasted good, I still felt guilty for killing him.

After the meal, I cleaned up and took the paper bag full of trash out to the garbage can. When I opened the lid, I saw the newspaper moving. Out of curiosity, I removed the paper, which covered the fish head; to my surprise, its eyes were still open, and its mouth moved.

"Oh . . . my . . . God! Oh my God! Oh my God!" I yelled as I threw the lid down on the ground. "The fish! The fish! Hey, Don! The fish is still alive!" I ran back to the camper with the bag of garbage still in my hand.

Don heard the commotion and ran to meet me at the doorstep. "What's going on, Linda?" He asked.

"Don, Don, Don!!!" I was in shock and was about to faint. "The fish," I said, "the fish is still gasping for air, and it's still alive!"

"What?" Don asked with his jaw wide open, and he rushed toward the garbage can.

"The fish's mouth is still moving," I said as I followed him. "His eyes are still open and were staring at me." I continued, "Oh my God, Don! Do something!" I was shaking and was about to cry. I felt bad and guilty before we ate the fish, but after I saw him, I was horrified.

Don opened the garbage can, looked inside, raised his eyes, and dropped his jaw in amazement. "Well, we can't eat fish fresher than that!" He said, laughing. "Half of it is in our stomach, and the other half still alive." He laughed again.

"Don! I don't think that's funny," I said as I bent over, held on to my stomach, and gagged. "I feel sick in my stomach right now, and I'm about to throw up, thinking about what you just said," I cried, and Don laughed harder. "Please! Shut up, Don! Please!"

"I am sorry," he said.

"Let's take him out of the garbage can and put him back in the water," I suggested, "where he can die in his own element. Who knows, he might just survive with part of his tail missing."

"Okay," he agreed, "let's do it. I hope you're right."

We took the carp out of the trashcan and carried him back to the water. The fish tried to swim for a couple seconds, but without a tail, it quickly sank to the bottom. I felt so bad, sad, and guilty for torturing and destroying an innocent life. I went back to the camper with tears pooling in my eyes. I looked at the leftover fish in the sauté pan. *I can't eat this anymore*, I thought. *I have to throw this away.* However, being conservative with food, I couldn't bring myself to do it.

Instead, I carried the pan of cooked fish to a much larger and fancier camper next to ours. I knocked on the door, and all four of the middle-aged occupants, two men and two women, came to the door. I looked at them, smiled, and asked, "Do you eat fish?" I showed them the leftovers of brown sugar–glazed sautéed fish.

"Umm, looks yummy," one said.

"Let's try it," another one said. I handed the pan to one of them and instructed, "You can warm it up on the stove for a few minutes before eating. It will taste better hot. You can give the pan back to me later, when you're finished."

"Thanks!" they all said.

I left feeling better, because I didn't waste all of the good food.

That afternoon, one of the women brought back the pan and said, "That was the best fish I have ever eaten in my whole life! It was so fresh and delicious. We all loved it. Thanks again." She continued, "Oh, if you have the time, can you give me the recipe?" she asked.

"I'll try," I replied, "but I never cook with a recipe. I'm glad you guys liked the carp."

"What! That was carp?" she responded in shock. "I didn't think carp were edible. I never heard of anyone ever eating them before. I'll have to go back and tell my friends about this." And she ran back to her camper.

I stood at the door, watched her, and thought to myself, *It was very fresh; in fact, half of it was still alive and swimming in the lake while you were eating its tail. And by the way, you're welcome.* I smiled, took the pan inside, and closed the door.

Chapter 4

HEAVY LOAD

DON AND I liked the Smokey Mountains and the lake so much that instead of going on to Florida, we decided to stay and look for a permanent home. We bought a newspaper and looked for a three-bedroom house in the area, but found none suitable. Don suggested we should look for some land, buy a mobile home, and park it there; when we moved, we could take our home with us. I gave him a very confused look.

"What kind of home are you talking about? How could you move a big heavy home with you?" I asked.

Don smiled and replied, "It's a home that's built on wheels."

"This I'll have to see," I said.

"Sure, baby!" Don was happy to show me something I had never seen before.

I put things away, and Don went to the lake to pull the boat out of the water. When he came back, we locked up the camper and took off.

"Do you know where we're going, Don?"

"Of course I do. We're going to Knoxville, Tennessee." He smiled cheerfully. "Right before we left, I asked around and was told they have mobile homes there."

"How far is Knoxville from Florida, where we planned to go?"

"Quite a way," Don replied.

"Oh well," I sighed, "we'll get to Florida someday, I guess."

"We will, baby. I assure you, we will," Don promised.

An hour or two later, Don pulled into a large parking lot filled with lines and lines of huge elongated boxes.

"Here we are, baby," Don announced.

I was looking around for a home with a normal frame and gabled roof but saw none.

"Where are the homes, Don?"

"Right there," he said as he pointed to some metal boxes.

I was surprised and a little disappointed.

"Now I see how they can be moved," I said. "These are boxes on wheels, not homes on wheels."

As we got out of the car and walked toward the first box, a salesman caught up with us and opened the door to one of the mobile homes and invited us in. I was surprised by how it looked inside; it actually looked larger and nicer than most real homes I saw in Ohio. The room was painted a light shade of green, had wall-to-wall carpeting, and was filled with beautiful furniture. It had two bedrooms, one on each end, each with their own bath. There was a nice-sized living room, dining room, and a large kitchen, with a connecting laundry room in between. After a few days in the small camper, the mobile home looked enormous, and I really liked it.

The salesman took us around and showed us several more homes and told us how much each of them cost. Without hesitation, we decided to take the best, most expensive one—the very first one we had laid eyes on. We made financial arrangements and used most of our life savings to pay for it in cash.

"Now we own a home, but where can we buy the land to park it?" I asked Don.

"We'll have to find it," Don said, "and bring our home to it."

"And where can we find a piece of land?"

"I don't know yet, but I'll talk to the salesman and ask him to connect us to a realtor."

The salesman called a realtor friend of his, and a half hour later, he showed up. He took us to a small town, fifteen miles north of Knoxville, and showed us a wooded property near the top of a mountain. From the property, we could see miles and miles of rolling hills. Don loved it. When we asked the realtor about the size of the property, he told us it was more than three acres. We took his word and didn't survey it. Later, we made financial arrangements and paid for it in full. Unfortunately, the three-plus acres we paid for turned out to be just a little more than one acre, but it was too late. We had made a mistake we had to live with.

There were even bigger problems: the land had no electricity, no water, no sewage, and no driveway connecting it to the road. We searched for days and found a construction company who could level a spot big enough for our home site and construct an entry driveway from the main road to the trailer.

Next, we hired another company to install electricity, water, and a septic tank. Connecting electricity was no problem. Having the water run uphill was not an easy task, but digging a septic tank into the rock was a nightmare. It took the construction company many days and a lot of broken equipment just to dig a hole big enough for the septic tank to fit in. At one point, the workmen gave up and threatened to quit. Don and I had to beg them, offering them more money. Reluctantly, they agreed and continued digging. Days turned into weeks and then months.

The project took us so long the company where we purchased our trailer asked us to pay rent for parking in their space. While waiting for the workmen to finish their projects, Don and I purchased necessities for our new home. The long wait, however, caused tension between us, and we fought and argued with each other over the smallest things. Our dream vacation was turning into a nightmare. I wished we had kept on going to Florida instead.

Finally, the land was cleared, the water pipes and septic tank were installed, and the driveway was finished. The only thing left was to bring our mobile home up to our well-prepared land. We hired a moving company; they brought over several bulldozers and a tall crane. I watched them maneuver our home uphill with extreme skill, which was not easy. At times, I thought we were going to have a runaway home, but thank God, we made it.

After all of the chaos settled down, I asked myself, "Now what?" Don was thirty-four years old, born and raised in America, and one of the youngest of seven siblings. He had married when he just turned seventeen, and he'd joined the air force months later. He knew very little outside of his military life. On the other hand, I was twenty-three, a foreigner, who spoke very little English, and had some street smarts, but I knew nothing about this new country, which was why many mistakes were made.

The first day in our trailer, I cooked three bags of instant noodle soup, on a brand-new stove, and sat three bowls of hot soup on the brand-new dinner table for our first meal.

"Here we are, in our beautiful home, on a perfectly scenic property," I said as I looked at Don while we were eating. "What are we going to do from here? Since all of our savings are tied up in this place," I sighed, "we have very little left. I don't know how we are going to eat and buy necessities." Don frowned and thought about it for a few seconds, as if he had never thought of it before.

"Well, I guess I'll have to look for a job."

"What kind of job will you be able to find in this place? Cutting wood? But where can you even find a job just to cut wood?" I asked sarcastically.

"I don't know," he replied. "I have to try something if we want to eat." Then his eyes lit up. "I'll go to the store and get a newspaper right now. There should be a lot of jobs advertised, and I'm sure I'll find one." He gave me a kiss, went outside, got into our car, and disappeared. Hours later, he came back with a bag of canned food and a stack of newspapers. While he looked for a job, I tidied up. After everything was in place, I started our dinner. I opened several cans of soup, poured them into a cheap aluminum pan, and sat it on the stove. While waiting for the food to heat up, I turned to Don.

"I'm so tired of eating canned food," I grumbled. "My dream was to come to America to eat different foods—the kind I don't have to cook. But after all of the instant TV dinners, bags, boxes, and canned food over the past few months, I wish I had fresh food, even if I had to cook it myself. Now, as I think about all of those fresh weeds and bugs I used to eat when I was younger, they sound good to me." I stopped talking to catch my breath and forced myself to smile. I felt bad for nagging, walked over to where Don sat, and gave him a peck on his cheek. He looked up at me and smiled.

"Right now, I wish I could have some of those weeds and bugs myself," he said.

EDDIE WAS IN the first grade, and it was hard on him because of his limited English. After he was forced to transfer to another school because of segregation, it was even more difficult for him. Although he struggled with his language, he seemed happy and loved the mountains, where there was plenty of room to play with friends.

Don's son Steve came to stay with us during the summer school break that year. Although we didn't have money, Don saved as much as he could to buy Steve a motorized mini dirt bike. Steve loved it, and he spent entire days driving up and down the mountain. I could hear his bike motor from miles away, and sometimes, I heard him crash as well. When he came home with scrapes, cuts, and bruises, I always helped him clean up his wounds and told him to be more careful the next time. I was only ten years older than he was, and our relationship was like a big sister to a younger brother. He had just turned fourteen, and I knew it would be four more years before Don finished paying for his child support. Lucky for us, Don stopped paying his ex-wife's alimony, since she had remarried. Sometimes, it was hard for us to come up with Steve's child support money, but I didn't mind, because I loved Steve. He was a sweet boy.

Since I was home doing nothing, I bought two toy poodle puppies; I intended to breed them to make money. Raising the two puppies was fun but harder than I expected, because of the cost of veterinarian bills and dog food. So instead of raising them for profit, we just kept them for pets.

IN AUGUST OF 1971, I discovered I was pregnant, and Don still did not have a job. We both worried about money but were happy to have a baby. We both wanted a baby, and I went through a lot of harsh medical treatment to be able to get pregnant.

When I was in Vietnam, a doctor told me my chances of getting pregnant were small. He said I had a cold uterus, and if I wanted to get pregnant, I needed to warm it up with an electrical shock. I took his advice and did as he suggested. I went to his office every day, two hours each day, five days a week, for six months to get treatment. Each time I went there, the doctor made me lie on a wooden bench and endure light shocks from a wand inserted deep in my womb. The treatment was horrible; it was hot, with a light tingling shock, and it itched. At the time, I wondered if I could take a minute more of it, but the vision of a beautiful baby came to mind, and I continued the unpleasant treatment. When I discovered I was pregnant, it was worth every minute of suffering in the doctor's office.

We desperately needed money for food and for the new baby, so I wrote to my family in Vietnam to ask them for help. I told them to sell the property we owned, which would provide plenty of money for us to live on with our newborn child while Don continued his search for a job.

My mother wrote back that the house wasn't worth much because of the bad economy at the time. She wanted to wait until I came home, and then I could sell it myself. I think my mother wanted to hold on to the property, hoping it would force me to return to Vietnam. I knew she hated the thought of me being so far away from her. I didn't blame her for wanting to hold on to the property; that meant she was holding on to me.

She didn't know how desperate my family was, and I didn't want her to know the truth about how my life had turned out to be in what was supposed to be my dreamland. I didn't want her to worry about me. Furthermore, I wanted Mother and the rest of the people in my country to think there was no hunger in the United States, just as I once thought.

We were so desperate that we had to sell our camper, pawn our wedding rings, and buy food at a discount grocery store. To make ends meet, I stocked up on a lot of chicken backs, necks, and feet because they were the cheapest. To me, they were also the tastiest parts of the chicken, so I didn't mind.

I was six months pregnant when Don took Eddie and me to go drift fishing, even though it was bitter cold. We ate everything we caught, regardless of its size or species. To make sure we caught enough to eat, Don and I often used more than one rod each.

We were on the boat as it drifted with the current, and for hours, nothing bit. "I need to pee," Don announced with a pained expression.

We were used to relieving ourselves from the side of the boat, and I said, "Go ahead. I'll watch your rod and reel for you." He looked around and saw no one nearby. He felt confident enough to unzip his pants and begin peeing.

Suddenly, his fishing rod bent, and it looked as though he had a big fish pulling on it. But before I could help him, both of my rods bent too. I told Eddie to hurry up, reel in his line, and help me with one of mine. While Eddie reeled in one of my rods, I reeled in my other one. I glanced at Don and saw him with both of his rods in his hands, one with a fish on it.

"Help me, Linda, help me!" he yelled. "I think we drifted into a school of fish!"

"I know we did, but I can't help you!" I yelled back as I continued reeling mine in. "I have fish on both of my rods as well, and Eddie is helping me right now."

"I can't hold on to the rod while I am peeing!" he shouted.

"I am sorry, but the way the fish are biting, you should be glad you don't have one on your other rod too," I joked.

"Thanks a lot, Linda!" Don replied. I could tell by his expression that he didn't think my joke was funny. I think he was irritated because he had to control both of his rods at the same time.

We were busy concentrating on the fish and didn't realize our boat had drifted farther down the river, close to a bank where dozens of people were fishing, until they began applauding Don's fishing techniques. I believed Don was embarrassed. I just hoped he zipped up his pants.

FINALLY, DON FOUND a job working for Jim Robbins Seat Belt Company as a personnel manager. He had to work hard every day and often worked overtime without extra pay. Most of the time, he went to work before I woke up and came home after I went to bed. I was pregnant, stuck at home on top of a mountain, with no money, food, or transportation and nothing to do. The only friend I had was an old woman, who lived down the street. She was sweet, but she was a very private person and didn't care much for company, so I seldom visited her. I tried to grow vegetables, but nothing grew on rocks. And the few plants that did sprout were killed by the cold weather and lack of water. I wished we had kept on going to Florida, where the weather was sunny and warm.

During that time, when I had too much time on my hands, I would translate my diary from Vietnamese to English. It became my obsession. English is not my native language, and it was not easy for me to express myself in English the way I did in my diary. As I translated my thoughts and my feelings, I hoped and dreamed that one day my work would become a book. I wanted nothing more than to share my story with the world.

Although Don had a job, the conditions were not to his liking, and he started drinking again. The situation took a heavy toll on our marriage; we fought more than we talked. During one of our arguments, I asked Don to let me go back to Vietnam.

"I can't take this place anymore," I cried. "I want to go back to my own country, where I can have good food and can be surrounded by friends and family."

Don was surprised at my request at first, but then he shouted, "Go right ahead!"

"I will!" I yelled back. "But I need an airline ticket, and you will have to buy it for me."

He snapped, "I'll do it as soon as I have enough money!" Then he went back to his bottle. I went back to the bedroom and cried.

I was sure Don got tired of listening to an unhappy pregnant woman nagging and complaining. I didn't blame him for finding comfort in a bottle, pills, and cigarettes. I felt sorry for both of us and just wished I had enough money to go back to Vietnam.

The month of January brought heavy snow and freezing rain almost daily. I felt lonely and trapped. Besides working on my diary, I had nothing else to do, so I decided to make a bird trap to entertain myself. I looked around the house and gathered all the equipment I needed: chicken wire, rocks, sticks, and twine. I was ready.

I bent a large piece of regular chicken wire into a funnel shape, about four feet tall and three feet in diameter at the bottom. I put the large end on the ground and weighted it down by tying rocks around the rim. Next, I used a foot-long stick to push one side up, to make an entrance for the trap. Then I tied about fifty feet of string on to the bottom of the stick. I led the long string over the porch, through a partly open back door, and into the house.

I used cooked rice and crackers as bait and placed it under the funnel. I sat inside and watched the trap through the sliding glass door. When I saw birds go deep inside the funnel to eat the bait, I pulled the string, the stick fell, and the birds were trapped inside. They tried to get out by flying up toward the small end of the funnel and were stuck. In normal circumstances, I would have kept them for pets. But instead, I snapped their necks and put them in a brown paper grocery bag and stored them in the refrigerator. When I had a dozen or two, I cooked them. They were delicious marinated in lemon grass, ginger, hot pepper, and soy sauce and then sautéed in a wok and served with rice.

I saved all of the beautiful blue, red, yellow, and brown feathers for decorations. Each time I looked at those feathers, I felt guilty, but I also felt justified; our survival came before theirs.

ON MARCH 5, 1972, before I had a chance to fly home, our daughter was born. I named her Brenda, which sounds like my name, Linda. But Don wanted to name her after Saint Teresa, so we did, and we used Brenda for her middle name. We hoped Saint Teresa would come to help us with our problems, and she did. Teresa brought joy and happiness to both of us. We loved her more than our own lives. I catered to her every wish and was too busy to feel sorry for myself; the desire to go back to Vietnam disappeared.

Eddie, Don, and me with one-week-old Teresa

Don worked hard but was paid very little. The money he did make paid for Steve's child support, and with what was left, he paid for his alcohol, pills, and cigarettes. So I continued to trap birds and buy the cheapest food in the grocery store. I tried to grow vegetables, but it was so much work with little reward. Still, I felt lucky to have something to do to keep me occupied.

Besides breastfeeding Teresa, I also made baby food for her. I believed it was tastier, cost less, and was better for her. I saved the few vegetables that grew between the rocks and used them just for her, because they grew without pesticides or chemicals. I also used fruit and meat to make her baby food. I cooked chicken, pork, or beef, then added celery, carrots, green beans, and potatoes. When everything was soft and tender, I pureed it by hand into a paste-like consistency, added a little salt and pepper, and stored it in small containers. I kept them in the freezer or refrigerator until needed. When they were almost gone, I started the same process over, usually once a week. Teresa was a very fussy eater; she did not like store-bought baby food. I tried to feed it to her several times, but she spit it out or threw it up. I didn't blame her; I would have done the same.

Eddie was a very good brother. He loved Teresa and kept a watchful eye on her all day long. He tried to keep her from hurting herself or getting into something she wasn't supposed to. Teresa loved her brother as well. When Eddie went to school or went outside to play, she would call or look around for him; sometimes she would cry until she saw him.

Eddie at seven years old and Teresa at eight months old

DON FOUND A half dozen Vietnamese students who attended school in Knoxville and invited them to visit us at our home. He must have felt sorry for me and wanted me to have some friends. I was lonely and welcomed any company; it didn't matter who or what language they spoke. I cooked Vietnamese food for them, and we became friends. They visited us often, until they finished their studies and returned to Vietnam. After that, we never heard from them again. Little did I know we would not be there much longer either.

I went back to the doctor for my first visit after giving birth to Teresa.

While checking me over, the doctor smiled and asked, "What are you going to name this one? Oops?" he grinned.

"What!" I exclaimed in shock. "I'm pregnant? But I'm breastfeeding, and I heard a woman can't get pregnant while breastfeeding."

"Whoever told you that was wrong," the doctor smiled. I frowned.

"Well, doctor," I said in disbelief, "we seldom have sex, because my husband is almost never home."

"Well, Mrs. Baer," he said smiling, "the fact is you are pregnant, and you only need to have intercourse once to get pregnant. Now I'll ask you again, are you going to name this one Oops?"

"I guess I'll have to ask my husband about the name," I said. "I can't wait to tell him."

"Good luck," the friendly doctor said as he walked out of the room. When I told Don the news, he was happy and worried at the same time, just as I was.

As 1972 ended, I was expecting our third child after the New Year. We decided to take a trip to Ohio for the Christmas holiday to visit Don's family. After a light breakfast, we locked up the trailer and took the two dogs to a neighbor, who agreed to watch them and our home while we were gone. Don drove to Interstate 75 and headed north.

Poor Don, the bursitis in his right shoulder started acting up again, and he had no choice but to drive in pain toward Fairborn, Ohio. Meanwhile, he had to put up with a hyperactive, talkative seven-year-old Eddie, a fussy ten-month-old Teresa, and a tired eight-months-pregnant woman. The long trip turned out to be a bad idea, but thank God, we made it in one piece.

Two days later, after the kids opened their Christmas presents, I was helping my mother-in-law prepare eggs and bacon for breakfast. While the kids were playing with their toys on the floor and Don messed around with the record player, looking for Christmas music, the phone rang. My mother-in-law answered it. "Hello, hello," she said. "Yes, they are here." Then she handed the phone to Don.

Christmas morning with Eddie, me, Don's mom, and Teresa, before we received the bad news.

"Hello, yes . . . What? Who is this?" He listened for few seconds and frowned; then his jaw dropped. "Oh no! Are you sure?" he exclaimed as he shook his head and hardened his lips.

His mother and I saw a shocked expression on his face, and we knew something bad had happened. We came to his side and listened intently. He turned to us, covered the telephone receiver with his hand, and said, "Our trailer burned down."

"What?" I exclaimed.

"How did it happen?" his mother asked, but Don couldn't answer either one of us. He held a finger to his closed lips, signaling for us to be quiet. His mother and I couldn't believe what we just heard. My stomach was heavy, and my feet were tired from standing. I had to sit down and wait for Don. When he finished talking, he hung up the phone and then explained.

"Our home is gone," he sighed. "It burned to the ground. This is all we need; you are going to have a baby in a month, we have no money, and now we have no home. I don't know what we're going to do." He came over to where I was sitting, bent down, and hugged me. He sounded like he was going to cry, so I stood up and hugged him.

"Don't worry, baby. If there is a will, there is a way," I comforted him. "God put us here, and he'll take care of us, no matter what." Don looked at me with a sad face.

"I know we'll be fine, honey. We'll make it one way or another."

To lighten the conversation, I wiped my tears, smiled, and said, "I didn't like the place anyhow. At one point, I wanted to burn it down myself. Now it's gone, and we are free to continue our trip to Florida after all."

Don looked at me with a half smile and said, "I know, *minh oi*, I know." We gave each other a brief kiss. Don let go of me and told us what our neighbor thought had happened.

"Our neighbor saw several teenagers hanging around our property the night before," Don said. "She believes they may have broken into our home, drank, did drugs, and perhaps accidentally set it on fire. Of course, it might have been an electrical short, or we could have forgotten to turn off the stove before we left. No one knows for sure."

When Christmas dinner was ready, Don's big family gathered around two tables full of food. Everyone was chatty and enjoying their meal, until Don's mother mentioned our misfortune. They reacted with concern and encouraging words: "If you need anything, just give me a call." We thanked them with our sad smiles.

The next day, we made the long trip back to Tennessee.

Don drove up the hill, where our beautiful dream home once stood. It was sad to see it replaced by a mountain of black ashes. The only things left were partially burned wood poles and twisted metal ribs protruding from the rubble. I knew all of our possessions were gone—the most painful of which were our pictures and my diary translation, which I had worked on for almost two years. I just hoped I could get some of the pictures back later from our relatives.

We got out of the car and walked around to investigate. I poked at the kitchen area and found a large discolored Chinese bowl, the only salvageable thing in the whole place. I took the bowl from the ashes, cleaned the black residue off with my fingers, and kept it. We left the pile of ashes and went to talk to several of our neighbors, but nobody knew exactly what had happened. They all seemed to think what our neighbor had said on the phone—kids had accidently started the fire. We thanked all of them for their information, and they also offered encouraging words: "If you need anything, just call me."

I wanted so badly to say, "We need money, food, blankets, clothes, and anything you can afford to throw our way; I would greatly appreciate it." But instead, we left in silence. We were desperate and didn't know where to go or what to do.

Don rented a one-room apartment nearby and squeezed all four of us into it. Teresa slept between us, in the same bed, and Eddie slept on the couch. There was no room for our two dogs, so we gave them to the neighbor who had been taking care of them.

A couple of weeks later, while having lunch, I asked Don, "Why can't we leave this place? We have nothing holding us here. We have no family, no friends, and no help from anyone. We stayed here because of the natural beauty, but we never had a chance to enjoy it; now it's become our burden." I looked at Don for his reaction, but he didn't say a word and kept on eating. So I made a suggestion, "How would you like to move to Florida?"

Don looked back at me, gave my question some thought, and smiled. "You're right, we have nothing holding us here. How would you like to go back to Vietnam?"

"Are you serious?" I replied excitedly. "Vietnam sounds very good to me." But after thinking about it for a moment, I had second thoughts. "I have no idea what the conditions are like in Vietnam right now or what is happening with the war. In the past two years, I've been too preoccupied with our own problems to pay attention to the war in Vietnam. But I don't care; I want to get out of here. This is the most boring, loneliest place I have ever been!"

Don looked at me with sympathy and replied, "I'm so sorry I put you through this. You're right. We have got to get out of this hell and go back to Vietnam." He grinned.

I was so excited. I got up from my seat and ran to Don and hugged his neck. "When can we go?" I asked.

"I have a friend named Paul, in Oklahoma, who was my boss when I worked for Lockheed; now he's a manager of an army contractor in Vietnam, called LSI. The company trains Vietnamese airmen how to maintain American airplanes." Don continued with a smile, "He told me whenever I wanted to return to Vietnam, just let him know. I'll give him a call right now and see if the offer is still good."

Don called Paul; they had a brief discussion, and after Don hung up, he turned to me and announced with a big, happy smile, "I've been offered a job in Saigon as a personnel manager."

"Wow! You did it again, sweetie. You are magic, and I am so happy to get out of here," I said as we hugged each other.

"I am so happy too," he said and squeezed me.

"Oh, be careful, Don! Don't hug me too tight. You might hurt the baby in my stomach."

"Oh, so sorry, little baby," Don said as he rubbed my stomach. "How fast can we move?"

"We can move today if you want to!" I replied.

"I'll call Paul back and let him know we are ready to move immediately," Don said.

We soon learned I couldn't fly overseas because I was nine months pregnant. After a long conversation over the phone one day, Don hung up and told me he accepted a temporary job working for Paul in Oklahoma City.

"My job will be to recruit new workers and send them to Vietnam," he explained. "We will have to stay in Oklahoma until the baby is born, and then we can move back to Saigon."

"I understand," I said.

Don made a few phone calls. He confirmed our apartment and was able to make arrangements for the phone and electricity to be turned on before we got there. As soon as Don hung up, he called his mother;

she wanted to be with us when the baby came, as she was when Teresa was born. Don told her we were moving to Oklahoma City and gave her the new phone number and address. Then we began packing to prepare for our journey.

We woke up early the next morning and squeezed everything that was left of what we owned into our old Barracuda. Poor Don; his bursitis shoulder flared up even worse, and it was difficult for him to move his right arm. I was about to give birth and had an eleven-month-old child in my arms, so I couldn't do much to help Don. Eddie tried to help, but there wasn't much a seven-year-old kid could do either. Somehow, we managed to get our possessions into our car, and then we were ready to take off.

But when Don turned the key, the car's engine started acting up. Don unbuckled his seatbelt and got out of the car. He opened the hood and checked the engine. A few minutes later, he got back inside and announced, "The stupid car's radiator is acting up again, but I can't do anything about it right now."

"What happens if the car dies in the middle of the freeway?" I asked.

"Well, we'll just have to take a chance and hope it doesn't happen until we make it to Oklahoma," Don replied.

Don drove the car with his left hand on the steering wheel and the right one pushed against the roof of the car to suppress his bursitis pain. I was having contractions, and I felt as if I was about to have the baby any minute. I just hoped I could hold it until we reached wherever we were going. Don had to stop often for gas, food, and bathrooms, as well as to rest his shoulder.

He was very concerned about my condition and often asked me how I was feeling. My answer was always, "Don't worry about me, honey. I'm fine." I was not about to tell him how I really felt. I didn't want him to worry about me; he needed to concentrate on driving. Each time I had a contraction, I let out a soft moan, turned my head, and hid my pain, hoping Don wouldn't hear or see the expression on my face. A couple of times, I felt the baby was on its way out, and I had to ask Don to look for a hospital. But then the pain subsided, and we were able to keep going.

That evening, we reached Little Rock, Arkansas, and Don pulled into a small motel for us to stay overnight. The following morning, we stopped to have breakfast and then continued our trip. Don looked at the map and told me, "We have only three hundred miles left to go."

"With our car's condition and the slippery road, it might take us all day," I commented.

That afternoon, our old Barracuda acted up worse; the engine roared like thunder, and grey smoke billowed from beneath the hood. Don had no choice but to continue to crawl along.

"I think our Barracuda is giving up on us," Don said with alarm.

"I hope not," I replied.

Right after I finished my words, the car made several loud pops, more smoke belched out, and then the engine stopped running. Don steered the car to the shoulder, and we all got out. I was carrying Teresa above my protruding stomach, and Eddie was hanging on to me. Don opened the car's hood and more smoke poured out.

"What's wrong with our car, honey?" I asked Don.

"Our car just died! Can't you see?" he snapped.

"What are we going to do now?"

"I don't know," he murmured and shook his head. "I don't know."

I started having another contraction, and I tried to put Teresa down to ease the pain, but she curled up her legs and screamed. She didn't want to step on the cold, unfamiliar road and was afraid of all the large trucks whizzing by. Don couldn't carry her because of his shoulder, and Eddie was too young to help. I had no choice but to let her stay put.

I looked at Don, and he looked back at my tired face and said, "I'm so sorry to put you through this, and now I have to leave you guys and go for help. I want all of you to get back away from the road while I hitchhike into town to rent a car. You and the kids will have to stay here until I get back."

"Okay, honey," I replied.

Don smiled and made a joke, trying to cheer me up. "Just don't have the baby while I'm gone." I thought that if he only knew what kind of pain I was in, he wouldn't have joked about it, and I was not about to tell him the truth; I didn't want him to be any more worried. I tried to smile and assured him that I would be all right.

"I hope I am not going to have the baby all by myself." I could tell Don didn't want to leave us, but he had no choice.

"I'm so sorry, honey," he apologized again and gave each of us a kiss on our forehead. Then he walked away with a sad face and heavy feet.

"Everything will be fine, baby!" I yelled to him. He turned around and gave me a half smile.

Don waved at several vehicles, and one stopped to pick him up. After Don was gone, I moved the kids farther away from the dangerous road. It was hard for me to walk in knee-deep snow with two babies, one in my arms and the other in my stomach. We struggled toward a tree stump, and I asked Eddie to help me clean off the snow. I sat down on the chilly seat with Teresa in my lap. It was so cold that I had to ask Eddie to go back to the car to get us a blanket. I used it to cover all of us, and we huddled to keep warm in the bitter cold of early February.

My stomach continued to hurt, and I kept hoping that I was not going into labor. A number of cars did stop to offer their help, but I told them I was waiting for my husband. A couple of hours later, Don returned with a white rental car; I saw him make a U-turn and pull up behind our Barracuda. He opened both of the cars' trunks and moved the heavy things from one car to the other. I stood holding on to Teresa and watched Don rub his shoulder and make faces as he continued to transfer our things. I wanted so much to help him, but I couldn't. When Don was done loading our things into the rental car, we got in and left our old Barracuda parked on the side of the road.

"We don't have much farther to go; I'll arrange to have our car towed tomorrow. But right now, it's late, and I have to get you guys to our apartment, just in case the baby decides to come today."

I looked at Don and gave him a big smile. My heart felt for him; I loved him so much. At that moment, I knew Don and I would always be at each other's side to take care of each other. I closed my eyes and prayed for us all.

Oklahoma City seemed somber, dreary, dark, and uninviting; perhaps it was just because of our situation. There were few tall buildings and hardly any trees; the few trees I did see had no leaves and were covered with heavy snow that just added to the dreariness. Don turned into the parking lot of a two-story apartment building, and we poured out of the car. I carried Teresa, and Don opened the trunk, pulled out our luggage; Eddie ran around, playing with snow.

"Hey, Eddie!" I yelled out. "Quit running around and help your father!"

He ran toward Don, picked up a small bag, and, together, we marched slowly into the office. Don talked to the manager behind the desk and explained our prerental arrangement. The man took us to a second-floor unit. I looked around the partly furnished one-bedroom apartment.

"It's nice, but small," I said.

"It's not too bad," Don replied.

The manager showed us around, gave us the keys to the apartment, and left. I put Teresa down and prepared her milk. Don and Eddie returned to the car to carry in the rest of our possessions. When they brought in the last load, we ate peanut butter and jelly sandwiches for supper.

"It's late, and I'm so tired," Don sighed. "Let's leave everything where it is and go to bed. We'll straighten it all out tomorrow."

"I agree," I nodded.

Still in our old dirty clothes, we jumped onto a naked mattress in the middle of the room. Teresa was between Don and me, and Eddie was on the other side of Don; we covered ourselves with a blanket and went to sleep.

The phone ringing woke us, and Don jumped up to answer it. "Hello! . . . Hello!" he said, then waited for a few seconds and asked, "Where are you?" He was silent for a few more seconds and then continued, "You're at the airport? Now?" I sat up and watched him as he raised his eyebrows and acted surprised. He looked down at his watch, and I looked at mine. I saw it was nine, but I couldn't tell whether it was nine at night or nine in the morning, until I looked out the window and saw the sun was up. I realized I'd overslept. "Okay, Mom, stay right there and I'll pick you up," Don said and hung up the phone.

I was shocked to hear that his mother was at the airport. I knew she planned to come for the baby's birth, but I didn't know she was going to come so early. I guess she just wanted to surprise us. It was a good thing Don arranged to have the phone installed early and gave her the number; otherwise, she would have been stuck at the airport.

"Do you know where the airport is?" I asked.

"I don't know, but I'll find out."

"How?"

"At a gas station," he replied.

"Do you want a cup of coffee before you go?"

"I don't see how you can find coffee among all those boxes," he smiled. "I'll get some at the gas station. Besides, I don't want Mom to wait any longer than she has to." He kissed my forehead, smiled, and said, "Don't have the baby while I'm gone."

"I'll try not to." I grinned and pushed him out the door.

Later, Don walked in with his mother while the kids and I were having breakfast. Eddie and I stood up to hug her.

"I am happy to see you, Mom," I said.

She smiled and replied, "I'm glad I'm here too."

"Well, Mom," Don said, "I have to run around today to take care of the car. Linda will fill you in on the rest of what happened to us yesterday. I'll see you guys later." He kissed each of us, told the kids to be good to Grandma, and left.

"I'm happy to see you here early," I said, smiling.

"I wanted to be here early to help you settle down before you go to the hospital; I figured it would be soon."

"Thank you so much, Mom."

She and I spent the rest of the day talking, eating, putting things away, and organizing the apartment. Don's mother had finally accepted me as her daughter-in-law; I loved her.

Don called several times to check on us, but he didn't come home until almost time to go to bed. That night, I had contractions all night long. I got used to the pain, though, and paid it no attention until four in the morning, when it got a lot worse. Suddenly, I had the urge to push.

"Hey, Don! Wake up!" I yelled. "Get ready to take me to the hospital." But he was too tired and couldn't keep his eyes open long enough to hear me. My pain became severe, and by five o'clock, scared and hurting, I had no choice but to really wake Don up.

"How bad is it?" he asked and was about to fall back to sleep when I raised my voice.

"It is very bad, Don! If you don't take me to the hospital right now, I'm going to have the baby right here!" I squeezed my stomach and moaned. This caused Don to sit up straight.

"How close are the pains?" he asked, alarmed.

"They are five minutes apart; you need to take me to the hospital immediately!" Don jumped off the bed, put his clothes on, woke his mother, and told her to keep an eye on the kids, while I put on my house robe. He grabbed the keys and the bag I had prepared for the hospital. I gave his mother quick instructions about the food and milk for Teresa, said goodbye, and headed for the door.

I held on to my stomach with my right hand, while Don held my left and helped me downstairs. Even with Don's help, I could barely walk. It took us awhile before we reached the bottom of the steps. We moved carefully over the icy parking lot to our snow-covered car. He opened the car door for me to enter first and closed it; then he went to the driver's side, got in, and shut the door. He turned on the engine but realized he couldn't see out because of the snow. He turned on the wipers, but they wouldn't budge. They were stuck to the ice. He turned on the wiper fluid to free the wipers, but the container was either empty or frozen. He turned everything off except the engine and bolted out of the car. He went to the windshield, panicked, and tried to remove the snow with his hand. He soon found out it was not just snow but thick ice as well. He couldn't remove it with his bare hands alone, so he ran to the trunk to look for something to remove the ice. He found nothing. He then ran madly around the parking lot, looking for something to remove the ice, but he came back to the car empty-handed.

Meanwhile, my labor pains became more and more intense. I yelled at Don to hurry up or I would have the baby in the parking lot. In desperation, he reached into his pocket, pulled out his comb, and started scraping violently.

I couldn't take it anymore. I rolled down my window, stuck my head out, and yelled, "Hurry up, Don! Please, hurry up! I think the baby is coming out. Please hurry up," I cried.

"I am hurrying! Just hold on for a minute!" he yelled back.

"I can't hold on any longer," I murmured, and from the inside of the car, I could hear him grumbling to himself.

"Come on! Come on!" he growled as he scraped harder. "Damn it! Come on!"

"Don! I feel the baby's head is coming out, and I can't stop it," I screamed.

"Hold on, Linda. Don't push!" he shouted. "You better not push!"

"I can't help it!" I cried and moaned.

When he was able to clear a small hole, just big enough for him to see through, he abandoned his scraping, jumped inside, took hold of the steering wheel, and drove out of the parking lot as fast as he possibly could.

"I don't think I can hold on any longer," I moaned again.

"I am sorry, but you have to try harder to hold on and not push, baby."

"I can't!" I cried in pain. "I felt the water break, and the baby's head is coming out. I feel the urge to push right now!" I told him.

"Hold on, baby. Try to hold on. Don't push. I think we're very close to the hospital."

Thank God, he was right. Within minutes, we were at the emergency entrance of Saint Anthony Hospital. Don parked the car and ran to my door; as soon as the door swung open, I slumped to the ground. I saw several people run from the hospital toward me, but I couldn't tell who they were or what was going on. The only thing I remember was telling them that my baby was coming out and I couldn't stop it. They put me into a wheelchair and rushed me through a throng of people to the delivery room. I was lifted from the wheelchair to a bed, and someone checked my stomach, while others ran around, preparing for my delivery.

"Where is my husband?" I asked one of them, when I didn't see Don in the delivery room.

"He must be moving the car, or maybe he's outside in the waiting room," one of them answered.

I remembered when Teresa was born, he didn't want to go into the delivery room with me; he said he couldn't bear watching me giving birth because he couldn't stand to see me in pain. I thought he might want to avoid seeing me in pain again with this child. After checking me over, the doctor administered an epidural, to help relieve the pain. Within a few minutes, my baby was born. He was the largest baby born to the smallest mother in the hospital that morning.

Me, Eddie, Mom with one-week-old Nicky, and Don holding an eleven-month-old Teresa

To me, he was the cutest and the most perfect baby ever born. A couple of hours later, a nurse wheeled me to a room where Don was already waiting for me. He smiled, happy to see me. The nurse gave me some instructions about how to use the button to call her if I needed and left the room. Don got up from his seat to close the door behind her, walked to my bed, smiled, and gave me a kiss on my forehead.

"Everything will be okay from now on, baby," he said as tears pooled in his eyes.

"We have a handsome baby boy and he looks exactly like you," I told Don.

"Poor kid," he said with a smile and gave me another kiss. Quietly, we held each other's hands and let tears of joy roll down our faces. We named him Nicholas but called him Nicky for short.

When Nicky was three weeks old, Aunt Lola and her husband, Uncle Ray, came to visit. Their intent was to take our car and our possessions back to Indiana, to be stored there while we were overseas. Our little apartment was tight and now occupied by eight. It was chaotic but cozy, and I loved it. During this time, Don's mother, aunt, and uncle kept an eye on the kids and gave me the opportunity to study for my citizenship exam; I needed it to obtain an American passport. Within one week, I had both.

Nicky was not yet five weeks old when we prepared to leave the United States. We packed our clothes and all the necessities for the kids into three suitcases. The day we were ready to go to the airport, we gathered our things and said goodbye to his mother, aunt, and uncle. Together, we marched downstairs with red eyes. Don's mom followed us to the parking lot, where we exchanged more hugs and kisses. Before I entered the taxi, she took off her white sweater and draped it around my shoulders.

"Here, this will keep you warm," she said.

"Thanks, Mom. I love you," I said, with tears streaming down my face.

"You are welcome, and I love you too," she said. "Don't forget to write as soon as you arrive in Saigon."

"Yes, ma'am. I won't," I said and gave her another hug before I got in the taxi. We all waved goodbye as the taxi pulled away.

Chapter 5

LIFE ON EDGE

TRAVELING WITH TWO infants was not easy. They were only eleven months apart, and both drank milk from bottles but at different times. It seemed as if I was constantly mixing their formula and feeding them. And after the feedings, I had to change their diapers; it wore me out.

Don tried to help, but other than holding them, he couldn't do much.

After a layover at the Los Angeles International Airport, we boarded a Boeing 747, which took us to Vietnam. Thank God the airplane was large and our seats were in the front row. The attendants attached two baby cribs to the wall in front of us, and they were heaven sent. The gentle rocking of the airplane coaxed the babies to sleep for hours. It was a blessing for us and those who sat nearby. I was able to rest without a baby in my arms for a change.

It took us over thirty-five hours, including various stops in different countries, to reach Tan Son Nhut Airport, in Saigon. Once there, we took a cab to the Continental, a luxurious, multistory hotel right in the heart of the city. A few days later, through an old friend of mine, we found and moved into a nice French apartment at the corner of Cong Ly and Yen Do Streets, near Don's work at Tan Son Nhut Air Force Base.

It is good to be back home again, I thought, *in my own element, where I can speak my language, eat my food, and be close to my family.* I felt smarter when I talked to my own people; they understood what I said and didn't raise their voices or their eyebrows at me or make me repeat myself a half-dozen times.

One day, when I was at the supermarket in Knoxville, Tennessee, a well-dressed middle-aged lady approached me while I was at a vegetable bin. She looked at me from top to toes, as if I were an alien, and then she pointed to a pile of Chinese cabbage and asked, "Do you Filipinos put this vegetable on your noodles?"

"What kind of noodle dish are you making?" I was trying to be helpful.

"You know! The kind you people eat."

"I see. I am sorry, but Asians have many different types of noodles, and by the way," I said, smiling, "I am not from the Philippines."

"Well, you look Filipino," she chided. "Well then, tell me how to make Chinese noodles or eggrolls," she asked in a louder voice, as if she were talking to someone in the next aisle. "You do know how to make Chinese noodles and eggrolls, right?" she shouted.

"What kind of eggrolls or noodles?" I asked. "Asian people have many different types of eggrolls and noodles, depending on what country they are from." As I explained, she raised her eyebrows in confusion. I continued, "Even with Chinese food, since China has so many regions and many different versions of these dishes, I can't tell you which one or which kind of noodle or eggroll you want to make. Do you know the name of the specific dish that you want to make?" I asked, but she didn't answer and just narrowed her eyes, wrinkled her face, and shook her head. By then, she must have thought I was crazy or stupid, because she acted like she didn't understand a word I said; it must have been my English. In confusion, she raised her voice again, but my hearing was fine. Knowing she might be a little confused, I tried harder to explain.

"I make Vietnamese spring rolls and summer rolls," I said. "If you want to make them, I will give you my recipes."

After she asked me to repeat each sentence several times, she said, "Well, I don't know the difference between you Vietnamese, Chinese, and Filipinos; you all look alike." I kept on smiling and tried to help her with the food, but I guess I was beyond her understanding. I wished she could have spoken my language instead.

Her remarks reminded me of my brother Bay, when he was younger. My husband asked Bay to go with him to the base to watch the airplanes take off and land, which Bay loved. He refused to go, so I asked him why.

"Because I am afraid of being lost," he replied.

"How could you get lost? You are with your brother," I said.

"I know, but when Don mingles with other Americans, they all look alike, and I'm afraid I wouldn't recognize him."

"I understand," I said, smiling. "That is funny, because American people say the same thing about Asians." We laughed, and I continued. "If we just peel off the outer layer of our skin, I am sure we will all look alike."

"That would look funny," he said, " but I wouldn't mind if we all looked alike."

"Oh no!" I shook my head. "We would be even more lost and confused; we couldn't tell the difference between our loved ones and our enemies, but that could be good as well, because there would be no war or prejudice in the world."

"That would be good if we had no wars."

"Yep, I agree." We both laughed.

Whenever Don and I were in public, it didn't matter which country we were in, we were always being stared at. I'm sure it was because we weren't the same race. I felt uncomfortable from those glares at first, until I shared my feelings with Don.

"The reason they are looking is because you are a very beautiful woman," he said.

"Awww, you are sweet and know just what to say," I grinned. "Perhaps you are right; we are a good-looking couple." We both smiled.

NOW THAT I was back in my homeland, I missed America, my adopted country, and my loved ones, even the ones who made fun of me; I couldn't wait to go back there to see them.

My parents were happy we were back in Vietnam. My stepfather was close to eighty but still practiced Chinese medicine and was in good health. Mother had problems with arthritis in both knees, and it was difficult for her to walk a long distance. She was eleven years younger than my stepfather, but her health was not as good as his. Still, she had to work hard, helping him with his medicine, which was a complicated process, and she had to do her daily chores.

But my parents were very happy and content; they lived in a large two-story home, built on five beautiful acres of land filled with fruit trees. Their property bordered a large river. I had bought the land for them and helped them build their house and furnish it before I went to the United States in 1971.

My stepfather and mother with Teresa and Nicky in 1974

My brother Kinh was twenty-one years old and in the Vietnamese military. While on military leave, he'd been married by parental prearrangement to a girl he'd met only once. After their wedding, he'd had to return to his unit. When he heard I was home, he took a break and came home to see me. I took him to a coffee shop, and we had a long conversation.

"On my wedding day," he said, "I could hardly recognize my own bride from the bridesmaids."

"Why?" I laughed.

"Because they all wore the same traditional white dresses, and the only way I could figure out which one was my wife was by the veil on her head." We both laughed, but deep inside, I felt sorry for him and for many others who had to experience the same custom.

Nho, my sister, also married by prearrangement, but she was lucky to have known her fiancé before they were married. He was a nice home town boy, who came from a very good family.

My brother Bay was about sixteen and was very happy we were back. He came to live with us and went to an auto mechanics school.

Khai, my eleven-year-old brother, still lived with my parents, but he came to visit me often. Other than my siblings growing and some marriages, my family had not changed much. Vietnam, however, had changed a lot during the two years I'd been away, especially in regards to the war and the military situation. We didn't know it until we went back to Saigon, but most of the American soldiers had returned to the United States, and the fighting was mainly between North and South Vietnam.

DON HAD A high-paying job working for Lear Siegler in personnel and training management, and I continued with my high-end black-market activities; I was more successful with it than before I'd left Vietnam.

Together, we made plenty of money, much more than we needed. My stepfather knew of the money we were making and advised us to invest in land and property. He was concerned that if we didn't invest it, we would waste it all; we took his advice and bought a house in downtown Cat Lo and a fruit farm near him. The farm that my father advised us to buy was about three acres and had established fruit trees, including cotton-apple, longan, mango, and coconut. It also had five small ponds, full of tilapia and catfish. My plan was to add a pig and chicken farm to create jobs for my relatives.

*Don, Eddie, Nicky, Teresa, and me having
our good night kisses before our bedtime, 1974*

Don and me at my parents' home in Cat Lo, near Vung Tau

Meanwhile, the war between the North and South still raged on. It not only killed people on both sides but it also destroyed our spirit, our dignity, and our self-respect. Those of us who were prosperous shut ourselves off from it just so we could breathe and survive without guilt. We closed our eyes, covered our ears, and tried not to see or hear what was happening to our country. We pretended there was no war and there was no tomorrow. For many, tomorrow was a dream that could sometimes turn into a nightmare.

In war-torn countries such as ours, there are no winners. Everyone loses, even those who claim to be victors. What do people gain? Dead relatives, broken homes, and a country torn apart. Many lose their lives.

IN 1972, WHILE *we were still in America, North Vietnam and the United States finally reached an agreement to end the Vietnam War. The agreement called for a standstill cease-fire, permitting both North and South Vietnamese troops to remain in their territory, for the gradual withdrawal of American troops, and for the creation of a Council of Reconciliation, through which the Vietnamese would resolve the political questions. President Thieu reluctantly accepted this agreement only after receiving secret assurances from President Nixon that the United States would respond with force to any violations of the treaty. Withdrawal of American soldiers began while negotiations were underway, even though the Paris accords were not formally signed until*

January 27, 1973. The last American troops returned home on March 29, 1973, leaving behind a small contingent of American civilian technicians (Don was one of them) and embassy personnel.

Although President Nixon had warned that Americans might be sent back to Vietnam if the truce was violated, the American Congress virtually eliminated that possibility by passing legislation that prohibited further expenditure of funds for US military operations anywhere in Southeast Asia.

THE KIND OF business I was in and the money Don and I made allowed us to rub shoulders with high-class society, the wives of high-ranking military officers and politicians, including President Thieu's wife and her friends. To me, they were just customers.

Besides our high-ranking Vietnamese military friends, we were also friends with Americans and their wives, who worked with Don. We all lived the life of luxury, with fancy clothes, nice jewelry, good food, good wine, and expensive cars. I hired three live-in maids—one to clean, one to cook, and one to care for my babies.

My black-market business brought many people in and out of my home daily. Some were buyers and others were sellers. I bought and sold gold, diamonds, cars, stereos, cigarettes, American money, grocery items, and things that were not available otherwise, such as chocolate, canned food, peanut butter, and jelly. I sold the grocery items mostly to American civilians, who were afraid to eat Vietnamese food or couldn't shop in the commissary.

The unsettled conditions in our country got worse and caused most of us to feel uneasy about going out; we were afraid of terrorist bombs and explosions, so I had parties in my home and invited friends to join us. We ate, drank, and danced to loud music from our fancy and expensive stereo. Of course, part of it was that I wanted to show off my status and good taste and to advertise my business as well.

Sometimes, the loud music bothered our neighbors, and they called the police. When the police showed up, I asked them to join the party.

They would partake with their guns swinging in their holsters. These could have been the very same officers who handcuffed me and put me in jail for doing absolutely nothing wrong when I was younger. When I had money, the police loved me, and I could do no wrong, even though I was as guilty as sin.

Don and the kids at Saigon Zoo

Perhaps my wine and food tasted good, or perhaps they turned a blind eye to my activities because I gave them money. Whatever the reason, the police ignored my activities and allowed me to continue to practice my illegal business.

BEFORE WE LEFT for America in 1971, Don sold our Toyota Corolla to his friend Chuck, who worked with him at Lockheed. Chuck paid Don with a bad check, and to avoid paying taxes, he never bothered to register the car in his name. He used the car for illegal drug trafficking and was caught. The courts impounded the car.

Unknown to us, the car was still registered in Don's name. When we were back in Vietnam in 1973, Don purchased another car. When he went to have it registered, the Vietnamese government charged him for the crime associated with the first car. I found a lawyer and gave him money to pay the fine, hoping to get our impounded car back, but it was hopeless. Each time my lawyer and I went to the legal office to see about our car, they gave us the run around. I think one of the high court officials took our car and either sold it or kept it. We never saw the car again, even after I paid thousands of dollars in fines and back taxes.

The real shock came when the police served Don with a warrant for illegal drug trafficking and demanded he pay the equivalent of twenty-five thousand dollars or spend three months in jail. When I saw the warrant, which was in both Vietnamese and English, I thought it was some kind of a joke. I had paid the fines and thought everything was settled. I almost threw the warrant away, but instead waited for Don to come home to show it to him.

When Don walked through the door, I handed the paper to him, laughed, and said, "Hey, Don! Look at this stupid paper."

Don read it and exclaimed, "Oh my God! I don't believe this!"

"Believe what?" I asked in alarm.

"The stupid government!" he grumbled. "After all of the trouble we went through to pay fines and not even get our car back, now the damn fools say I am going to jail for dealing drugs unless I pay twenty-five thousand dollars in fines." Don was angry, and I was worried.

"I didn't believe it either," I said. "I thought it was some kind of a joke."

"Oh no, this is not a joke. I will be going to jail if I don't pay those fools."

"We did pay them," I said.

"I thought we did too."

We looked at each other, shook our heads, and I said, "Well, we'll have to get a lawyer again."

"Those stupid, idiotic fools!" Don said again as he walked to the bedroom to change clothes. I followed him.

"We didn't get our car back yet," I said, "and I think they are just dragging the matter out for as long as they can so they can rip us off for more money."

"Stupid fools. All of them are stupid fools, including that lying lawyer of ours." Don's jaws tightened in anger. "Wherever Chuck is, I hope he feels guilty for what he's done to me and my family; what a friend he was."

I shook my head and said, "I doubt it; I don't think his kind ever feel bad, but I would never have thought he would do this to us."

I went back to the same lawyer I used before and told him what happened. I showed him the warrant. He read it and said, "I'll take care of it."

"I hope you will do it right this time," I warned.

"I thought I did it right the last time, but I guess someone cheated, and it wasn't me."

For months, I was at the lawyer's office almost every day and spent thousands of dollars on his fees and the government fines. We hoped everything would be over and done soon.

IN 1974, THE *Communists developed a plan for the final takeover of the South. Although South Vietnamese resistance was fierce at times, they were unable to withstand the determined invasion from the North. At the same time, the Watergate scandal and Nixon's resignation in August further cemented America's position of no more military involvement in Vietnam.*

The North Vietnamese Army began successful attacks in the Central Highlands, and the key cities of Hue and Da Nang fell. From that point on, the fall of South Vietnam was inevitable. Thousands of American civilians and South Vietnamese began preparing for a hasty evacuation.

THE WAR TURNED from bad to worse. The Viet Cong attacked nightly with rockets and mortars, which hit not only the countryside but the city as well. Even though the South fought hard, they could not stop the determined Northern invasion. Realizing what was coming, American companies began closing down, and those Americans who married Vietnamese women were getting ready to leave. Don and I also worried about our family's safety, and we planned to leave the country as soon as possible. Many of our friends and their families had already gone. They all left in a hurry, and we didn't have a chance to find out where they went. I realized I might never see or hear from them again. Our luxurious life and our glorious parties were short-lived.

The North Vietnamese Army was inching closer to Saigon, and there were no defenses left; that was when the real panic began. Don and I wondered if we would even make it out of the country in one piece.

On April 3, 1975, Don came home early and announced, "We have twelve hours to leave. Get the kids ready, and don't take anything except our clothes."

I knew we had to leave, but twelve hours? "Why do we have to leave so suddenly?" I asked.

"The American Embassy ordered my company to close down, and all of us must evacuate. They gave us only a few hours to board the first plane out of here. They are afraid we might get stuck here if we don't go now," Don explained.

"What about our property and my family in Vung Tau?" I said as tears pooled in my eyes. "No one knows we are leaving, and when they find out, they will die, especially my poor brother, who just went home to see my parents on his school break. When he returns, he will be so shocked to find out we are gone. I can't leave Vietnam until I let my family know first."

"No! You can't," Don said. "We don't have time."

"I wish we had a phone so I could call someone," I said.

"I know, but we don't. And your family doesn't have a phone anyway."

"You're right," I said sadly.

I gathered all three of the maids and told them what was going on. They were very surprised, even though they knew we would have to leave them soon. They helped me pack, and none of us had a dry eye.

"Don't pack too much, because we can't carry it," Don warned. He began taking out some of his clothes from one of the suitcases.

"Just pack our good clothes," I said to the maids. "Everything else we'll have to leave behind, including our furniture and personal belongings. You guys take what you can and leave the rest for whoever wants it. When my family gets here, it will be too late."

I thought of my family and felt a sharp pain in my heart. Tears soaked my face as I packed. "My poor mother, brothers, and sister," I said. "They will be so sad when they come to see us and find an empty apartment."

Don saw me crying, came to me, and said, "I'm so sorry, but we have no choice."

"I know it, but I wish we did."

I stayed up with the maids, talking and crying all night; the atmosphere in my living room felt more like a funeral home. I loved my maids; they were so good with the children and so loyal to me. I knew I could never find people like them again; besides, even if I could, I wouldn't be able to afford them in America. I would miss them, and I knew they would miss us too.

The next morning, they helped feed the children, and then I ran to the neighbors to say farewell and leave a message for my family.

"Please, Phan," I said, "when my family comes, tell them that we had to evacuate; I will write them as soon as I can."

"I will tell them for you," she said as she began to cry.

"Thank you," I said with tears streaming down my face as I rushed back to my apartment to get ready to leave.

South Vietnam was being overrun by the North, and the administration of US President Gerald Ford began planning for the evacuation of American citizens. On Friday afternoon, April 4, 1975, a C-5A Galaxy was to make the first flight of Operation Babylift, carrying the first group of embassy employees, orphans, and some civilian contractors from Tan Son Nhut Airport to Clark Air Base in the Philippines. Passengers were to be transferred to charter flights and welcomed by President Ford upon arrival in San Diego, California.

Our family was scheduled to board that first flight.

Because of our big family and our luggage, we had to wave down two taxis. Don helped the drivers with the luggage while I counted my money. I saved enough to pay for the two taxis and gave the rest to the maids. Most of it was Vietnamese currency, and I knew it would be worthless in the United States. We all hugged and then we left.

On the way to the airport, I could see smoke from the previous night's rocket attacks and terrified people on the move. The traffic jam was bad, and we were moving very slowly. My driver was losing patience, so I started a conversation with him.

"I am so sorry that our country and our people have to go through this mess," I said.

"The war would not be so bad," he said, "if the politicians who were involved would just get together, go to an open field, and fight with each other until they were all dead; that would be fine with me. I don't want them to use my family or me as pawns in their chess games for power, and I don't want them to take our young men and use them as cannon fodder." He choked up but continued, "They are being killed for no reason at all." He wiped his tears. "All I ever wanted was peace and to be able to feed my family."

"I am sorry; I feel your pain," I said as I looked out the window.

It took us hours to get to the airport. When the taxis finally stopped in front of Tan Son Nhut Airport, we rushed out. I paid both of the drivers, and we gathered our kids and our luggage and ran into the building toward the boarding desk. When we reached the ticket counter, the clerk told us we were too late; the Operation Babylift C-5A we were supposed to be on had already taken off. Don and I were so upset, but there was nothing we could do. We took our children into the waiting room, hoping to get on the next flight. I looked around and saw many other evacuees who also missed the same airplane.

A few minutes later, the kids said they were hungry. I asked Don to keep an eye on them while I looked for food. I found a French bread vendor and bought five Vietnamese baloney sandwiches, one for each of us. We used our luggage as a table and chairs. While eating the sandwiches, I watched people and their reactions to the evacuation. Everyone in the waiting room showed signs of fear, anger, and anxiety.

Through their conversations, I discovered that many of their loved ones left earlier on the C-5A. They were also upset about missing the plane.

My children, on the other hand, seemed happy and content; they couldn't care less about what was going on. I smiled as I watched my innocent children talking, laughing, and chasing each other around a pile of luggage, with their half-eaten sandwiches in their hands.

There was a loud boom, and several people ran outside. Don and I were curious to see what was going on and followed them. Not too far from the airport, we saw a large pillar of grey smoke coming up from the ground. We all assumed it was just another rocket or mortar explosion. Some onlookers stayed outside to watch and talk, and others, including us, came back inside.

Moments later, we heard a siren, and all ran back outside. Ambulances and fire trucks raced toward the plume of smoke. We all just watched in confusion.

After a while, a middle-aged man came to our waiting area and made a somber announcement. "I am sorry to bring you bad news, but the C-5A Galaxy crashed shortly after takeoff from Tan Son Nhut Airport." We all looked at each other in shock.

This is the same C-5A that my family was supposed to have been on; it crashed a few minutes after this picture was taken on April 4, 1975.

"There were many casualties. We're not sure how many, but some passengers and crewmembers did survive." He paused long enough to control his emotions, and then he continued. "I will let you know more later, when I have more information." As he was about to leave, people in the room started asking him questions, but he just shook his head.

"We will let you know more when we know more," he said, and then he left.

Many in the room, whose relatives may have perished, started to cry. Our children stopped what they were doing, sat down on top of the suitcases, and watched those who were mourning for their loved ones.

Don turned to me, grabbed my hand, and whispered in my ear, "Almost everyone in this room, including our family, was supposed to be on that plane. If not for the bad traffic, we might have ended up dead."

"Thank God for the bad traffic!" I said. "I thought I would never be grateful for Saigon traffic."

That evening, we learned more details about the C-5A crash. Somewhere over the ocean, the airplane's tailgate blew open and forced the pilots to turn around for an emergency landing at Tan Son Nhut Airport; it crashed within a mile of it. The plane was filled with 328 passengers and crewmembers. One hundred and fifty-five of them died, including 79 Vietnamese orphans, 5 crewmembers, and 71 civilians. Most fatalities were in the plane's cargo area, where we probably would have been, according to Don. We were very lucky.

It was late in the evening when there was an announcement that there would be no more flights out of Vietnam that day. We had waited all day. Some of the passengers stayed right where they were and waited, while most of us left the waiting room to find a place to sleep for the night. We dragged our suitcases and our children out to the gate, waved down two taxis, and told them to take us to a nearby hotel. We planned to rest there until the next morning. Since I gave all of my Vietnamese money away earlier, I had to use the dollar bills to buy sandwiches and pay the taxi drivers. I knew we would need more Vietnamese money, so I had to return to my neighborhood, where I knew I could get money changed at a good rate.

"I don't want to pay for everything in dollar bills," I told Don. "It will cost us twice as much. I'm going back to our apartment to change the dollars for Vietnamese money, if you don't mind."

Don shook his head and said, "I don't think you should go back there. It's too dangerous."

"I have to go back and get some money to buy food for the kids." I explained, "Small business owners will not take the dollars, because they don't know what to do with them; some taxi drivers around the airport might accept dollars, but it will cost us twice as much, if not more."

"Okay then, just be careful," he warned, "and please hurry back, because I will worry every second you're gone."

"I will. I promise," I said.

I walked to the street, waved down a cab, and told the driver where I wanted to go. Traffic was not as bad as it was in the morning. When the driver drove up to our old apartment, I climbed out and said, "Don't leave; wait for me here. I will be back."

"Okay," he agreed.

As soon as my neighbor saw me, she said, "Your mother and your brother were here just a few hours ago. When I told them you had already gone, they both cried and left."

"Oh my God!" I exclaimed. I missed the chance to see my mother and my brother. It could have been my last chance to see them. I felt horrible, but I tried to control my emotions and asked the lady to change the money for me. I was too tired and upset to tell her anything about the day. I took the stack of money she handed me and stuck it in my pocket without counting it; I thanked her and walked away in tears.

I climbed back into the cab and asked the driver to stop at a food stand, where I bought us banh mi sandwiches, five loaves of French bread, some cured meat, and a dozen cans of soda. I made sure we had enough for the night's dinner and for the next morning's breakfast as well. When I got back to the hotel, we ate our sandwiches and then went to bed.

The next morning, we got up early, hoping we could get to the airport and catch the first available evacuation flight out of there. The kids told me they were hungry, but I told them they would have to wait until we got to the airport; I didn't want us to be late again. They were very good kids and listened to me without complaint. I looked at their hungry faces and felt sorry for them, so I broke up a loaf of bread and handed each of them a piece.

When we got to the airport, there was already a long line of people ahead of us. We lined up and followed the slow-moving mob inching toward the security desk. While we waited in line, Don and I ate our sandwiches and kept looking at each other with thankful smiles. We were both relieved, knowing we would be out of Vietnam and out of danger soon.

The kids, however, didn't care if we stayed or went back to America. The only thing they were excited about was flying in an airplane; they couldn't stand still and kept jumping up and down. Now and then, I had to caution them to calm down. When it was finally my turn, I walked up to the desk first. I showed a clerk my passport, which contained pictures of me and our three kids.

Our 1974 passport picture. Clockwise: Eddie was nine, I was twenty-eight, Teresa was three, and Nicky was two.

Everything went well; the kids and I moved forward, stepped to the side, and waited for Don, who had a separate passport because of his job.

Don gave his passport to the clerk, who looked through some files and began questioning him. Minutes later, I saw her call for her boss. When he came, I could tell from their expressions they were having a serious discussion, but I was too far away to hear them.

I looked at Don, and he looked back at me with a worried frown. I knew something was wrong and tried to listen to their conversation, but the kids were making too much noise, and I couldn't hear. "Stay right where you are," I instructed the kids. "I have to find out what's happening." I didn't wait for their response and walked toward Don.

"What's going on, Don?" I asked with deep concern.

"Oh, just some stupid paperwork about the back taxes on our Toyota," he replied with a hint of a smile. "There's nothing to worry about. Just go back and keep an eye on the kids."

I nodded my head. "What paper are you talking about? I thought we had everything taken care of by our lawyer before we left," I asked.

"Well, it looks like the lawyer and Chuck got me in trouble again," he said, shaking his head.

"I don't understand what you are talking about. We paid thousands of dollars in taxes and fines, and everything was cleared by the Vietnamese courts. Our lawyer told us this was over and closed."

"The problem is," Don grumbled, "we were too trusting; we trusted the people who were not trustworthy—our lawyer and Chuck, my so-called friend. Now, let me take care of this, and you go over there and take care of our kids."

"Okay," I said as I nodded my head. "I just hope everything will be cleared up soon, because I don't want to miss another flight."

"Oh no, we are not going to," Don replied with confidence.

I went back to attend to the kids but kept a wary eye on Don. I noticed he stopped talking to the clerk at the desk and moved aside to let other passengers pass through. I assumed he was waiting for his papers to be processed. Minutes later, two Vietnamese policemen came to Don, pushed his hands behind his back, and, to my horror, handcuffed him. I ran to the police and asked them in Vietnamese what was going on.

With an arrogant attitude, one growled, "This is none of your business!"

Before I had a chance to respond, the other one asked, "And who are you?"

"I am his wife," I answered, "and I want to know why my husband is being handcuffed?"

"Your husband here is trying to escape the country without paying court fines and back taxes," he snorted.

"Oh my God!" I exclaimed. "We cleared all of that up with the courts months ago. I gave my lawyer the money to pay for all of it. Now, please let my husband go," I demanded.

"You might have given money to your lawyer, but your lawyer has not paid the court," he said sarcastically. "You probably just paid your lawyer's fees and not the court."

The other policeman chimed in, "Do you think we let people come to this country, live off of our blood, sweat, and tears, not pay their taxes, and then try to get away with it, like your husband?"

If it were true, the police would have had a right to be angry, but we had paid for everything we owed, plus much more. If they only knew the truth, they would be angry with their government and not with us, but it was impossible for me to make them believe me.

Our three children saw what was happening to their father and came running toward him. At first, they were just curious, until the police escorted Don away from the desk toward the exit door. That is when the kids started to cry, and I did too. Don tried to say something to us, but we couldn't hear him over the noise. The policemen ignored all of our crying and led him toward the door, in front of hundreds of staring eyes. The kids and I were terrified and didn't know what to do, so we just cried and followed behind them. As he was about to exit the door, he stopped and came back to us. We held on to each other and continued to cry.

"You guys have to leave Vietnam without me," he said as tears spilled from his eyes.

"No! I can't, and I won't!" I screamed. "We are not going anywhere without you."

The policemen began pulling Don away, but Don pulled back and pleaded with them.

"Wait!" he said to the policemen. "Please let me talk to my wife and kids for a minute, before you take me." I'm sure the police didn't understand a word Don said, but I believe they could read his body language and facial expression. They stopped pulling and let him talk to us.

"Honey, I know this doesn't look good for us right now." He paused, shook his head, and looked as though it were taking all of his strength to get his words out. "You and the kids have to leave without me for now. I want you guys to get on the plane and get out of here while you still can. No matter where you might go, I'll catch up with you. Just take care of each other and wait for me."

"Oh no! I will never leave here without you! Besides, there is no more time left. If you don't get out right now, you may never have another chance," I sobbed.

"I know, honey! I know, but right now I have no choice. I promise you, I will find a way to get out of here."

One impatient policeman barked to Don in Vietnamese. "Enough, American!" He jerked Don's arm. "Now you will go to jail!" Poor Don. Although he didn't understand a word the policeman said, he knew what the hard jerk meant. He ignored the police and continued, "You have to take the kids and leave me, baby; you have no choice." Don turned to the children. "I want all three of you to go with Mom, and I will catch up with you guys later." Don bent down and kissed each of the kids on their heads and gave me one on my tearful cheek and said, "Please take the children out of this hell, and I will see you soon."

The kids hadn't understood what was happening until Don talked to them; they realized their father was not coming with them, and that was when they started to scream at the top of their lungs. I stood like a crying statue, watching them, while the two strangers led my husband away. I wondered when or if I would see my beloved husband again.

After Don was out of sight, I had no choice but to take the children and our suitcases and get on the plane. The problem was the children didn't want to go without their father, and I had a hard time moving them. Besides that, I had only two hands, but there were five suitcases and three unmovable kids. I looked at everything and tried to figure out what to do. A couple of good Samaritans saw my situation and decided to help me carry my luggage while I pushed the kids along.

We boarded a C-141 StarLifter, a military aircraft normally used to transport equipment. But since it was an emergency evacuation, they had to use it to take American citizens out of Vietnam.

Right before we entered the plane, I looked back and, to my surprise, saw Don standing just a few hundred feet from us, with the two policemen at his side. As soon as the kids saw their father, they tried to run back to him, and the partially smooth boarding process ended. As soon as I was able to catch one child, the other escaped. I asked a stranger to help me, and we brought them back inside and held them down.

The plane did not have seats, and everyone had to sit on the floor between lines of ropes, tied horizontally to the aircraft wall to form a straight line. After we sat down, a crewmember tied our waist to the ropes. The two younger ones didn't want to be tied down and became more distressed. They screamed as they tried to untie the ropes. I was too tired and upset to do anything with them; I just let them do whatever they wanted. A man sitting next to us knew the kids wanted their father, took pity on them, and began talking to them. To my surprise, they listened to the stranger and calmed down some. I sat there with red, swollen eyes, watching my children softly sobbing as they tried to see their dad through the window. Thanks to the tight ropes, which held them in place, they couldn't move; then they turned to me with a barrage of questions.

"Why is Daddy not coming with us?" three-year-old Teresa asked with tears still dampening her face.

"Where is my Daddy? I want my Daddy!" two-year-old Nicky yelled.

"Why did the police take my Daddy to jail? Are they going to kill him?" Eddie sobbed.

"No, they are not going to kill him," I murmured.

"When can I see my Daddy?" Eddie asked. "I don't want to go without him."

I didn't have an answer for them, because I didn't have one for myself; I wished I did. The roar of the engines grew louder, and it made me even sadder, because I knew we were leaving Don behind. It was bad enough to go without him, but to leave him in the middle of the war, which was just about to collapse into chaos, was unbearable.

I closed my eyes, and in the depth of my heart, I prayed, "God! Please protect my husband, and let us see each other again." I repeated my prayer until it became my mantra; I didn't know if it could be answered, but it felt good to pray.

As the plane taxied down the runway, I peeked through a small window and saw Don still standing there, with his hands cuffed behind his back and his head bent down to his chest. I thought it must be painful for him to stand there and watch helplessly as his wife and children were taken away to some unknown place without him. At first, I wondered why the police had softened and allowed him to watch his family fly away, but then I had an idea why.

The plane was in position to take off, and the engines roared louder as the plane hurtled down the runway. It gained speed and then lumbered into the sky. As the airplane climbed higher, my tears ran down even faster. Thank God the kids were interested in flying and temporarily forgot about their Daddy, and I had a few moments to think.

Where are we going? I wondered. *And when we get there, what are we going to do without Don?* I closed my eyes and prayed again; first, I prayed for Don's safety, and then for us, for our journey to wherever we might end up. I hoped Don could get out of Vietnam; otherwise, I might never see him again. I was afraid it would be just a matter of hours before South Vietnam was conquered. The more I thought about it, the more frightened I was about Don.

"Please God, get my loving husband out of Vietnam today, before it's too late! Come on, Don! Come with us. I can't live without you. Please, try to get out of there now!" I repeated this mantra until the kids distracted me with their questions.

Later that day, we landed at Clark Air Force Base in the Philippines, and one by one, we followed each other out the door. I held on to my two youngest, and Eddie was right behind me.

"Why is Daddy not coming with us, Mom?" Eddie asked.

"Waaah!!! I want Daddy! I want my Daddy!" Nicky started.

"I don't want to go down; I want to fly back to Daddy." Teresa pouted and yanked her hand away from mine.

I tried hard to guide them down the steps, but they didn't budge; I had to pick both of them up by their waists, walk down the steps, and sit them down on the ground. As soon as their feet hit the ground, they stomped, screamed, and jumped up and down.

"I am not going anywhere until my Daddy comes," Teresa yelled.

"I want Daddy! Waaah! Waaah! I want my Daddy!" Nicky screamed and cried.

I was in tears as I tried to grab their hands to take them to the waiting bus, but they just stood in the same place, screaming and crying as they twisted and turned their bodies, avoiding my guiding hands. I looked at them and shook my head in confusion. I was physically and mentally drained and didn't know what to do with them. I realized I needed to come up with some quick answers to calm my children, so I wiped my tears and acted strong.

"Hey! I forgot to tell you guys something," I lied in an upbeat voice, with raised eyebrows. "I just now remembered what your dad told me before we left." I smiled big. "He told me to go ahead and he would meet us in a hotel. The Vietnamese government wants your Daddy to stay behind and help people with the evacuation of Vietnam."

Thank God! It worked. They immediately stopped crying and looked up at me with hope in their eyes. I looked at my children's swollen eyes and couldn't believe what had happened to us. I just wished it was a nightmare we would all soon wake up from.

I never had to make decisions about where to go or what to do when Don was with us. But he wasn't there, and I was lost and confused.

Just then, a man in uniform came up to me when we were just about to get in a line to board a bus.

"Are you Mrs. Baer?" he asked. I was surprised. No! I was shocked.

"Yes!" I replied. "But how do you know my name?"

"Your husband called from Vietnam," he said with a smile, "and asked us to help you and your three children."

I was so relieved to know Don had somehow managed to get to a phone and call ahead; I knew then he was safe.

"I will take you and your children to a hotel on base," he said, and then he looked at the kids, rubbed their heads, and smiled.

"What about my suitcases?" I asked.

"I'll bring them to you later," he responded.

"Thank you so much," I told him.

"You are most welcome; it is my pleasure." He winked at me and smiled.

I realized then that Don was with us. Although he was not there in person, he knew I needed help and sent someone to help me.

"Thanks, honey!" I closed my eyes, reached for his soul, and then sent my love back to him. I loved him so much, and I knew I wouldn't rest until we were together again.

My children and I followed the man to an already packed bus with its engine running. The uniformed man waved to the bus driver and signaled for him to stop and let us on. When the bus door swung open, Eddie climbed up the tall steps; then the man picked up Teresa and placed her on the bus floor, where Eddie held on to her. Then he picked up Nicky and walked up the steps himself. I climbed quickly up right behind him.

I couldn't see from where I was, nor was I aware of how much time had passed, until the bus came to a complete stop. Since I was right at the doorstep, I got off the bus first and saw that we had arrived at a motel. As people began to pour off of the bus, I gathered my kids. They seemed surprisingly calm. It might have been because of the stranger, who talked to them and distracted them from thinking about their

Dad, or maybe they believed my lie and thought their Dad would be at the hotel; either way, it was a good thing. Our military helper took us to one of the motel rooms, furnished with two beds, one bath, and a small color television. The man turned on the screen, smiled, and said, "Stay here, watch television, and relax. I will bring you your luggage." I thanked him and he left; later, he returned with our suitcases.

The children were interested in a TV show until I said, "Hey, you guys, let's take showers. Who wants to go first?" I asked as I opened the suitcases to retrieve their clothes.

"I'll go first," Eddie volunteered.

"I'm hungry!" Nicky whined. "I don't want to take a bath until I eat."

"No," I said, "you take your bath first, and I will take you out to get something to eat later."

"No! No!" He screamed. "I want to eat first."

"There's no food in the hotel!" I exclaimed. "We'll have to go out to find a restaurant before we can eat." To avoid another two-year-old tantrum, I decided to take them out to eat before bathing them, so I closed the suitcase.

"I just hope we can find an open restaurant nearby," I said.

"We don't need for them to be open, Mom," Nicky said. "We can open it ourselves."

"No, son, it doesn't work that way."

"Why not? I am strong and I can do it," he said as he pumped himself up. I looked at him, smiled, and thought, *How can I explain to a child that we can't just go to some closed restaurant and open it up ourselves?* So I decided to play along.

"We might have to, Nicky," I said. "Are you going to help me?"

"Okay, Mom. I am strong and I can open everything," he replied as we stepped out, and I closed the door behind us.

The kids and I walked around for a while, looking for a place to eat, but found none, so I intercepted an elderly couple who were walking toward us, with toothpicks still hanging from their lips.

"Excuse me! Do you know if I can find some place to eat around here?"

"Yes, you can. Right over there," she said. She pointed to a building a few blocks away.

"We just came from there, and they have very good food," the man said.

"Thanks!" I replied.

I followed their directions, found a nice cafeteria, and we marched in.

"Hey, Nicky! It's already open," I exclaimed with a smile. "You see. We didn't have to open it ourselves. Boy! Aren't we lucky today?" I kept the smile on my face to hide the pain in my heart and to keep my children happy and calm. I ordered four good hot meals of soup, sandwiches, and pasta. As we ate, I wished Don were there with us.

After dinner, we took our time strolling back to the motel. Once again, I opened the suitcases and pulled out the clothes we needed for a shower. "I'll go first," Eddie volunteered again as he looked through the suitcase to find his own clothes. I waited for Eddie to get out of the shower, and then I gave the two younger ones their bath and dressed them. I told them to watch TV, and I went to take a shower myself.

While in the shower, I heard all three of the kids screaming.

I turned the water off, wrapped a towel around my soaking wet body, and before I had a chance to get out of the bathroom door, I heard Eddie yelling.

"Hey, Mom! I saw Daddy! I saw Daddy!" he said and ran back to the TV room. I opened the door and followed him, where I saw all three kids jumping up and down, pointing at the TV. "I saw Daddy! I saw Daddy!"

I looked at the TV, but there were only some local news reporters talking about the evacuation of orphans out of Vietnam. I looked at my watch and saw it was after ten in the evening. It was too late for a flight to land. "You guys must have seen somebody who looked like Daddy, because it's too late for Daddy to be here today. Besides, your Daddy told me he had to stay to help with the evacuation. He said he would be here later, but I don't think he meant today." I lied, because I didn't want them to start acting up again. I went back to finish my shower. But the kids began screaming with excitement again.

"Mom! Mom! Come here!" Teresa yelled. I ran out again but only saw the same news reporters. I told the kids to stop teasing me and let me finish my shower.

After my shower, I dried my hair in front of the TV, just in case the kids really did see Don. Suddenly, the kids screamed, "There he is! There he is!" I looked at the screen and saw somebody who looked a little bit like Don, but the kids insisted it was Don. I looked closer at a man who was carrying two handicapped children, one in each arm. The man walked down the steps, holding two kids.

"Did you see Daddy, Mom?" Eddie asked.

"I saw somebody who looked like Daddy, but I'm not sure it's him," I said with some doubt. Meanwhile Teresa and Nicky continued to jump up and down as they danced and clapped their hands. They really believed their Daddy was on the way to see them. The TV showed the same news footage again and again. I looked closer at the man and realized it was Don.

"That does look like Daddy," I said. "Well! Let's hope it is Daddy. But why in the world is he carrying two handicapped children?"

"Mom! That is Daddy!" Eddie said. "He told you he had to stay behind and help evacuate refugees, and that's exactly what he's doing."

"But if it is Don, how did he get out? And who are those handicapped children? If it is him, where is he? Is he here in the Philippines? Or is he still there in Vietnam?"

Wherever he was, I was happy to see him on TV. His image brought temporary relief to my aching heart. It was almost midnight. It was late, but none of us could sleep, and I didn't want to force the kids to go to sleep either; I needed their company. A few minutes later, I changed my mind. I turned the TV off and said, "It's late; let's get ready for bed, in case your dad comes early in the morning. We have to get up to greet him."

I was doubtful, but that's what I told them. The kids were tired and fell fast asleep. I watched my children innocently sleeping and thought of their future. I wondered what they would grow up to be, and if they would remember any of the frightening experiences we went through together. Whatever happened in our future, I hoped and prayed that the love we shared that day would forever stay in our hearts.

I laid my head down on the pillow and thought of Don, of our journey, and of what we had been through together since we met. There were many times I thought we would never see each other again, but luckily, we always found each other. I hoped this separation was like all the others, just temporary, and we would soon be back in each other's arms once again.

I remembered when Don was still in the air force and was sent back to America for medical evaluation. He spent three months and ten days in a military hospital. I wondered if the air force would ever release him and let him return to Vietnam. Although we continued to write to each other, our future was cloudy and uncertain; we didn't know what was going to happen to our relationship. In one of my letters to him, I wrote,

> Dearest Don,
>
> It has been so long since I saw you, talked to you, or held you in my arms. I miss you so much it hurts; it is like a sword piercing my heart each time I think of you. I am lost, sad, and lonely without you. The world seems different since you left me. I don't know how long I can survive without you. I think if the war doesn't kill me, then the pain in my heart might. Dearest Don, if I can't be with you in this life, I hope to be with you in the next one. I love you with all my being and will love you for eternity.

His response was:

> My precious Linda,
>
> Hi, how are you? I hope you are better than I am right now. Believe it or not, I am sitting here reading your

letter while listening to our love song, "The Letter" by the Box Tops. I've been thinking about getting out of the air force and hitchhiking back to you, and then I received your letter. I can't stop crying.

Whether you know it or not, I can't survive without oxygen, and you are the air I breathe. You are the food that nurtures my soul. Without you, there would be no life. My life was empty until you came to me. I existed, but I was not alive until I met you. You brought me joy and happiness. Never in my life have I known such feelings. I love you more than life itself, but if I can't be with you, it will be the end of my world. I will come back to you, one way or another, if I want to live again. Please wait for me.

Forever yours,
Don

Don did get out of the air force through medical discharge and returned to Vietnam as quickly as he could.

I hoped he would once again come back to me and to our children. The memory cheered me, and I dozed off.

A loud and urgent banging on the door woke everyone up. Before I had a chance to get out of bed, the frightened kids came running to my arms. "Open the door!" someone yelled. "Open the door!" I was scared and held my children close.

"Linda! Open the door! It's me," the man's voice yelled.

The loud knocking continued. "It's me, Don!"

"Oh my God!" I yelled as I let go of the kids, and we all ran to the door. As soon as the door sprang open, Don stepped in, and we immediately embraced. We were all so happy to be together again.

I let go of Don first and asked, "How did you get out? Who were those kids you were carrying?" All three of the kids wanted Don's attention.

Eddie finally let go of Don and jumped on the bed, but Teresa and Nicky still clung to Don's neck.

"Oh, those were two orphans I helped carry to the airplane," Don said. "By helping them, I got out of Vietnam."

"How did you escape?" I asked. "I thought they took you to jail!"

"I wasn't in jail," he said. "I told the policemen I would give them money to pay the fines, and they uncuffed me. I gave them all the US dollars I had and told them to pay my fine and taxes for me. They assured me they would and let me go. Of course, I knew the money went straight into their pockets, but I had no choice. Besides, there will be no government record soon anyway."

Don continued to tell us how he had escaped the horror. "Shortly after I paid off the police, I looked for Bill, an American friend of mine who worked at the airport. When I found him, I explained my situation and asked him for help. He said there were several C-141s lined up at the back gate, ready to take orphans to Clark Air Force Base. He also told me your plane went there too. I asked him if I could use the phone, and he took me to one of the offices, where I was able to call the base to ask them to please help you guys. Obviously, they did.

"After I made the call, Bill put me in his Jeep, flew right by the guards through the back gate, and dropped me off. I thanked him and walked up to one of the C-141s. The pilot agreed to take me, but I had to carry two handicapped orphans, who were victims of polio. I agreed, and that's how I escaped from Vietnam." Don smiled with relief.

"Thank God," I replied, and I turned to look at the kids, who were still hanging on to Don. He promised to never leave us again.

After a couple of days in the Philippines, we returned to the United States.

Chapter 6

HIGH EXPECTATIONS

ON THE MORNING of April 30, 1975, just days after we escaped from Saigon, North Vietnam took over the South and renamed the capital city of Saigon Ho Chi Minh City. The Vietnam War was finally over.

Don and I went back to Ohio so our children could have their grandma, aunts, uncles, and cousins near them. We purchased a used car and a small old house with three bedrooms and one tiny bath, on a busy street right outside of Wright Patterson Air Force Base, where military planes flew overhead every few minutes. It was unbearably loud.

Don found work with the VA as a college veteran's counselor and traveled to different parts of Ohio for days at a time. I was left at home with three kids and no transportation. If I needed to go grocery shopping, I had to call a taxi or wait for Don to come home.

Although we lived close to his family, we seldom saw them. The kids and I didn't have the transportation to go visit them, and they were too busy to visit us. I just wished we lived in a different place, where I could walk to the stores. I needed a car, even a small old one, to use for shopping, to take the children to a park, or to go to the doctor if there was an emergency. But I knew we couldn't afford it. The money we once had was invested in properties or had paid for government taxes we didn't owe and for the crooked lawyer we trusted in Vietnam. We had just bought our home with what little we had left. I wondered if we still owned the property in South Vietnam. It would be sad for us if we lost all of our life savings. Once again, all of our money was tied up in land.

At the time, Eddie was ten years old and in third grade. Teresa was three, and Nicky was four. They were too young for school, so I homeschooled them; they were doing well with math and reading. Although they seemed to be happy, I believed they still needed more activity outside of the house. What they needed were friends their own age, but there were none in our neighborhood. Our yard was too small, and the street was too busy for them to play outside. Our poor children were cooped up inside the house watching Sesame Street most of the day.

The situation was very hard on the kids and me, and I often complained to Don; my nagging caused us to argue all the time. Our constant fighting put pressure on our marriage, and Don started drinking heavily again. At one point, we almost called it quits. Thank God, we came to our senses and took steps to save our marriage.

We decided to sell our home and move away from Ohio. Don called a friend he used to work with in Vietnam and asked for his help finding a job. Before we could sell our home, Don received a job offer from Iran Aircraft Industries (IACI) to be their senior advisor, so we decided to move to Iran.

The company allowed our family only one month to get ready. We found a realtor and turned our home over to him to sell. We took enough clothes for the five of us and put everything else in storage. Before leaving, we took our children to say goodbye to Don's family. When we told them we were going to Iran, none of them knew where it was. One of Don's brothers-in-law heard the word Middle East, shook his head in disgust, and said, "You can't pay me enough money to go to such a stupid place, with dirty people riding camels."

"Why are they stupid and dirty?" I asked.

"Because they all eat weird stuff, have a weird religion, and smell like camels."

Here we go again, I thought, *people making rash judgments about others because of their religions, customs, cultures, and looks*. We are all different, but prejudices have no basis in fact or reason. This was the same man who always made fun of my food. His wife and many others in Don's family, however, loved my cooking.

None of them seemed surprised at our announcement. In fact, they didn't show much emotion at all. After a few brief hugs, we piled into our car and left. As we drove away, I wondered if they really even liked us. It didn't matter to me, though. They were Don's family, and I loved them.

WE TOOK ADVANTAGE of the free time and drove to Florida, my dreamland, since the previous time I was in America, I hadn't had the chance to see it.

It took us two days to travel from Fairborn, Ohio, to Tampa, Florida. We drove around for hours, just enjoying the city. Later, we ended up in Clearwater, a small town near St. Petersburg, and rented a tiny old shack near the beach. It had only one small bedroom, with a tiny kitchen and bath, but we loved it.

We spent most of our days on the beach, fishing, crabbing, hunting for seashells, or just relaxing on the sand. We loved Florida and promised each other we would live there when we returned from Iran.

Nicky was three, Teresa four, I was twenty-nine, and Eddie eleven, in Florida in 1976

It was sad when the month ended and our vacation was over. We sold our car, left our little shack, and were on our way to Tehran, Iran.

It was a long flight from Florida to New York, and after hours of delays, we caught a flight to Rome, Italy, where we stayed for three days. I was glad we decided to visit Italy, because I loved the Vatican, with all the ancient art and old buildings, especially the churches. We loved the city and Italian food, but the taxis fell into another category. We didn't speak Italian and had trouble telling the drivers where we wanted to go.

Don, Nicky, Teresa, and Eddie (clockwise) at the Coliseum in Rome

They took advantage of it, often taking us on wild goose chases, and charged us unbelievable fees. We decided walking was much cheaper, if we knew where we were going. One day, we took a taxi to the Sistine Chapel. After admiring the church, we walked around sightseeing and later became lost. Don had to hail a taxi and gave the driver a piece of paper containing the street name and the address of our hotel. He took us around the city for an hour or more; at one point, I told Don I saw the same building twice.

Don didn't believe me; he smiled and made a remark. "I guess all of the old buildings look alike." After he commented, I kept quiet and stared out the window, until it was his turn to notice.

"I thought we went through here before," Don said, but before we could say anything, the driver dropped us off at our hotel and charged us fifty dollars. Don paid the driver, and he sped away.

"I'm hungry," I told Don. "We need to find something to eat. I'm sure the kids are too."

"How about the restaurant inside the hotel?" Don asked.

"I don't like the food they serve in their café," I said, shaking my head.

"Well, I don't like their food either, and I'm hungry too," he said and pointed to his left. "Let's go that way."

"Okay," I said. The kids were excited about the food and took off running ahead of us. We walked to a corner just a block from our hotel and saw a familiar building. We both realized it was the same place we entered the taxi about an hour earlier. He and I looked at each other and shook our heads in disbelief.

"If we'd only walked a few more yards, we wouldn't have had to pay fifty dollars for a taxi," I said.

"Well," Don said with a big smile, "when in Rome, we do as the Roman taxi drivers do." We both laughed.

"At least we were on an unexpected sightseeing tour, and it was worth the money," I said, and we both smiled.

We went to a restaurant and ordered a pizza and spaghetti. But when the food came, they looked and tasted nothing like the Italian food we have in America. The pizza's crust was paper thin, and the spaghetti hardly had any meat in it. Although the food was okay, it was not what we expected. After the meal, we went back to our hotel and flew to Iran the day after.

Chapter 7

MIDDLE EAST TRAUMA

ON SEPTEMBER 3, 1976, we arrived at Mehrābād International Airport. One of Don's colleagues, an employee of IACI named Jim, came to meet us. After exchanging greetings, Jim told us he would take us to a nice furnished apartment the company had rented for us. Jim helped Don put our suitcases in the back of the van, and the kids and I squeezed into the back seat. While Don talked to Jim and the kids had their own conversation, I gazed out the window. Tehran was interesting, but like most large cities, it had traffic problems, with noisy horns, and was crowded.

The car turned slowly into Pahlavi Street. I saw two rows of large trees with broad green leaves and wide branches reaching out across the road to touch each other. It created a huge tunnel-like canopy covering the entire street. As the car entered the canopy, I noticed the bottoms of the large tree trunks were painted white, and the roots were exposed to running water ditches alongside the road. They were beautiful.

Jim turned off Pahlavi into Tahlavi Street and parked in front of a tall building; he stepped out first and then opened the back door for us. Don helped the kids out on his side, and we all followed Jim into the building. We walked into a large foyer; I looked up and realized the building had three levels. Jim opened the door to the lower apartment. While Jim and Don brought in the luggage, the kids and I spread out in different directions to check out our new home. There were three bedrooms, a living room, a dining room, and a large kitchen. I walked down the split level and found a huge bath with two different kinds of toilets, one in each room. There was an American standard, and the other was the Persian type, the one you have to squat over. It had a water hose protruding from the wall, which was used to wash up afterward. I was familiar with the Persian type; we used them in Vietnam.

After saying thanks and goodbye to Jim, we all went outside to a nice sunken garden in the backyard.

"I love this place! So far, so good," I told Don as he came near me.

"It looks nice," he said, with a satisfied grin.

Within a short time, we found a school for the kids. I filled the apartment with more furniture and planted the garden full of vegetables, herbs, and flowers.

The company issued Don a car with a private chauffeur, Hossain, who took Don to and from work and wherever he needed to go. When Don didn't need the car, he sent Hossain back to the house to take us anywhere we wanted to go. Hossain was available twenty-four hours a day, seven days a week, with no days off. Don and I loved him and let him off whenever we didn't need him.

The children loved their English-speaking schools and all of their teachers. Don was happy with his job, and I developed many friendships with women from all over the world; some of them had husbands who worked at the same company as Don.

THE OWNER OF our apartment building was an old Iranian plastic surgeon, who occupied the second floor. He was about sixty-five and lived with a young girl, who was one-fourth his age, and their adopted five-year-old boy. The young girl, named Fati, later became my friend; we taught each other languages and shared our cooking recipes.

The doctor, however, was a very flirty old man. One day, I was home alone cooking and cleaning. While I was at the sink washing the dishes, he came down to see me and asked me something in English, but before I had a chance to turn around, he came up behind me and grabbed my breasts with both hands. Shocked, I quickly turned around and slapped him hard with my soapy hand. I cursed him out in Farsi, and he apologized to me in English. Then he went back upstairs to his apartment.

When Don came home, I told him about the doctor's advances toward me. Don went to the doctor's flat and confronted him; he apologized to both of us and promised he would never touch me again.

Everything went smoothly after that, and I never told Fati about the incident. The boy they adopted was around the same age as my children, and they played well together. Besides teaching each other cooking and speaking our languages, we took our children to parks and shopping. Sometimes Fati took me to the homes of her family or friends, where I learned more about Iranian food, customs, culture, traditions, and the Islamic religion.

Don, me, and Eddie, with Teresa and Nicky, at the zoo in Tehran.

I got together weekly with the women I knew who had husbands working for IACI. We took turns having parties at each other's homes, normally on Friday or Saturday afternoon. The parties were to entertain our husbands, get our children to play together, and give us women a chance to chitchat. Some weekends, instead of partying with friends, we took our children to the park or the zoo, or we went fishing and picnicked in the Alborz Mountains by ourselves.

One weekend, a group of Iranian friends who worked with Don asked him to go with them to the Caspian Sea for a short break. Don accepted their invitation and asked me to prepare food for the trip. Instead of using the chauffer, Don decided to drive the car himself and gave the driver the weekend off. Don didn't trust his driver to take us. He thought he drove too fast on dangerous roads. One time, he did let Hossain drive us to the Caspian Sea, but when he came too close to a cliff, Don almost had a heart attack; he vowed never to let anyone else drive us up there but him.

The Caspian Sea was not too far from Tehran, but the road was rough and dangerous. It was narrow, winding, with many potholes and falling rocks. Our Iranian friends were used to it, and they drove fast—so fast that they left Don struggling far behind. Now and then, all four of the drivers ahead of us pulled over, got out of their cars, walked around, and waited for Don. As soon as Don drove up to them, the men came running over to make fun of Don's slow driving.

Nazam walked up to Don's window and exclaimed, "I thought Americans drove fast! What in the heck is the matter with you, big boy?" He finished his words and everyone laughed.

"Not this American," Don replied to his friend as he got out of our car. "Especially with my wife and kids in the car." Don retaliated with a big smile, "I'm not driving too slowly; you guys are just driving way too fast!" They all laughed again.

We loved this group of friends; they were fun and crazy but very polite. We all walked around, admiring the mountain peaks for about ten minutes, and Don made a suggestion.

Me, Teresa, and Nicky in the Alborz Mountains, on our way to the Caspian Sea

"Since you guys know this road well and are driving much faster than I am, why don't you go ahead, and we'll catch up with you at the Caspian Sea. What do you think?"

At first, they refused to leave us behind, but Don insisted, and reluctantly, they agreed.

Don waited until they disappeared behind the mountains and then moved our car to a safer place. While Don and the kids walked around enjoying the majestic views, I went to the back of the car and prepared lunch; I didn't care much for viewing the scenery. I like mountains with tall trees and flowers, but these had neither. Other than a few low bushes scattered around, it was bare, rough, and unfriendly, and there was nothing of interest to me.

I made chicken and lamb shish kebab sandwiches for everyone and handed them out along with cans of soda, and then I sat on a rock to eat mine. While watching my family enjoy their food and drinks, I noticed Nicky holding a half-eaten sandwich in one hand and his stomach with the other; he was bending over, with a pained expression on his face. My first thought was my poor child might have food poisoning. I put my sandwich down and ran to him.

"What's wrong, honey?" I asked.

He reached up and whispered in my ear, "My stomach, Mommy," he said.

"What about your stomach?" I asked. "What does it feel like?"

"I need to go to the bathroom!" he moaned.

"Number one or number two?"

"Number two, Mommy," he winced.

"That's okay," I said. "I'll take you behind the bush and let you use the bathroom, okay?"

He looked at me as if I had just lost my marbles and yelled, "No! I don't want to! I want to go home!" Then he started crying.

"No, Nicky. We can't go home right now," I said. "We are hundreds of miles from home. If you need to do number two badly, you'll have to do it over there." I pointed to a bush nearby and tried to talk him into it. "I have a napkin; you can use it to wipe yourself."

"No! I don't want to do it here," he bellowed.

When Don heard Nicky and me arguing, he finished his sandwich and came closer to see what we were fussing about. I told Don what was happening, and he convinced Nicky to use the bathroom behind the bush. It worked. Nicky took the napkin from my hand and handed Don his half-eaten sandwich. I went back to finish my sandwich and then tidied up the car. A few minutes later, I heard Nicky screaming bloody murder again.

"What now?" I grumbled. I stopped what I was doing and rushed toward him. Eddie and Teresa eyed me as I walked by. When they heard Nicky cry, they stuffed the rest of their sandwiches in their mouths and took off running. I smiled at them as they ran past me.

They got to the scene before I did. When I arrived, I saw Eddie, Teresa, and Don laughing as hard as Nicky was crying. I was confused and asked Don what was going on.

"Oh, I just ate Nicky's sandwich!" Don exclaimed through hysterical laughter. "I am so sorry."

"You are not sorry, Daddy. You are laughing," Nicky cried.

"Why did you eat Nicky's sandwich?" I asked Don.

"I don't know!" he said. "I thought he gave it to me."

"No, Dad!" Nicky screamed. "I did not give it to you! I just asked you to hold it! And you ate it! Waah! Waah! Why did you eat my sandwich, Daddy?"

"I am so sorry, son," Don said with a sad face. "I don't know why I ate your sandwich. I guess I was distracted by the beautiful mountain views; I was not thinking, and I am sorry. I promise I will get you a much bigger one when we get to the Caspian Sea, okay?" Don then gently rubbed Nicky's head.

"Okay, Dad," he sobbed. "Just don't eat my next one."

"I promise you I won't eat your next one," Don said with a remorseful expression. He held out his hand, Nicky took it, and we all returned to the car. We drove off slowly, making our way to the Caspian Sea.

Although the Caspian Sea was not too far, it took us many hours to get there, because of the bad road and Don's slow driving. We also stopped often to picnic and sightsee.

The sun was going down, and Don crawled along the cliff even slower than before. Now and then, he had to move out of the way to let other faster cars pass. It was getting dark, and we still had some ways to go. After the sun disappeared behind the mountains, Don was barely creeping along. I thought, *If I get out of the car, I can walk faster than he's driving.* He was so nervous about the road condition he began to sweat, and his body odor started to permeate the car. I smiled when I saw the kids in the back seat holding their noses.

"Hey, Dad, am I going to smell like you when I grow up?" Eddie asked.

Don laughed and said, "No, son, you won't smell like me, unless you have to drive at night on a dangerous road, with a wife and three kids, in a hot car without an air conditioner; then you would probably smell like me." We all laughed.

I saw another four-door sedan with dim lights pass us, going dangerously fast near the cliff. I turned to Don and asked, "I wonder how many people have died on this road?"

"A lot, I'm sure," he replied.

"Then why do they take such chances?" I said.

"Perhaps they are not too smart; they think if they don't die now, they will just die later, or perhaps they think their life isn't worth living," Don said.

I knew Don was being sarcastic; he talked as if he didn't like the fast drivers because they made him look bad for driving too slow, but I asked the question anyway.

"Oh, do you really think they are stupid?"

"No, Linda, I was just kidding."

"No, Don, I know you were not kidding!"

Don raised his voice, "I told you! I was just kidding; I'm not serious! I don't think people want to kill themselves intentionally. They are not that stupid." He was mad, and I was offended.

"But why?" My voice was even louder than his was. "Why are you saying bad things about people? It's not nice," I snapped.

"About what people, Linda?!"

"Well, Don! I don't like the way you are talking to me," I shouted.

"How am I talking to you, Linda?" he shouted back.

"You are not being nice to me, because you keep calling me Linda."

"Well, have you been nice to me?" Don asked.

"No, but I'm not as mean as you!" I pouted.

"Well, Linda, sounds like the pot is calling the kettle black," he said.

The kids were quiet and listened to us fight for a while, but they grew bored and started singing, "Up the mountain, through the prairies, to the ocean . . ." The same song we all sang on a long car trip. Don and I realized how stupid our fighting was and started singing along with the kids. "To the . . . o . . . ce . . . an . . ."

It was very late when we arrived at the motel. There was nothing for miles, except lines and lines of new cheap-looking motels along the beach. Don parked in front of the office, which did not look much different from the other buildings. Before he got out of the car, he said, "You guys stay right where you are and let me go pick up the key." A few minutes later, he came back and drove us up to one of the units.

He parked, and we jumped out. Don walked up to one of the doors and opened it. He turned on the only light, which was a single light bulb dangling from a wire in the middle of the room. We followed him inside. There were four single beds, sitting on a sandy cement floor. While Don and Eddie went back to the car to bring in our suitcases, the two younger ones followed me as I investigated.

At the end of the room, there was a small area with a curtain hanging from the ceiling, which I assumed might be the bathroom. I walked to it and found a small light bulb on the end of a long electrical cord hanging over the Persian-style toilet. I reached over and turned it on, but it was so dim I couldn't see to count my own fingers. There was no bathtub or shower, just a water pipe sticking out from the wall with a showerhead attached to the end, and it pointed to an open spot on the cement floor, right next to the toilet; I presumed it was our shower. After Don and Eddie brought in our suitcases, we were too tired to bathe and all went straight to bed.

The following morning, we joined Don's friends and went swimming. In the afternoon, we got together and had a fun cookout. The day after the barbeque, we all went our separate ways.

Don and I found our way to a boat dock, rented a six-passenger boat, and hired a sixty-year-old man named Hasan to be our fishing guide. Hasan didn't speak English, so I had to be the interpreter. While Don and I put on our life jackets, Hasan helped the excited kids put on theirs and then helped them onto the boat. Don took all the fishing gear and jumped on board. I climbed on after him with a tackle box in my hand. Don sat in the front of the boat, the kids sat in the middle, and I sat in the back of the boat. When everyone was settled, Hasan went to the back, sat near me, and started the engine. While he maneuvered the boat along the swift-moving river, he said, "I will take you to a place where you can catch catfish that could weigh a hundred pounds or more." It sounded good, but I hoped I wouldn't hook one that big.

"Do you eat catfish?" I asked him. He stuck out his tongue and shook his head.

"No! Iranian people don't eat those trash fish," he said and continued to shake his head and make faces.

"Why? Catfish are good to eat," I said, laughing.

"No! They are not," he argued. "They are the dirtiest fish in the water; they eat garbage and dead things from the bottom of lakes and rivers. How could you eat them?"

"I guess you are right!" I said.

"I heard Americans also eat pigs and cows!" he said and again shook his head in disgust.

"Yes! We do eat them," I said. "We don't just eat the meat, but we eat the intestines too." Hasan stuck his tongue out even farther this time, shook his head, and acted like he was about to vomit; that made me laugh even harder.

"You react to those who eat pigs and cows as they react to others who eat horses or dogs," I said. Hasan slowed the boat down, and our conversation ended. I looked around at the beautiful green savanna surrounding us and wished the people in this world would be more open-minded and accept others' differences without being critical and judgmental.

As the boat docked, Don jumped off and helped pull the boat up on land. We got out of the boat, and while Hasan looked for a bush to tie his boat to, we took our fishing equipment and prepared the hooks.

Hasan walked over, making faces at us, and signaled for Don to stop what he was doing.

"What stupid fish eats plastic?" he said in Farsi. "You have to use live frogs if you want to catch these catfish."

I was trying to interpret what Hasan said, but I didn't understand the word frog and couldn't make out what Hasan was trying to tell us. In desperation, he got down on all fours and started jumping around like a frog, making a "ribit, ribit, ribit" sound with his mouth.

"A frog!" I said, and we all laughed. We understood him, and I asked, "Where can we get live frogs?"

He pointed to Don, himself, and the boat and motioned for Don to come with him. The kids understood his hand signals and wanted to go too. After they left, I stayed behind to straighten up our fishing gear and untie the plastic lures.

I finished my job and waited for them to come back with frogs. I wondered why it was taking so long, and I decided to look in the nearby bushes for frogs myself. In the first bush, I saw a huge green bullfrog lying motionless in the grass. I came closer to him, and he tried to jump away. I chased him down and finally caught him. I took him back to my fishing gear, hooked his top lip to a large hook, and tied it to a fifty-pound line.

The frog was too heavy for me to cast out, so I laid my rod down on the ground, stepped on the handle, picked up the frog with both hands, and threw him into the swift moving water. "There is no way a fish in this small body of water can eat a huge bullfrog," I said to myself. "But since there is nothing else for me to do, I'll give it a try. Who knows, a shark from the Caspian Sea might come by and eat it."

I smiled when my fishing line began moving. *It must be the frog or the current*, I thought, but then my rod began moving fast toward the water. I rushed to pick it up and set the hook. Whatever was on my line was heavy. *It's probably hung up on a log*, I thought. But the log began moving! I knew I had something big on my line. My heart was pounding as I fought and fought with it until its head came up to the surface.

"Oh my God!" I exclaimed when I saw the giant head of a weird-looking catfish. I tried hard not to lose him, because I knew no one was going to believe me otherwise. Thank God, I was able to drag the monster to the bank, and to my surprise, it wiggled and followed me out of the water. I continued to drag it away from the river until I felt it was far enough for me to stop to catch my breath. I was shaking like a leaf as I stood looking at the four-foot monster with a foot-wide head. I'd never seen such a weird thing in my life. It must have been the fish Hasan described earlier.

I stood in silence, staring at the strange fish while it stared back at me. Cold chills ran down my spine as I let my imagination get the best of me. I felt as if I was in some strange dream, and the fish was from some horror movie. After all, I didn't pull him out of the water; he wiggled and followed me up here by himself. I began feeling uneasy and scared and started backing away from the fish. I couldn't wait for Don and the kids to come back. Half an hour later, they still had not come back, and I began to worry.

I hope their boat didn't sink, I thought. *If it sank, they will drown and I will be left here to die.* The more I thought about it, the more I worried. I saw the weird monster start moving, and I stepped back even farther. I felt relieved when I heard the sound of a boat motor coming closer and closer. I hoped it was Hasan's boat bringing my family back from frog hunting. I ran to the edge of the water but couldn't see anybody through the tall king grass.

Minutes later, I saw Don's head popping up and down with the waves. The moment I saw him, I immediately waved and yelled, "Hey, Don! I caught a big fish this big." I stretched my arms all the way out to let him know how big the fish was. When he saw my outstretched arms, he smiled and held up his thumb and forefinger, suggesting the fish was four inches long instead of four feet. I shook my head and continued holding out my arms. He shook his head to let me know he didn't believe me and again held up his thumb and forefinger.

Hasan docked the boat right in front of me. Don jumped off first and then helped the kids onto dry land. As soon as their feet hit the ground, I ran ahead of them toward my fish and stopped just a foot from the giant. When they saw the fish, they immediately stepped back and screamed. Don's eyes were wide open, and his mouth dropped. When everyone recovered from the initial shock, Don asked, "How on earth did you manage to land this thing?"

I gave him a proud smile and bragged, "It wasn't easy!"

"What did you catch it with?" Don asked. "Or did you really catch it?" And then he squinted at me in doubt. "Are you sure the fish wasn't sick and crawled up here by itself to die?" Don looked at me with suspicion. "Did you find it up here?"

"What do you mean, Don?" I was irritated. "Do you think the fish was already up here? You don't believe I caught it?" I said as I raised my eyebrows and gave him an angry look. "Is that what you think?"

"Let me put it this way," he softened his voice. "It's just hard for me to believe you caught this fish because it is so big." He smiled when he realized I was getting mad and tried to smooth it over. "What did you catch it with?" he asked.

"With a frog," I said and pointed to the half-dead frog nearby. The kids immediately ran to play with the frog. "Did you guys catch any frogs?" I asked.

"Only three small ones," Don replied.

"Well, that's good enough to start with," I said. Teresa didn't want to fish; she just wanted to play with the frog. Before Don helped Nicky with the frog on his hook, Eddie was already fishing at the edge of the river.

"I want to catch a big fish just like Mom," Eddie announced as we approached him. I believed he could do it, because he loved to fish, and who knew, he might catch a bigger one.

Teresa and Nicky with his catfish near the end of 1978

Don and Hasan with our stringer of Wels catfish

By afternoon, we had caught a long stringer of fish, but none were as big as mine.

I planned to take all of them back to the motel, where I could clean and filet them and then take them back to Tehran to share with friends.

Hasan ate carp and other fish that had scales, so I gave all of those to him. He took the fish I gave him and put them in one of the boat compartments.

We gathered our things and got in the boat. I sat next to Hasan again, and we talked while he guided the boat along the snake-like river.

"I was thinking," I said with a smile, "Iranian people don't eat catfish; is that why they grow so enormous?"

"It's because of our religion," he explained. "We eat carp but don't eat any fish without scales; we also don't eat pigs, cows, or shellfish, because they are dirty." He shook his head again and stuck his tongue out.

"How funny," I said. "Most Americans don't eat carp but are happy to devour everything else you mentioned."

"We think American people are dirty and are cannibals," Hasan said, "because they all eat cows, horses, and pigs and other nasty things, like shrimp, catfish, oysters, and clams; I heard sometimes they even eat them raw." He once again stuck out his tongue and shook his whole body in disgust. I just looked at him and smiled.

"Do they eat dogs and cats too?" he asked.

"Oh no! Most of them don't. I don't eat dogs or cats either."

"That's because you are not American," he said. I thought Hasan was a little confused, but it was hard for me to explain to him who was eating what.

Hasan reminded me of the time I was in the United States when an American woman asked me if I ate dogs.

"No, I don't eat dogs," I said to her with a smile.

"How about cats and horses?"

"No! I don't eat them either; they are my pets," I said.

"I heard all Asians eat dogs, cats, and horses, but you don't?" she asked.

The poor woman was obviously confused, and I felt sorry for her, just as I did Hasan and many others who had preconceived notions about other races and cultures.

I was lucky enough to have had the chance to live in many different places. I learned their customs, cultures, and traditions, which were so different from mine. The most important thing I learned was to not judge anyone and to not make fun of their food. There are no bad or dirty foods; the differences are in our religions, countries, regions, customs, cultures, traditions, and tastes.

When we were back on the dock, Don paid the boat rental and gave Hasan a big fat tip. We packed up our car, and Don drove to the restaurant for dinner and back to our motel just in time to hit the sack.

DURING MY YEARS in Iran, I learned to speak Farsi and cook Persian food; I believe I did well at both. I was communicating with Iranian people and bargaining with them in the stores. While Don was at work and the kids were in school, I spent most of my time working in my garden, cooking, cleaning, and washing clothes. When I had time, I went shopping for clothes and food or went to a nursery for more flower seeds and plants. We were happy, and life was good for us.

At least, it was until religious radicals and the government decided to fight for control. The country split into two groups; the power struggle between them threw the country into revolution and chaos. Their differences spilled into the streets of Tehran. Each side demanded power, and demonstrations became street battles; peace in Tehran was lost.

The last time we went to the mountains, Don took a wrong turn and ended up in a small village. It was late, and the kids were hungry, so I told Don to stop at one of the small street vendors.

Don parked the car, and I told everyone to stay inside while I went for food. I walked up to the porch where a half-dozen middle-aged men wearing turbans sat at a table smoking their Persian pipes; they all stared at me as I approached.

I was polite and asked them in Farsi if they had anything for my hungry children to eat. They waved their hands and motioned for me to get lost. I was confused and thought I might have said something that upset them. I repeated myself to make sure I didn't make a mistake. This time they all stood up and, without saying a word, motioned for me to get off their property. I was confused and scared and went back to the car. I'd never seen Iranians acting that way toward me before. They were usually polite and loving. I went back to the car and got in.

"I don't know what's going on," I said as I sat down. "I don't understand what's happened to these people! They are acting weird." I closed the door behind me, and Don moved on.

"I saw them shooing you away," Don said.

"Yes! And I don't know why."

He drove to another vendor, and the same thing happened. It didn't matter what I tried to say; they were aggressive and refused to talk to me or sell me their merchandise. Don drove around to find more stores, but soon we were lost and driving around in circles. I asked him to stop at one more and let me try again, but again, I was rejected. When I asked them for directions back to Tehran, they refused to give them to me. I began to worry; I crossed myself and started to pray. "God, please protect my family. Don't let them be harmed, and please guide Don out of here before nightfall. Please."

Meanwhile, the hungry kids continued to complain, but there was nothing I could do except tell them I would find food for them soon.

Don drove by a bread company where they made fresh Persian nan. As we drove up, we could smell the fresh-baked nan; it made our mouths water. I told Don to stop, and instead of going by myself, this time I took all three of my children into the bakery with me, hoping for sympathy.

I smiled and greeted the two bakers in Farsi and asked, "Hello, mister. Can I buy some nan for my hungry children?" They didn't answer me right away and just looked at us. I saw one man whispering to another under his breath. I couldn't understand what they were saying, but I could tell they didn't want to sell bread to us. I took advantage of the silence and begged, "Please, sell me some nan for my starving children."

They looked at the kids for a few more seconds, and one asked roughly, "How many loaves?" We loved nan, and I wanted to buy a lot of them to take home.

"Twenty loaves," I responded.

"Na!" he said it with an attitude and his head tilted upwards. In the end, I got a quarter of what I asked for, and I was happy just to get that much. I paid him, thanked him, and took the bag full of hot nan. The kids tore into the bag before we even made it to the car and then quickly asked for more. I gave Don a piece of nan as we drove away. We came home late that night, but we were safe.

The next day, when Don came home from work, he said, "My Iranian friends told me the people in the village where we bought the nan yesterday are against all foreigners, especially Americans. They said we were lucky to get out of there alive, much less get bread."

"Well," I said, "there are good and bad people in every town of every country; we just happened to stumble into a good man who would sell us bread."

The next day, I was on the way home from the Karoush supermarket when I saw a group of half-naked men covered in blood, marching toward me on the opposite side of the street. They were reciting some religious chants as they swung heavy chains over their shoulders and from side to side. They beat themselves violently, causing blood to flow. I was horrified and stood in stunned silence. I glanced at an old man standing with a cane near me and asked him in Farsi, "Excuse me. Please tell me, are they prisoners being punished?"

He gave me a stern look and said, "No! They are men of God and are not being punished," he declared in English.

"Oh, I am sorry," I said.

"They are volunteering to suffer," he said. "They are heroes; they do this to erase your sins and mine." Confused, I looked at him and said nothing. I thought, *Wasn't that Jesus's job? Didn't he already claim to be our savior, according to the Christian Bible? Didn't he die on the cross to wash our sins away a long time ago? Well, double saviors are better than one.*

"Do you know what is on the end of those chains?" he asked.

"No, sir, I don't know," I responded in English.

"Well, you should learn," he snapped. "Those chains have razor blades attached, so they can cause more pain and make more blood flow. More blood will wash away more of ours sins."

"But why do they have to do that?" I asked. "Why can't they just let us take care of our own sins? We did it; we should be paying for it ourselves," I said.

"You don't understand, do you?" he growled. "They do this so we can all go to heaven."

"Wow!" I remarked in feigned excitement, "We are all going to heaven, and we will have a big party there." I had a stupid grin on my face, and he looked at me with disapproval.

"What religion are you, anyway?" he demanded.

Oh no! I thought to myself, *Not again. I've been through this before in Vietnam, and I'm not about to be that dumb again.* I was caught twice in the middle of demonstrations between Buddhists and Catholics in Saigon and was questioned about my religion. Both times, I gave the wrong answer and was beaten. After that day, I vowed to keep my religion to myself. Instead of answering his question about my religion, I just thanked him for the lesson and walked away.

I thought to myself as I walked home, *Why must there be so many religions and so many Gods? Why can't there be just one God? If God is as powerful as some claim, he or she could easily bring peace and happiness to one small world like ours.* That was just my thought, but in reality, I knew better. I knew there was no way that our world could settle down with just one king, one president, or even one God; that's because of our pride, greed, and selfishness. We divided this little world of ours into too many countries and religions, and one leader could not satisfy us all. Poor God, he or she must be going crazy from splitting himself or herself into so many different believers and followers. The more I thought about it, the more confused I became, and this small brain of mine couldn't handle it anymore. I opened the door and entered my apartment.

As time passed, there were many more demonstrations in the streets. Some were political, while others were religious. It was getting so bad that sometimes I had to keep my children home from school to avoid danger. Our family seldom left the house, and when we did, we only went shopping for food; other than that, we kept our door locked tight.

I noticed those nice people at the stores stopped being friendly to me. They also stopped being friendly to each other, their own people. No one looked at each other in the eye, nor did they smile with each other, as they used to. They seemed mistrustful and afraid of something or someone. Their fear and mistrust were probably justified, because no one could tell their friends from their enemies. Iran changed for the worse, and for the first time in almost three years, I felt uncomfortable.

Fatima, my housekeeper, was a fifty-year-old woman who had worked for me since I first arrived in Iran, and I loved and trusted her with my life. She and I were very close, or so I thought. She taught me to speak Farsi and cook Persian food; in return, I taught her English and to cook everything I knew. She always complimented me about how smart and pretty I was; we shared tears and family secrets, and we laughed at each other's jokes. She brought me gifts, and in turn, I bought her clothes and jewelry, but no one ever saw them, because she always covered herself from head to toes with her chador.

Fatima had to cover herself when another man was around, even with Don. When Don was away at work, she took her chador off, but as soon as she heard the key rattle in the door, she grabbed her chador, draped it around herself, and put a loose piece of the black material into her mouth to hold it in place as she did her chores.

I thought how uncomfortable it must be for the women who wore chadors; how could they do their work wrapped like mummies all day in all of that material?

"Why do you have to cover yourself all day, especially inside the house?" I was curious and asked Fatima one day.

"Because of your husband," she replied. I looked at her for a second and thought, *Oh no! What did Don do?*

"What did he do to you?" I asked.

"It is not just your husband," she explained, "but any man. After women marry, no other man can see her but her husband."

I looked at her, wrinkled my eyebrows, and asked, "We wear clothes, don't we? How could another man see us if we wear clothes, unless we took off our clothes in front of them?"

"Well, we do wear clothes," she said, "but clothes don't cover all parts of our skin."

"What skin? I wear my normal clothes, and I don't show any of my skin," I said.

"How about your feet, your arms, and your face?" she asked as she pointed to each part of my skin that was naked.

"Oh! So it's not just the private part but the whole nine yards," I said.

"What is the private part, and what is the whole nine yards?" she asked.

"Oh, it's just slang," I said, and we both laughed.

I was thinking to myself, *If I was born and raised here, I might get used to the chador too.*

After the revolution began, I noticed even Fatima began acting different. She was quiet and seldom smiled or talked. I was concerned and asked her about it one day.

"What is going on with Iranian people? And what is wrong with you? Lately, everybody seems to be quiet and unfriendly."

"Iranian people are tired of the Shah and his wife!" she snapped. "We want to get rid of them."

"Oh! Why? I thought the Shah and his family were nice people; what happened? What went wrong?"

"Nothing, and yes, everything," she replied.

"What is the matter, Fatima? You seem different. You seem distant and sad all the time. Are you and your husband getting along?" I had asked her this question before, and she always shared her family problems with me. This time she talked without looking at me.

"You people don't want to know," she raised her voice and barked, and I was surprised with her new tone. "The religious people want to bring the Ayatollah Khomeini back from Iraq," she said.

"I heard that from my friends," I replied. "But why do the Iranian people want to do that? I thought the Shah was a good man; I like his wife and his children too," I said.

She extended her bottom lip and rolled her eyes.

"You foreigners don't know anything! You people work for the Shah, get paid by the Shah, and he takes our blood, sweat, and tears to pay you people." I was shocked into silence as I listened to her with my eyes wide open and my jaw dropped. "Our country is getting poorer, while you foreigners, especially you Americans, are getting richer." She stopped to catch her breath and continued, "It's time for us to take down your Shah, take back our country," she declared, "and rebuild our Muslim religion."

When she was finished, I went over to her, looked straight into her eyes, and asked, "Just when did you start to feel this way about me and my family? I thought we were close friends; I didn't know you resented us Americans, especially me."

"I have always felt like this about you people," she replied. "You Americans have too much money, and you look down on people in other countries. We don't like Americans. We want Americans to get out of Iran." She paused to catch her breath. I frowned as I listened to her in disbelief.

"Fatima! That is very surprising to me. It is very sad for me to know how you really feel about me, about my family, and about American people. I hate to think you were here with us only for the money and nothing more." Like her, I stopped to catch my breath and continued, "I thought of you as a true friend, and I really love you, Fatima." I walked away in tears, and she went back to her chores. She quit early that day and never returned to my house.

About this time, our chauffeur began to miss work often; we believed he was taking part in the demonstrations. Don decided to let Hossain go and drive the car himself.

Not long after Fatima and Hossain left, Nazam, a close friend of Don, invited us to his house for a party. Before the party started, Nazam took us aside and whispered, "You guys need to leave Iran while you still can." He looked at us with concern as he continued to whisper. "The Shah is sick, and he has already left the country for his treatment, but we know he is not coming back. The Ayatollah Khomeini, however, will come back, and everything will change. I'm afraid you guys might be stuck here if you don't leave now." Don and I listened to every word. "It doesn't look good for the IACI Company and all of us who worked for the Shah either." He paused for a second and looked away. "I too plan on taking my family out of Iran, but I'm not sure where we are going yet."

"If you decide to come to America, look us up," Don said.

"I will," he said.

We thanked Nazam for his friendship and his honesty. He shook Don's hand and gave me a hug, and then we all returned to the dining table.

After our conversation with Nazam, Don and I were nervous for the rest of the party. We left his house early that night.

On the way home, Don and I talked and made our plans. He said he was going to quit his job in the next few days, and I decided to pack up and get ready to leave Iran. The following day, Don went to work. I stuffed all the clothes I wanted to keep into five suitcases and planned to sell the rest. While Don was working and running around trying to get our passports and airline tickets ready, I hung a sign in front of our door in English and Farsi, which read, "Family going back to America, selling everything." I sold our furniture, appliances, Persian rugs, shoes, and clothes, all in a couple of days.

Don quit his job, and we were ready to leave, but we couldn't get our exit visas and the passports stamped; the embassy was too crowded, because everybody was trying to leave Iran at the same time. Don got his visa and passport done a day after I sold everything, but the kids and mine were not ready yet. Besides the passports, we still couldn't get our airline tickets, because the airport counters were closed, and we couldn't go anywhere without boarding passes.

Don woke up and left the house early each morning but always came home disappointed. Meanwhile, the demonstrations were getting worse. One day when Don was out trying to make our travel arrangements, I could hear them outside on the streets howling and chanting. As I listened to them, my nerves got the best of me, and I started to panic. I stuck my head outside to look for Don and saw an aggressive demonstration with people of all ages and genders walking toward me, shouting something at the top of their lungs. When I saw some of them flipping their tongues up and down to make noise as they danced, I realized they were celebrating. I stepped back inside, watched them through the milky glass door, and waited for them to pass. A few minutes later, I opened the door and stuck my head out again.

What is going on? I thought. *What are they celebrating about?* For some reason, this worried me even more. *Where is Don? I hope he comes home before too late.* I kept the door ajar, just wide enough for me to look out and watch the slower participants at the back of the group.

I saw a cheerful and smiling woman walking toward me, so I stepped out and asked her, "What is happening? Why is everyone celebrating?" When she saw me, her face immediately turned sour and irritated.

"You should know!" she snapped. "The crazy Shah is gone, and the Ayatollah Khomeini is on his way home! If you didn't know that, you should have gone with the Shah." I smiled and she frowned.

"Thank you. I will," I said. She shoved me aside and walked away, so I went back inside.

While I was in the kitchen trying to find something for the kids to eat, I heard Don rush into the house; I was relieved and made a sarcastic comment.

"About time you're home!" I admonished.

"Linda, help me!" he urged. I turned to look at him and saw that half of his face was covered in blood.

"Oh my God!" I exclaimed. "Don! What happened to you?"

"Don't worry," he said. "I'm okay. One of those fanatics smashed my window right in front of the American Embassy."

"Come here," I said and grabbed his hand and took him to the kitchen sink. "Let me clean off your face. I hope you didn't get glass in your eyes."

"No, I don't think so," he said.

"Which side do you think would do this to you?"

"The driver's side," Don replied, and I laughed.

"No. Do you think it was the ones who support the government or religion?" We both laughed.

"Where are the children?" he asked.

"They're in the backyard, playing," I replied. "They would be freaking out if they saw your bloody face. What happened, and who broke out your window?"

"As I was leaving the embassy, I stopped at an intersection and was about to turn. I happened to look to my left and saw a man standing there with a large chain in his hand. He stepped forward, glared at me, raised the chain, and *kwamp*! He shattered my window. I turned away to avoid the hit, and when I was about to speed away, he swung the chain again. The second time, he barely missed my face. I hit the accelerator and roared out of there as fast as I could."

"You're lucky the window was closed. Otherwise, you'd be in bigger trouble."

"I'm in bigger trouble right now," Don blurted out. "I think the shattered glass cut my back and my butt, and I think they are bleeding right now."

"What do you mean?"

Don turned around, and I saw blood soaking through his shirt and pants.

"Oh, my goodness! I'm so sorry. I didn't know that your back was hurt too. Please take your clothes off. I want to see how bad it is."

Don took off his shirt, dropped his pants. He was covered in tiny cuts.

"Why don't you take a shower, wash off the glass, and let me bring you some clean clothes?"

"That's a good idea," he said.

Don ran to the bathroom, and I found him some clothes.

"Hurry up! We need to go!" I said through the shower curtain.

"No! We can't go yet!"

"Why can't we?"

"Because I just got your passports stamped, but I wasn't able to get our airline tickets yet."

"Why?"

"Because no one was working at the ticket counter. I waited there for hours, but nobody showed up."

"Oh no! What are we going to do now?"

"I don't know," he said. "Let me finish showering, and I'll figure something out."

As Don showered, I decided it would be best if we took our family to the airport and waited there until we could get tickets. I was scared it was too dangerous for us to stay in the apartment. When Don finished his shower, I told him what I wanted to do.

"I want us to go to the airport, whether we have tickets or not. I'd rather wait there than here! You go ahead and finish what you are doing, and let me go upstairs to say goodbye to our friends."

"Okay," he said. "I totally agree with you. And by the way, thanks for helping me with my wounds."

"It's okay, I'm happy you're all right," I said as I walked out to the foyer, closed the door behind me, and walked upstairs.

A few minutes later, I came back down and then went to the backyard to call the kids.

"Hey, children! Come on inside. We are leaving right now."

"Where is Dad?" Eddie asked.

"He's inside."

"When did Dad come home?" Teresa asked.

"He just got home."

The kids were happy to hear their father was home and came rushing inside to look for him. When they saw Don, they ran to him and gave him a big hug. While they ate, I went out to the front door to hail us a couple of taxis. It took forever; the kids got impatient and ran in and out of the door to check on me. I was beginning to get very frustrated and wondered where all the drivers were. Their absence only added to my growing fear.

An hour later, we loaded our suitcases into two taxis and were on our way to the airport. I sat in the taxi, praying and hoping we wouldn't run into a demonstration. Who knew what they might do to us, especially to Don. My fears materialized just as we approached the airport; we were caught right in the middle of a large group. Lucky for us, most of the demonstrators just stared at us as we drove by. I wondered, *Where are they coming from, and where are they going to? If they think they are going to heaven, they have a long way to go.*

When we finally arrived at the airport, we found our way through the gate and to the passenger waiting room. Many families were already there. The ticket counters were empty, and I thought the clerks must be out demonstrating too. I asked around and discovered some passengers had tickets, while others didn't. It made me feel better to know we were not the only family without tickets.

We waited and waited, but the ticket counter still didn't open, and for two days, we saw no airplane land or take off. We ate whatever we could find, including cucumbers, raw onions, and crackers, and if we were lucky, we had fruit, cookies, and bread. But food was not the problem; the real problem was cleanliness and sanitation, which posed the most serious threat. We washed ourselves in the bathroom sinks, but that was far from a shower or a bath, and since we were nervous, we sweated a lot. When I walked by people, I could tell they all smelled, including us.

The kids often asked, "Why are we still here? When are we going? Why hasn't the airplane come yet? When are they going to be here?"

Don and I had to come up with some believable answers to keep them from worrying. I was sitting on a long bench, next to Don, watching our children running around playing with the other kids. I turned to look at Don and sighed. "I wonder if we will ever get out of this place?"

Don reached over and squeezed my hand. "Don't worry, baby. I got you into this place, and I will get you out of it, one way or another." He smiled and winked at me. I smiled and moved closer to him. Together, we sat watching our kids.

"What are we going to do, and where are we going to live when we get back to the States?" I asked.

Don looked at me in surprise and replied, "You don't remember? We bought property in Florida."

"Yes, I do," I replied, "but I thought it was just land for investment and not a home!"

"Well, we will build us a home when we get there," Don assured me.

"Do you know where our property is located?"

"No, not exactly, but I know it's somewhere between Tampa and Orlando, and I know you will love it." He smiled.

"Okay, I guess I will," I said as I shrugged my shoulders.

Don bought sixteen acres of land on Lake Panasoffkee through a realtor we had never met. We had a picture of a forest bordering the water, and that was all. We had never seen it in person. I wondered about our new adventure in America and thought about all the other property we had invested in and what might have happened to it.

The sound of an airplane and raised voices brought me back to reality. I looked around and saw everyone was on their feet—some were yelling and screaming as they ran toward the terminal windows to watch the large bird land.

Our family was no exception; we jumped up and down and hugged each other. The bright lights at the ticket counters popped on, and their windows swung open. One by one, we lined up to purchase our boarding passes. After Don paid for our tickets and checked in our luggage, we lined up to board the plane. I could not have been happier to leave Iran, but at the same time, I was sad to leave under those circumstances.

As soon as the plane rose into the sky, I looked at my family and saw my children talking and laughing. I looked over at Don and saw him grinning. I smiled with satisfaction, and then I crossed myself, to pray for our safe journey back to the United States.

Chapter 8

CYPRESS KNEES

AS THE AIRPLANE'S wheels touched down in New York, everyone was roaring with excitement; we yelled, cheered, and clapped our hands to show relief.

"We are back to freedom-land, baby," Don smiled and squeezed my hand.

"Yes! We are back to our loving country. The number-one USA! Yay!" As soon as I could, I got up from my seat and kissed Don and the children to welcome them home.

We waited for the door to open and followed each other to the luggage carousel. After picking up our luggage, we dragged them along to find someplace to eat. Since we hadn't eaten a decent meal for days, we decided to look for the best restaurant in the airport, and when we found it, we stacked our luggage near the front door and walked in. After our delicious meal, we rested for a while before Don bought airline tickets to Florida. We landed in Tampa in the afternoon, and Don rented a car to take us to Lake Panasoffkee.

It took us over an hour on Interstate 75 before we reached our sixteen acres of wooded land, or should I say our untamed forest. Don and I walked around investigating, while the kids ran to the water's edge to watch a small alligator.

"Now that we're here, what are we going to do with this jungle?" I asked Don.

"It's too late to think about it right now; let's find a hotel and rest for the night, and we'll talk about it in the morning."

I called the children and told them to get back in the car, and Don backed out to the dirt road. It was not easy to find a motel in the dark countryside, in the middle of farmland. Don drove around and around for miles, but there was nothing except for open land with cows, horses, and pigs.

Don stopped at a one-pump gas station and asked. He was told we needed to go to the small town of Bushnell, about fifteen miles away.

"What? Fifteen miles away?" I exclaimed. "Where in the world are we, Don? This place looks like a jungle in Vietnam; I'm really disappointed."

"I know you are, but do we have any choice right now, baby?" Don asked, and I could tell he was not too happy about it either.

"I guess not," I grumbled, "but what are we going to do out here in the boondocks?"

Don didn't like my negative comments and replied, "Oh well, we'll find out, won't we?" Five miles later, we passed a town with one traffic light but no motel. Don continued for fifteen more miles to the next one and found a motel, barely big enough for the fleas. It had old red carpet and a rusted mirror on the ceiling; we had no choice but to settle down for the night.

The next morning, we went to a chain restaurant and ordered sausage-and-egg biscuits. Don and I had coffee, and the kids drank milk.

Panasoffkee Lake was very large, but there was nothing much around it but farmland. Country living was not my thing; I had been there and done that. It reminded me of the sad time when I was six years old, living without my father and mother, and had to fend for myself, eating bugs and weeds to survive. It also reminded me of my lonely time in our trailer up in the cold Smokey Mountains of Tennessee, where I had to trap poor little birds for food.

I loved Florida but not the alligator-gathering jungle of Lake Panasoffkee. I wished our land were closer to a city. Although I was sad about the location, I hoped my children would keep me busy so I wouldn't have time to be sad or lonely.

Within days, Don and I bought a large mobile home and parked it right next to a deep canal, where raccoons, possums, and snakes roamed wild, right underneath our trailer. Our intention was to use the trailer temporarily until we built a larger home and developed a commercial campground with an adjoining mobile home park.

The Lake Panasoffkee area had only a few hundred residences, most of whom were farmers and lived in mobile homes themselves; some were parked right on the other side of our canal. Our commercial plan was not for the residents that lived in the area but for the people from out of state who came to Florida to get away from the snow. Since we were close to Interstate 75, we hoped to entice traveling campers to our campground. This is how we would make our living.

Don found a school for Eddie, but the two younger ones stayed home, where I taught them myself.

We hired a well-known construction company and asked them to cut down trees, clear out the land, fill up the swamp, and level the entire area. They brought in hundreds of loads of dirt and dumped them into the swamp. Unfortunately, the swamp was deep; it seemed like the more dirt they filled it with, the more dirt was needed, and the more money we had to pay.

Meanwhile, we had to deal with the wild animals, which came out from the disturbed marshland and terrorized us. Each night, a family of raccoons visited our porch and tore into our garbage can. Don decided to get rid of them once and for all.

He bought himself a twenty-gauge shotgun and was ready to take on the whole group. He waited for the sky to turn dark and then went out to the porch to set the trap. He placed the garbage can right at the window, came back inside, and opened the window's screen to get ready. At nightfall, he told the kids to go to bed early and then loaded the gun. Everything was set and ready. He sat quietly behind an open window, with the shotgun in his hand, waiting in the dark for the raccoon family to show up. He didn't have to wait long. In the moonlight, the shadows of four creatures appeared from the marsh. I recognized them; they were the same raccoon family: a mother with three little babies, following each other and marching toward the trailer.

The mother arrived and climbed up on the porch first, and then she waited for her babies to come to her. She started to look and sniff around for a few seconds and then climbed up on the garbage can; her face was a foot from Don's face. I was sure she was close enough to smell Don's breath. I sat next to him and watched as he prepared to shoot. I expected a loud noise from the gun, so I closed my eyes, covered my ears, held my breath, and waited. Many seconds passed, and he still didn't pull the trigger. I opened my eyes to peer at him, with both of my hands still covering my ears; even in the darkness, I could see his hands shake. I nudged him with my elbow and whispered, "Shoot! Hurry up! Shoot!" The raccoon heard me. She raised her neck, trying to look inside. I held my breath to keep silent as I stared into her eyes. At one point, her face was on the gun's barrel, but Don still didn't shoot. I was perturbed, nudged him again, and urged him to shoot. But he still didn't. I couldn't understand why; he had the perfect opportunity and didn't use it. I turned to look at him and motioned for him to give me the gun, but he refused. The raccoon heard the commotion inside and stuck her head even closer to our faces. I tried very hard to stop myself from reaching out to grab her neck. She must have heard my thinking, because she immediately jumped off the garbage can and led her children back into the swamp.

Don laid his gun down, looked at me, raised his shoulders, and cocked his sweaty head to one side. "I couldn't do it," he said. "When I looked into her eyes and she looked back at me, I just couldn't pull the trigger." We stood up; Don put his gun away, and I went outside to clean up the raccoon's mess. Don closed the window, and we went to bed.

We took a break from our land development and drove to Tampa to shop and to find a good Thai restaurant; we all liked spicy food. After a delicious dinner, we walked into a pet shop, just to look around. An hour later, we walked out with a longhaired Chihuahua puppy and named him Titi, which means *small* in both Vietnamese and French. We loved the puppy, but the dog loved Eddie the most and followed him in every step.

One day, Eddie was on his bicycle, with Titi following beside him. I was doing something in the kitchen, when I heard Eddie scream. I ran outside to investigate and saw Eddie crying his eyes out, holding the lifeless body of Titi in his hands.

"Oh God! I killed him, Mom." When I came within reach, Eddie handed Titi's body to me.

"What happened, son?" I asked Eddie, who was sobbing so hard he couldn't answer me.

All he could do was murmur through his tears, "I killed him, Mom. I killed him."

"How did it happen, Eddie?" I asked. But when I saw him in so much pain, I didn't want to make a big deal out of it. I tried to comfort him because I knew how much he loved Titi.

"Mom, I didn't mean to hurt him," he cried. "He just ran right in front of me, and I couldn't stop. I am so sorry."

"Eddie, you didn't mean to kill him," I said as tears filled my eyes; I stroked the dog's head and continued, "Don't feel bad. It was just an accident. You didn't do anything wrong."

When he calmed down a little, I said, "Well, let's take him to the backyard, and I will help you bury him. How is that?"

"Okay, Mom," he answered softly.

At the base of a large cypress tree, Eddie and I dug a hole and buried our beloved pet. I made a cross from wild persimmon tree limbs and gave it to Eddie to put over the dog's grave. I returned to the trailer to continue my kitchen chores. Hours later, I looked out the window and saw Eddie still on his knees at the graveside. Poor Eddie, he must have been so hurt. I shook my head and felt sorry for him.

ONE NIGHT AFTER dinner, I was washing the dishes, and Don was watching television with the kids. After finishing the dishes, I took the trash to the porch and stuffed it into the garbage can. Instead of going back inside, I stood in silence, enjoying a few moments of solitude. I peered out at the swamp, and under a clear, bright, moonlit sky, I could see the wildlife activity in the marsh.

"Hey, Don!" I called from the porch, "Come here! Hurry up!" All four of them came running out.

"What's going on?" Don asked.

"What happened, Mom?" the kids chimed in.

"Look! Look!" I said as I pointed to an open area in the marsh. There were at least a dozen large hares jumping up and down, playing, and chasing each other. Don saw the rabbits, ran to our bedroom, grabbed the shotgun, and brought it out to the porch.

"Oh no! Not again," I said. "I don't know why you bought a gun if you're not going to use it. If I were you, I'd get rid of it." I was trying to shame him, and it worked. Don ran out to the marsh, and we heard one shot. Minutes later, Don brought a big dead brown rabbit to the porch. I was not surprised to see him come back with a rabbit; Don earned an expert marksman ribbon when he was in the air force.

It was late, so I placed the rabbit in a brown paper bag and put it in the refrigerator. I planned to clean and cook it the next day.

The following morning after breakfast, I was cleaning the dishes while all of the kids were watching television, and Don was outside with the workmen.

It was summer, and Eddie was home from school. He was watching a TV show with the kids, and I asked him, "Hey, Eddie, can you help me clean the rabbit?"

"Okay, Mom," the thirteen-year-old replied. "Tell me when you want me to help." And he turned back to watch the show. I put a large pot of water on the stove and prepared the meat cleaver, the chopping block, and a pan. The water began boiling, and I yelled at Eddie to bring me the rabbit. He ran to the refrigerator, grabbed the brown bag containing the dead rabbit, threw it on the sink, and turned to walk away.

"Oh no you don't!" I yelled. "You told me you were going to help me with the rabbit, remember?"

"Aww, can I do it later, Mom?"

"No, I need you to take the rabbit out of the bag now!" I demanded. "I'll bring the boiling water to the sink, and you'll help me dip the rabbit in it." Eddie picked up the bag, dumped it upside down, and tried to shake the rabbit out of the bag. But the bloody rabbit stuck to the bag like glue, so he had to shake it violently. He did this while still focused on the TV.

I stood watching and waiting for Eddie to get the rabbit out of the bag until I lost my patience and yelled at him.

"Eddie! Would you please stop watching the TV for a second and try harder to get the rabbit out of the bag?"

"Okay, Mom," he said as he shook the bag harder. I let him do his job and returned to the stove to turn it off.

"Oh my God! Oh my God! Oh my God!" Eddie screamed as he ran out the door. His reaction shocked me, and I ran out after him.

"Are you okay?" I asked as I pushed the door open. He nodded his head, indicating he was fine. "Did you burn yourself?"

"No!" He shook his head

I went back to the sink, picked up the rabbit, and was about to dip it into the hot water.

"Oh my God! Oh my God! Oh my God," I yelled as I dropped the rabbit back into the sink and bolted out of the door.

"Eddie, let's go tell Dad and see what he wants to do," I said, and together we ran to the field to look for Don. We found him at the construction site, talking to the workers, and called out to him.

When Don came within earshot, I said, "Hey, Don, you won't believe it, but the rabbit you killed last night was pregnant."

"Wow! One shot, six rabbits; I broke my own record," Don said, laughing. "That means there will be more rabbits for us to eat."

"I am not going to cook them, if that's what you mean," I said as I shook my head.

"Dad, we can't eat those poor babies!" Eddie frowned and looked at Don as if his dad were a cannibal.

"Well, let's bury them," Don suggested. "What do you guys think?"

Eddie and I thought it was a good idea.

Thankfully, Teresa and Nicky were glued to the television and had no idea what was going on. Don went to the sink, put the rabbits in a bag, and took it outside.

"Where do you want to bury them?" Don asked.

"I want to bury them next to our dog," I said as I grabbed a shovel, and we walked toward Titi's grave. Don put the bag down and started digging near the tree's trunk. Eddie and I stood there watching in silence. When the hole was deep enough, he laid the bag in it and covered it with dirt. He looked at us, smiled, and took the shovel back to the trailer. Eddie and I gathered tree limbs to make crosses. I ran back to the trailer for twine, tied six crooked crosses together, and stuck them in the ground, side by side, the large one for the mommy rabbit and the other five smaller ones for her babies. I felt bad for the rabbits, but I thought the line of crosses looked so cute. I decided to make a flower garden around the cypress tree to honor our dog and the rabbits after our home was built and I had more time.

THE PENINSULA WHERE we chose to build our dream home was surrounded by trees and water; everyone agreed it was a picture-perfect location. I couldn't wait to have parties and hang out with friends and family there. I learned to love the place, and I often imagined us sitting on our deck over the water, enjoying the sunrise and the sunset, watching the wildlife activity.

The day after the land was ready to start building, the workers took their noisy machinery away. I looked out the window and thought how nice it was to finally have a quiet day. From the kitchen, I saw two men, dressed almost identically in plaid shirts and overalls, walking around our property near the swamp, taking notes. Don wasn't home, so I went out to see what they were doing. As soon as I came close to them, one asked in his hillbilly accent, "Ma'am, is this your property?"

"Yes, it is," I replied.

"Do you have a permit from the government to fill up wetlands?" he asked.

I was confused, so I asked, "What do you mean by permit?"

The second man took a hand-rolled cigarette out of his toothless mouth, gave me his sternest look, and added as he spit on the ground, "Ma'am, if you don't have the government's approval, you can't touch the wetlands. You have to pay a hefty fine, or you could even go to jail." He then put the half-burnt cigarette back between his thin purple lips.

"I'm sorry," I said. "We didn't know."

"Sorry isn't good enough, ma'am!" The first one said.

"Well, what can we do about it now?" I asked.

"Let's see," the second one said as he looked back and forth at the newly filled swamp. I stared at the cigarette and hoped he didn't burn his lips. "Looks like you filled up a lot of wetland!" he declared. "A lot!" He slowly shook his head and then chuckled.

"Well, to avoid a hefty fine and jail time," the first one chimed in, "you'll have to take out every ounce of dirt you put in," he snarled.

"What!" I exclaimed. "You must be joking! There is no way we can take out every load of dirt we put in; it would take thousands of loads."

"Well! The more you put in, the more you must take out."

"That is impossible!" I shook my head.

"Well, then, we'll be back with a court order for you to pay the fines and a warrant for your arrest. What do you think, Bubba?"

"Sounds aw'right to me, Billy." By then, I was very upset.

"We are from the EPA, ma'am, and we're here to make sure people like you don't destroy the wetlands and natural habitats," Billy said, or maybe Bubba said; I wasn't sure.

"How much time do we have to fix this problem?" I asked.

"What do you think, Bubba?" Billy asked his partner. "Want to give them a week or two, maybe?" he said, and I interrupted them.

"There is no way we could take all of the dirt out in one or two weeks. It took us months to fill it in, and it will take more time to take it all out," I explained. "Please be reasonable."

They looked at each other; one spit his tobacco juices out and said to the other, "I think we should just go ahead and pursue the court order for her arrest. What do you think, Billy?"

Billy scratched a mosquito bite on his hairy neck and replied, "If that's what you want, Bubba."

I couldn't stand these two people any longer and said, "Can you please wait until I talk to my husband to see when and how we can do all of this? I'm sure he will be coming home any minute."

I made an excuse and walked back inside. I heard Don's car and was relieved to see him home. I looked out the window and saw the three of them talking. I said to myself, "I hope Don has better luck talking to those men than I did."

Half an hour later, Billy and Bubba left. Don rushed inside and slammed his keys on the table. I knew whatever they'd said wasn't going to be good.

"What did they say to you?"

"Those damn rednecks," Don grumbled. "They want us to take out every blasted ounce of dirt we put in the swamp!"

"I know. They told me the same thing," I said, "but how much time did they give you to take the dirt out?"

"One month," Don said.

"Well, at least they gave you one month; they only gave me one or two weeks." I rolled my eyes. "It took us several months to put the dirt in; now they give us a month to take it out. I guess that's fair," I said.

Don was very angry with the two visitors, and he shouted, "I was so happy to be back home in America, and now those idiots make me feel like turning around and going back overseas again."

"Oh no! I am not going anywhere!" I said. "I might leave this place and its project, but I am not about to leave America anytime soon." I shook my head. "I've had enough emergency evacuations to last me two lifetimes. Besides, we created this problem ourselves, so we can't blame anyone but us. We can learn from this mistake and move on. Our dreams might be crushed, and it may cost us a lot of money, but we learned our lesson." I stopped to catch my breath.

"You're right, baby," Don said. "But this is going to be a very expensive lesson, and it might mean we shouldn't be here after all. What would you say if I told you to pack up and get the hell out of this place?"

"I would say hooray!!! Hooray!" I was happy and grinning from ear to ear. "I think it's a great idea! The best one you've had in months."

"But before we can get out of here," he said, "we need to pull some stupid dirt out of the swamp." He exclaimed, "What a mess!"

The next day, we asked the same company who brought the dirt in if they could help us take the dirt out. They agreed to do it, but they wanted twice as much to take it out as they did to put it in. Their reasoning was that it was much easier to put in than take out. We had no choice but to pay them what they asked.

They started the following day. It cost us nearly everything we had, and we gained nothing in the end. We looked around and found a used twenty-five-foot camper loaded with everything we needed—our small home on wheels. Don also bought a large Pontiac station wagon and installed a hitch to pull the camper. The day before we left, I talked to Thelma, our middle-aged realtor neighbor, and asked her to watch our trailer while we were on vacation.

"Hey, Mrs. Thelma, can you please keep an eye on our home while we're gone?" I asked. "Don and I want to take our children on a long vacation before school starts," I explained.

"I'll be happy to watch your home for you," she said with a smile. "Just make sure you come back home, wherever you go." Thelma was joking, but she didn't know we might never come back.

"We'll try," I smiled. "Thanks, Thelma, and here is a key to our trailer," I said as I handed her the key. Don saw me talking to Thelma and came over to say goodbye. We hugged her and were about to walk away when Thelma waved her hand to stop us.

"Wait a minute; I have something to tell you," she said.

Don and I stopped to hear what she had to say.

"Do you know the heavyset old woman and her boyfriend, Barney, who lives over there, in the small trailer at the end of the canal?" she asked as she pointed to a trailer park across from our canal.

"Yes, we know both of them well," I said. "They came to visit us often, and we became good friends. We had dinner at each other's homes; I like them very much. Why, is there something wrong with them?" I asked in concern.

"No, there's nothing wrong with them," she said, "but yes, there's everything wrong with them." She rolled her eyes. "You guys might be friends of theirs, but they are not friends of yours."

"What are you trying to say, Thelma?" Don asked.

"Did you guys talk to them about your commercial development?" she asked.

"Yes," I said, "while we were at each other's houses; they asked us a lot of questions about our project, and we didn't mind sharing with them." Thelma looked concerned. "We told them all about our future campground and trailer park; they were happy for us." I was puzzled and asked Thelma, "Why? Do you know otherwise? Was something else going on?"

"As I was telling you," Thelma shook her head and repeated herself, "they are not your friends. You guys gave them way too much information. Rocky's friend, who works at the local EPA office, just told him your so-called friends, Barney and his girlfriend, went to the EPA office and complained about you guys destroying the environment and the animal habitat. That is why the EPA knew what you were doing and came to give you guys a hard time." My jaw dropped, and I couldn't say a word.

"That bastard," Don growled. "I can't believe what I'm hearing."

"How could they do that to us?" I said. "I thought they were good friends." I shook my head in disappointment.

Thelma was sympathetic and said, "I'm sorry you guys had to stop your development project because of some stupid, jealous people like them."

I looked at Don and said, "We don't read people very well, do we, honey?"

He tightened his lips, shook his head, and said, "We're just too trustful, baby."

"Well, thanks for letting us know what happened, Thelma," I said. "That is so sad. I hope I don't run into those two-faced backstabbers before we leave."

"Okay, forget about them. Go ahead and have a good time on your vacation. Just hurry home; I will miss you guys," Thelma said as she hugged us.

"We will miss you too," Don and I said, and we walked back to our trailer.

Our camper, station wagon, and mobile home in 1979

The next morning, we prepared to leave. The camper had a large queen-sized bed in the back, with a bathroom and family room next to it. The dining room furniture in front opened into a double bed. The kitchen, with a stove, sink, and small refrigerator, was located in the middle. Teresa and Nicky shared a double bed in the front, Eddie slept on the couch, and Don and I had the queen bed in back.

As we were getting ready to go, we turned up the radio. We sang along. Suddenly, the music stopped, and a radio announcer came on. "Sorry, we have to interrupt our program and bring you bad news; we just received information that fifty-two Americans are being held hostage by the Iranian government right now."

We stopped moving and listened in stunned silence until the announcer finished. I looked at Don. "Did you hear that?" I asked.

"Yes, I did, and I'm not surprised," Don said. "I'm just glad we got out of there when we did. I hope some of our friends are not among the captives."

I sighed and said, "We never know how our lives might turn out, do we?"

"You're right," Don agreed. "Can you imagine if we hadn't left when we did? We could be among the hostages."

"We're very lucky to be in America," I said. "And here we are bickering and complaining over a stupid piece of land while our people over there are behind bars or worse. Shame on us!" I tightened my lips and shook my head.

Don locked the trailer door and walked around the car and the camper, checking all of the tires to make sure everything was in perfect shape for the trip. The kids and I went back toward the canal to say goodbye to our dog and the rabbits, and then we scattered about in different directions. I walked to the peninsula, where we had intended to build the gazebo and our dream home. *Too bad*, I thought as I looked around. *But it's also a good thing. I don't think I'll miss all of the chaos around here.* When I returned, I saw Eddie kneeling in front of Titi's grave; teardrops stained his cheeks. I went over to him and pulled him close. Teresa and Nicky were close by, talking and pointing at a small alligator in the water.

"Hey, you guys!" Don called. "I'm ready to go; come on, let's hit the road."

We were all excited to go. From a distance, I could see Don smile as the kids approached him. I opened the door and hopped into the front seat while the kids all climbed into the back.

"Seatbelts on, everybody!" I demanded.

Don pulled slowly away from the grassy yard. Thelma came out to her porch and waved goodbye, and we waved back. Don beeped his horn as we turned onto the dirt road that led us away from Lake Panasoffkee.

Chapter 9

WESTBOUND

WE WERE ALMOST to Tallahassee and the children were singing, when all of a sudden Don exclaimed, "Oh no!" The kids and I just looked at each other, confused. "Look, you guys! There is a cloud of white smoke pouring out behind the car." We all turned to see.

"Not again!" I said. Don pulled off the road, and the smoke billowed out even more, and then the car stopped running.

"What happened, Don?" I asked.

"I don't know," he answered. "I'll have to take a look, but before I do, I want you guys to get out of the car and get as far away from the road as you can."

"Okay," we all answered and ran to a grassy area a good distance from the road.

Don opened the hood as more smoke poured out. He waited for a few seconds and then checked the engine. Minutes later, he came to us and said, "It doesn't look good. I think our transmission blew out. I'll have to call a tow truck to take it to a garage to get it fixed. I don't know how much it will cost or how long it will take, but we have no choice. We'll probably have to get a new transmission."

I saw a gas station farther down the road and pointed it out to Don. "Look, Don, there's a gas station within walking distance. We're in luck; we can walk there to get help."

"I hope so," he replied.

"But how do you know the transmission went bad?" I asked.

"Just the way the car acted," he explained. "I don't want you guys to go with me to the gas station. I want you all to stay right where you are while I arrange for a tow truck." Don walked away, and we found a termite mound to sit on and wait.

They towed our car to a garage, and, as Don predicted, it needed a new transmission. We had to stay in Tallahassee until our station wagon was fixed, so Don rented a car and drove us around Tallahassee.

We stayed in a hotel at night but went back to our camper, still parked on the side of the freeway, for food and to change clothes. Don left a note on the camper's door for the highway patrol, telling them we had car problems and to please not tow it away. Instead of feeling bad about our misfortune, we made Tallahassee a part of our journey, and we had a great time while we were there. Don discovered, after the fact, that if he had installed a five-dollar coolant on the front of the radiator to keep the water cool while pulling a heavy load, the transmission would not have overheated and blown out the gaskets. But too bad, the repairs cost us five hundred dollars instead of five dollars.

"Where do you guys want to go first?" Don asked when we got our car back and were ready to leave.

"It doesn't matter to me where we go," I said. "As long as our family is together, I am happy."

"Me too. I could be happy anywhere," Don smiled. "Our home is wherever we lay our heads, even right back there in the middle of nowhere."

"That's what I just said." I looked at him and claimed my statement.

"I know what you just said, and I was just agreeing with you." We both laughed, and the kids resumed their song, with Don and I joining in, "Up the mountain . . . down the ocean . . ."

During the first few weeks of our trip, we zigzagged up and down between Interstates 10, 20, and 40, hundreds of miles out of our way. We tried to visit all of the attractions—national parks, zoos, museums, and national monuments.

We didn't want to miss anything along the way. We saw so much natural beauty and learned so much about America and its history. We marveled at the differences we found in each state's culture and customs. We had so much fun on the road, and I didn't want to stop traveling.

Nicky, me, and Teresa at Grand Canyon, on our way to California in 1979

The kids loved visiting the Native American museums and memorials along the way, but when we were inside, we saw many horrible black-and-white pictures of a long line of people, uprooted from their own land and forcibly moved to a place unknown to them. One of the pictures showed some of them beaten and left to die. I looked up at Don with tears in my eyes and said, "I hope our children will remember this trip when they grow up and never forget these many valuable lessons they learned and what they have seen." We came into the museum with happy faces but left with a heavy heart.

In Arizona, Don noticed the gas gauge was on empty. We looked around for a gas station but saw nothing, except for miles and miles of desert.

"I should have stopped for gas an hour earlier," Don lamented, "while I had the chance, but I expected to see another one sooner than this."

A beautiful red coyote came out of nowhere, dashed across the road right in front of us, and Don had to slam on the brakes to avoid hitting it. He pulled the car to the shoulder, and we watched the coyote walk away.

"That coyote tried to commit suicide and kill us all," I said.

"No, he just wanted to see if he could run faster than the car, Mom," Eddie said.

"Too bad, we could have barbecued the coyote," Don joked as he looked at the gas gauge in alarm. "We are just about out of gas," Don declared with a worried frown as he turned the air conditioner off. "I don't think we can make it to the next town."

"Where can we get gas in this desert?" I said. "There is not a soul or any sign of civilization around here."

"Well, there might be someone," Don replied and pointed to what appeared to be a few tiny shacks protruding above the desert sand. "It looks like there's a small village not too far from here."

"I guess we can go there and see," I said.

"What choice do we have?" Don asked. "But I'll have to unhook the car from the camper, because pulling the camper would use more gas."

"Okay," I said, "but I want all of us to go with you."

"Of course, we're all going," Don said as he opened the door and got out. Poor Don had to work on the camper's hitch in the hot, burning sun. From inside the car, I could see heat waves undulating above the desert and Don sweating a river; I just hoped he didn't get a heatstroke. When he finished unhooking the camper, he opened the car door and jumped inside.

"It is hot out there!" he exclaimed.

"It's hot in here too," I said.

Don started the car, pulled away from our camper, and turned right onto an uneven dirt road toward the village. Although it was hot, we didn't turn on the air conditioner; we were afraid to use more gas. A couple of miles from the freeway, we approached an old rusty gate. I saw a large sign on it, which read, "PRIVATE DO NOT ENTER." I looked at Don as he slowed down.

"It must be a joke; how could the whole village be private?" I said. "Let's go inside and see. Even if it is private, we'll tell them we need gas, and I'm sure they'll understand."

"I agree," Don said. "Whoever they are, I think they'll help us."

Don drove slowly through the half-open gate, and a young man with brown eyes and long, dark hair appeared out of nowhere and ran in front of our car to stop us. Don rolled down the window just in time to hear him raise his voice.

"Where do you think you're going, white man?" he snapped and pointed to the gate. "Did you not see the sign back there?"

"Yes, I saw it," Don said, "but we are in desperate need of gas, and we couldn't go any farther. We need your help." Don was very polite.

"We don't have gas here!" he shouted. "You have to leave now or suffer the consequences! We don't have anything in here for a white man." He looked mad. "Don't you think you've taken enough from us? Just look at us; we are forced to live in the middle of the desert. Who helped us when we needed help? Now! I want you to get off of our reservation." I recognized the young man was a Native American, and I could tell he was angry.

He moved out of the way to let Don turn our car around. We went back to the freeway and parked the car behind our camper to wait for help. I hoped the people in the reservation wouldn't come out and take revenge, but if they did, I would understand; they believed the white man had been unfair to them.

Lucky for us, a kind highway patrolman stopped and helped us; he took Don to Flagstaff, bought five gallons of gas, brought Don back, and helped him pour it into the gas tank.

Don hooked the camper back to the car while we all waited. After he was done, we all piled into the car and Don followed the patrolman to Flagstaff. Don honked his horn, and the patrolman veered off. We rented a motel room, and the next day we took the kids to an amusement park. They had a great time on the highest roller coaster in the West.

A couple of days later, we resumed our journey and made it to California. Don drove to Sacramento to visit a friend and her family; during the day, she showed us around the city and we looked at homes. We had planned to live there permanently, but it was too hot for us, so we changed our minds. Ten days later, we decided to go to Canada to cool off.

"Is it still cold up there this time of the year?" I asked Don at breakfast.

"It's really cold in the winter," Don said. "But right now, it should be very comfortable."

After we ate, we prepared to leave. The children were already in the car waiting for us. We got in, and Don drove out of the parking lot, heading west toward the Pacific coast. We drew closer to Interstate 5, which runs north and south. As I watched out for our northern turn, I noticed Don had a serious look on his face, as if he was thinking about something important. Seconds later, he turned to me with a grin and asked.

"How would you like to go to Mexico?"

"Is it cold in Mexico?" I asked.

"Nope, it's not cold at all. It's warm the year round," he replied. "Do you want to try Mexico instead of Canada?"

"I don't care; wherever you want to go," I said. I shrugged my shoulders and declared, "I've never been to either one of them, and I don't have any preferences. But if we go south through Los Angeles, I would like to stop to see my stepbrother, Den, and his family."

"That's a good idea," Don said. "We haven't seen them for years, and I'd like to see them too," Don smiled. "Let's head for Mexico, shall we?"

And just like that, he turned south on Interstate 5 toward Mexico.

It was a beautiful day when we approached the northern part of Los Angeles. We found a nice campground, and Don parked our camper right next to a large swimming pool. After a late lunch, the kids asked if they could go swimming. I nodded my head and told them to be careful. They changed into their bathing suits, and to the pool they went. Don took a drink of water and turned to me with a smile.

"Would you mind if I took a quick trip to visit a friend of mine?" he asked.

"Okay, I guess. But who is it, and where does he or she live?"

"His name is Jim, and we used to work together in Vietnam. I don't know where he lives, but I have his work address. He works for Lockheed, and according to the map, it's not too far from here," Don replied.

"Okay. I like it here and don't mind staying here for a while."

He smiled and walked away to unhook the car from the camper. Then he came back inside to give me a kiss and said, "I'll be back as soon as I can." He went to the pool where the kids were swimming, waved goodbye, and left.

Don came back late in the evening, and before he said anything, I could tell he had been drinking from the way he smelled and the way his eyes looked.

"How was your visit?" I asked, a little disappointed and sad.

"Oh, it was good," he said. "My friend is in charge of the Lockheed overseas operations, and he offered me a job."

"What kind of job?" I asked. "I hope it's not another overseas job; I don't want to leave America again."

"Oh no, it's right here, working in management for Lockheed. I told him I would let him know after I talked to you."

He looked at me with red, glazed eyes and asked, "What do you think about living here for a while?"

"I think it would be fine, but what about our home and land in Florida?" I asked.

"We can just keep it until we go back there, and if we're lucky, we might not have to go back there at all." He winked and smiled at me, and by the way he acted, I didn't think he liked it back there either.

"I don't know about you, but I never want to go back to that mosquito-, raccoon-, and alligator-infested swamp again. Where and when would you start your job?"

"In Cucamonga, not too far from here, and I can start tomorrow," he said.

"Cuca . . . what?"

"Cu . . . ca . . . mon . . . ga," he said slowly.

Don started work the following day; I found a realtor and began hunting for a place to live.

Each day, I dragged my three children along with me, from house to house, looking for something to either rent or buy. Two weeks later, we bought and moved into a nice new three-bedroom, two-bath home in Rancho Cucamonga, near the foothills of the San Gabriel Mountains.

Chapter 10

TWO-FACED COIN

DON LIKED HIS new job at Lockheed. He bought himself a used car for work and gave me the old station wagon. The children started back to school after a long summer break, and I started a tiny garden in our small backyard. After I finished pampering the garden, I took care of the house chores. However, one can only do so much cooking, cleaning, and shopping for food.

I grew bored and enrolled in Chaffey College, in Rancho Cucamonga. I was in an adult educational program, where I studied English as a second language, to prepare me for the high school equivalency (GED) test. I was determined to pass the test so I could attend college. Within six months, I met both of my goals. I enrolled in an English and a math course and was doing well. Although I was busy, I still saved time for my garden and family.

Teresa and Nicky with my Asian gourds in California, 1980

I loved California weather, but I didn't like the earthquakes, mudslides, smog, pollution, or strong wind. We lived right at the foothills, and when there was a heavy rain, it often brought mud mixed with big rocks down from the mountain and created huge road blocks. Each time this happened, we were cooped up inside until the city cleaned up the mess. Sometimes, they had to use bulldozers to remove the large rocks. If there was heavy smog, caused by bad air pollution, we had to stay inside too. Even with all of these problems, I still loved my home and liked the city of Rancho Cucamonga.

My love of animals and the desire to be around them was never far from my thoughts. I looked in the newspapers in search of anything that could crawl, fly, or swim. I found one ad that said, "Moving out of town, selling everything, including three rabbits and forty ducks."

I couldn't wait for Don to come home so I could tell him about it.

"Hey, Don," I said as soon as he walked through the door. "Could I buy three rabbits and a few ducks?"

"What are you going to do with ducks and rabbits in this place?" he asked.

"I am going to raise them for food," I explained. I didn't tell him how many ducks for fear of him saying no. "The rabbits will give birth to more rabbits, and the ducks will lay eggs and make more ducks."

"Then what?" Don asked.

"Well, we can sell them or eat them," I replied eagerly.

"If that's what you want to do, it's okay with me," he sighed. He didn't like pets as much as I did.

I called the people who listed the ad and made some hasty and necessary arrangements. The next day was Saturday; we took our kids to the mini farm and bought all forty ducks and the three rabbits, a brown, a black, and a white one. We brought the animals home and realized we didn't have a fence to hold them. The six-foot wooden fence we did have wouldn't keep the ducks in, because the bottom of the fence was a foot above ground, and the small animals could crawl underneath it. I told the kids to stay home and watch the dozen boxes full of animals while Don and I ran to the hardware store to buy material to build a house for the rabbits and a fence for the ducks. For the next two weeks, we chopped, cut, sawed, dug, and banged nails into the wood. We made so much noise our neighbors probably thought we were building a factory. It was hard work for Don and me, but we finished the job. I asked the kids to help me let all the pets loose into their new home. I think the animals were happy to finally get out of the boxes. The duck fence was nice, the rabbits' house was cute, the children liked their animals, and I loved them all.

The duck house we built

The ducks and the rabbits, however, were not very good pets; the farmer raised them for food, so they were very unfriendly. We could not play with the rabbits, because they bit, and the ducks ran away when we came close to pet them. Those forty ducks did not stay small and cute for long. They grew like weeds and ate like cows. At one point, I thought they would eat us out of home. The more they ate, the more they pooped; the more they pooped, the stinkier our backyard smelled. I didn't know at first that ducks loved to bathe in their own drinking water; the more water I gave them, the messier they became. Soon, our backyard became wet and smelly, and the duck coop was full of duck poop. Every day, I spent so much time catering to the animals and spent more money on their food than I did on my own dining table. Months later, I still had not seen an egg or a baby rabbit. We found out later that all three of the rabbits were male, and the ducks needed more time to mature before they could lay eggs. My dream of raising ducks and rabbits turned into a nightmare.

ONE AFTERNOON, I came home from school, and when I walked into the kitchen, I found a window broken and glass scattered everywhere. I was confused at first, but then I realized we had been robbed. I ran to the phone and called Don.

"Hey, Don!" My voice was shaking. "You need to come home right now! Someone broke into our house!"

"Calm down, Linda," he said. "Calm down before you have a heart attack. I want you to get out of the house right now, just in case the thief is still in there."

His words terrified me. I slammed the phone down and bolted out of the front door. A few seconds later, I ran back inside and dialed Don again. "Come home, Don! Please come home!" I begged.

"I can't right at this moment. I'm in the middle of an important meeting. Just calm down," he said. "Just calm down."

"Calm down! Calm down! Is that all you can say?" I raised my voice and cried, "We were just robbed, and all you can tell me is to calm down?"

"Walk around outside of the house," he advised, "and look through the windows to see if anyone is still inside."

I slammed the phone down again and ran outside. I walked from window to window but saw nobody. I ran back inside, picked up the phone, and dialed Don again. "I don't see anything except clothes and drawers strewn everywhere," I said.

"If you're sure no one is inside, go ahead and call the police, but make sure you don't touch anything until the police arrive."

"Okay, but I wish you could come home now."

"You'll be all right; you're doing fine. Call me after the police leave."

"Okay," I replied.

I called the police, and two of them came. They walked around and asked me all kinds of questions, as if I were the thief. One took fingerprints from the broken window, while the other walked around the house with a pen and a notepad.

"Has your house been broken into before?" he asked.

"No, sir. My house has never been broken into before, sir, officer," I answered him nervously.

"Do you know what the thief took?"

"No, I don't. I called you as soon as I could; besides, my husband told me not to touch anything."

"Good advice," he said.

"I'll check later and let you know what I lost," I said.

"No, it's better for us if you do it now while we're still here," the policeman said.

I followed the officer from room to room, and I didn't find anything missing until I came to my jewelry box. Our coin collection from all over the world and my small diamond ring were missing. The value of the ring and the coin collection was not much, but their sentimental value was priceless. When the police left, I went to the backyard and discovered the gate was open; I looked at the rabbit cage and was surprised to see two of them were missing. I remembered I fed three of them before I went to school, but only the black one remained in the cage. I wished the thieves had taken all three rabbits and all the ducks as well.

MOST WEEKENDS, OUR family took a break from our busy schedule and spent time together in the mountains, picnicking and fishing for trout; it was always fun. When we got hot, we waded into the cold stream to cool off. We would also collect edible wild watercress, which grew along the edge of the water. I used it for soups and salads and sometimes sautéed it with meat or shrimp.

Picnicking and fishing with Eddie, Teresa, and Nicky, 1980

We often invited friends and their families to come with us. One of our best friends was Ron, our realtor, who was a musician in his church. Through him, we had purchased our home. We had a dozen people when we put our two families together. If we didn't go out to fish or picnic, we often went to each other's homes for barbeque.

Ron approached us one day and asked to borrow two thousand dollars. He said he was working on a real estate deal, which would materialize in one month, and he would pay us back in full. Since he was a good friend, a church-going person, and appeared to have strong religious beliefs, we trusted him and didn't hesitate to lend him the money. After the month was up, he said there were more snags in the deal, and he needed more money from us, three thousand dollars more. To insure the loan, he gave us a second mortgage on his house. We were somewhat hesitant about the second loan, but he sounded desperate, and since he gave us a second mortgage on his home, we thought we had nothing to worry about and agreed to lend our friend the additional money.

Months passed, and Ron hadn't paid us. When we asked him about the money, he always had a convincing excuse for not having it; again, we believed and trusted our friend.

Wading in the stream

Don came home from work one day and acted so excited.

"Hey, baby! I got a new job," he announced. "Do you remember when I applied to the Veterans Administration several months ago?" he asked.

"Well, not really," I responded. "Doing what?"

He smiled and said, "The VA Hospital in Sepulveda, near Hollywood, offered me a position in personnel management as a GS-11."

"What about your job at Lockheed?" I asked. "I thought you liked it."

"The government job is more secure, and I'll be making more money and can retire sooner. Besides, Lockheed wants to transfer me to Saudi Arabia, and I do not want to go back overseas right now, especially to the Middle East," he explained.

"I don't want to go back there either," I said. "Have you accepted the government job yet?"

"No! Not yet. I wanted to talk to you about it first. It sounds good, but I'll have to drive one hundred twenty miles a day, five days a week," he sighed.

"Wow! Sixty miles one way is a lot of driving," I said.

"I'm not too crazy about spending so much time on the busy Los Angeles freeways," he said, "but I think I'll like the job, and I want to give it a try. What do you think?"

"I think it's the best thing for you to do," I replied. "I wouldn't mind moving closer to your work, if you wanted me to."

"Are you sure about that?" he asked.

"Yes. Besides, it's near Hollywood, and we could see movie stars all the time." I grinned.

"But what are we going to do with our home and the animals?" he asked.

"Well! We'll have to figure that one out, won't we?"

A few days later, Don quit his job with Lockheed and stayed home to prepare for us to move.

Ron listed our house for sale. After we were done packing, we sat on the couch eating our sandwiches, waiting for the movers to take our furniture away. Don looked at me and said, "I wonder if Ron will really keep his promise and pay us back."

"We don't have to worry about it," I said. "Remember, he promised he will pay us, after he receives his realtor's fee. After he sells our home, he has no choice but to pay us with his sales commission. Besides, we hold a second mortgage on their house, remember?"

"For our friendship's sake, I do hope you're right," Don said.

We moved to Sepulveda and rented a nice house about fifteen miles north of Hollywood. Don liked his new job, and the children all went to a new school. Eddie was fourteen at the time, Teresa was seven, and Nicky was six. They were okay with their school but not too crazy about the new location.

I went to Mission Hills College in San Fernando. I took three different courses in interior design, food nutrition, and family counseling. I loved my school and the new friends I made. Don and I were so happy when Ron sold our house, but instead of repaying the loan, he kept the commission for himself. Months passed, and we still waited. When we asked him about the money, he came up with more excuses and then made more promises. We had no choice but to accept his word.

Lynn, his wife, called me one day, and I was so excited to hear from her. I thought it was nice for her to call, until she asked to borrow more money to buy herself a used car. She said she needed a car to go to work to make money to pay us back. Of course, we didn't lend her any more, but we were still friends, and we loved them. I just couldn't understand what they were doing.

SINCE WE LIVED near Hollywood, we often drove through Beverly Hills to check out the movie stars, hoping to see them in person instead of just in the movies. We did see a few from a distance. One day, Don kept driving until we reached Universal Studios. He parked our old station wagon in a busy parking lot, and we poured out. We went to see the Bionic Woman's reenactment show.

While hundreds of us sat waiting for the show to start, a stagehand came to me and asked if I minded going on stage and taking part in the show. I was confused and looked at Don and the kids. The whole audience and my kids were yelling, "Go! Go! Go! Go! Go! Go!"

Don grinned and said, "Go ahead!" I looked up at the friendly stranger and smiled as I reached out to hold his waiting hand. He smiled as he led me through the stage while the crowd cheered on. When we went behind the curtain, I saw a dozen people running around; I assumed they were part of the production crew. As soon as they saw me, they came closer and told me what to do. They gave me a quick lesson on how to hold on to a long rope and act as if I were trying hard to pull it with one hand.

When they were sure I understood, they let me go back on stage by myself. I grabbed the rope with one hand, as they instructed, and then stood smiling awkwardly in front of the rowdy crowd; I had no idea what I was waiting for. I looked down at Don and the kids; I rolled my eyes, feeling like a big dummy. I wished I had never agreed to do it. Suddenly, the stage light turned on so bright it blinded me; I saw nothing but a laser beam shown over my arm. It appeared on a big screen that my arm was made of steel. I saw a dozen strong men, collected from the audience, who all eagerly came to the stage. They grabbed hold of the other end of the rope, and I was in a tug-of-war with them. They were pulling very hard, but I used only one hand and acted as if I were pulling. In the end, I won. That was my five minutes of fame.

DON LIKED HIS job but didn't like the Los Angeles area. To him, it was too crowded and dirty. He often complained about the traffic, the earthquakes, the mudslides, and the smog.

"I can't stand this area any longer," he said one day after he came home from work.

"Why?" I asked. "We just moved here only a few months ago."

"I just don't like this area or this neighborhood; it's terrible. I'd like to move!"

"Move again? I don't want to move," I replied. "I like my school and the kids like theirs. Everything is so convenient, and the whole place is so exciting. I love it here."

"I know you like it here, but if I stay here much longer, I'm afraid my drinking might get worse."

I knew Don's drinking was bad enough already; I didn't want it to get any worse. I didn't know if I could handle it. I loved California, but I loved Don more.

Whenever we went out to eat or to a friend's house, Don always drank too much and often came home drunk. Sometimes, he would drive on the busy freeway with one hand on the steering wheel and the other covering one of his eyes.

One night, after we left dinner and were on our way home, I asked him, "Why are you driving with only one eye? Isn't it dangerous?"

"After a couple of drinks," he explained, "if I don't cover one of my eyes, I see too many centerlines, which confuses me; by covering one of my eyes, I can see better."

"I see. Then why do you always drink so much?" I asked.

"I don't drink too much, Linda!" he exclaimed. "I only had two or three drinks tonight, and that's not too much."

"No, Don. I watched you. You must have had at least eleven, and probably more; I lost count."

I was concerned for our safety and asked him if I could drive, but he refused. He told me he didn't trust my driving at night. I thought he knew what he was doing, and I never questioned him about his one-eyed driving again.

I turned to Don and asked, "If we move, where do you think we should go?"

"Anywhere on the East Coast." He smiled.

"Do you miss your family there?" I asked.

He looked at me and said, "Yes, sort of."

"I miss mine too, but they are on the other side of the earth," I said sadly. "At least yours are in the same country."

"Hey, I have an idea!" Don said. "Let's play the map game." Don explained, "I lay a map out on the table and let the kids turn it around and around while you and I hold hands. Then, with our eyes blindfolded, we point to the map. Wherever our fingers land, that is where we'll move. What do you think?"

"It sounds like a fun game, but I only want to do it with an American map," I said. "I do not want to go back overseas right now."

"Okay," Don said and got up to look for a map. I cleaned up the table and put the leftovers in the fridge. When the table was clean, I called the kids back to the room and explained what we were about to do.

They were very excited and couldn't wait for the game to start. Don came back with a map and spread it across the table. He and I stood on opposite sides, but hand in hand, with our eyes covered. The kids were laughing at us.

"We're ready. Let's go!" Don yelled. The kids started to move the map around.

"Go! Go! Go!" We all laughed and yelled excitedly.

"Here comes our new home," Don said.

We lowered our fingers, pointed to the map, and then took off the blindfolds; our fingers were on the state of Washington. We looked at each other and shook our heads.

"It's too cold," Don said.

Don and I had our eyes covered and tried again. This time, we landed on San Antonio, Texas.

"It's too hot," Don said, and we repeated the game.

Our fingers traveled from San Diego to New York to Chicago to

New Orleans; we couldn't find a suitable place. After a few more spins, I grew tired of the game, and so did the kids; they left the table and ran outside to play.

"Don, why don't you just move us to wherever you want to and forget about this silly game?" I was a little irritable and made a sarcastic comment, "You aren't going to be happy until we point to the place you want to go anyway."

"I want to move back to Florida," Don said.

"Okay then, Florida it is," I replied.

"Remember, we still have land at Lake Panasoffkee," he said.

"Oh no! Not back there," I pouted. "Can you imagine leaving an exciting place like this and returning to the boondocks?" I snorted.

"I don't mind; I love it there," Don said.

"Well, maybe you don't mind, but I do. If you want to go back there, you can go by yourself, without me and the kids." I was upset. "Besides, we can't go back there right now. Don't you remember, we called Thelma and asked her to rent out the trailer?"

"I know we did," Don countered, "but we can take it back whenever we want. That was part of the deal."

"Well, I don't want to," I growled. "I never want to go back to that awful mosquito-infested swamp!"

"Then what are we going to do with our land?" he asked.

"I don't really care," I snapped. "You can sell it, rent it, or give it away. It's bad enough that I don't have any friends, and there is nothing to do there; I don't like the idea of smelly cow manure and being friends with raccoons and alligators." I started to cry.

"Well, let's do the map again," Don replied. "And this time, I promise we will move to wherever our fingers touch the map; I don't care if it ends up on Canada."

"Are you sure?" I asked.

"Yep."

I called the kids to come in and start the game all over again. This time, they were less excited. I had to promise them they only had to do it one more time. The game began, and the kids barely moved the map. When Don and I undid the blindfolds and looked at the map, our fingers pointed to Charleston, South Carolina. We looked at each other and yelled aloud at the same time. "South Carolina it is!" All five of us were excited about South Carolina, even though the kids and I didn't know anything about the place or where it was located.

"There is a lot of history in Charleston," he said. "Before I went to Vietnam, I was stationed at Myrtle Beach Air Force Base, about one hundred miles northeast of Charleston. I've been to Charleston many times, and I love it. I know you guys will love it too; I can't wait to move there." He smiled and put the map away.

Don applied for a transfer to Charleston, and a few weeks later, they accepted him as a personnel management specialist at the VA Medical Center. We sold our smaller car and started to pack; I went to college to withdraw from my courses and to say goodbye to my teachers and classmates.

We hired a moving company to pack and transport all of our large boxes and furniture. We packed all the knickknacks and the rest into our station wagon and our camper. Right before we were ready to hit the road, Don called Ron for the last time, hoping he would pay the money he owed us. I asked Don to turn the telephone speaker up so I could hear what Ron had to say.

"Hello!" A man's voice answered after a couple of rings.

"Hey, Ron. This is Don. How are you?" Don asked.

"Hey, buddy! I'm fine. What's up with you, my brother?" Ron acted excited.

"Just want to let you know we are moving back to the East Coast," Don said.

"Oh no. Why, Don?" He sounded sad.

"I just like the East Coast better," Don replied.

"Where on the East Coast are you moving to, buddy?"

"Charleston, South Carolina," Don answered, and he continued, "I want to know if you can pay some of the money you owe us before we leave."

"Oh, sure I can. Just let me know when you leave, and I will meet you to give you the money."

"We are leaving here tomorrow morning," Don said.

"Since you guys are going east, you'll have to go through here; let's meet at a restaurant. What do you think?" Ron suggested.

"Let us know which restaurant, and we'll be there," Don said with excitement.

"I'll talk to my wife," Ron said. "And I'll call you right back." Don hung up the phone.

"Well, Ron is not such a bad guy after all," I announced.

"We should be ashamed of ourselves for doubting our best friend," Don said.

"Well, let's wait and see," I said. A few minutes later, Ron called back and let Don know the name and the address of the restaurant where we were supposed to meet.

It was December 8, 1980. Don pulled our camper behind our Pontiac station wagon, packed full with kids and possessions, and we headed out east on Interstate 20, toward Cucamonga.

We met Ron and his wife, Lynn, at a fancy restaurant. When we walked in, I saw not just two of them but their entire family. Ron's children, mother, and mother-in-law all sat at a long table. I was touched and so happy to see everyone. I thought it was a nice surprise.

My family joined them at the fancy table, which Ron had reserved for us. After we all settled in, Ron began to order several bottles of wine and many exotic appetizers, including escargot and calamari. When we were done with wine and appetizers, we ordered. Everything looked so expensive, so Don and I ordered the least expensive ones. When the meals were done, we were stuffed, but Lynn and Ron and their family still ordered dessert. A while later, Don looked at his watch and called Ron aside.

"Hey, Ron," Don said, "it's late, and we have to hit the road. How about the money?" Don asked.

"Oh, I don't have it with me," Ron said and then hugged Don. "You guys go ahead, and I will send it to you as soon as you give me your new address."

Don was silent for a few seconds and then said, "That will be fine, Ron." Don was obviously disappointed, but there was nothing he could do. Don returned to the table and sat next to me. A waiter in a black tuxedo brought the bill to our table and gave it to Ron.

"Hey, Don," Ron said as he handed the bill to him. "Can you take care of this? I forgot my wallet at home. Sorry, buddy." Ron grinned and tilted his head to one side.

"Okay, Ron," Don said with an unhappy face.

I understand my husband, and I could tell by the way he talked and looked that he knew he had been duped.

Nevertheless, Don and I were very courteous to Ron and his family. We hugged and kissed them as though nothing had happened. I gave Ron a hug, and Don shook his hand as we left the restaurant.

Before we entered our car, Ron said, "Don't forget to send me your new address as soon as you get to South Carolina."

"I won't forget," Don replied. We waved to them as Don drove out of the parking lot. I looked back and saw them talking and laughing with each other. I think they were proud of themselves for tricking their best friends into paying for their meal, with no intention of paying us the loan. I could tell Don was upset, and he said nothing for a long time.

"Everything will be okay, baby," I comforted him.

"It's so wrong, Linda," he said with a sigh. "I just don't understand how people can do things like that and sleep well at night."

"People like them have no conscience," I said.

"You're right," he said. "I just wish I had known it in the beginning."

"How can we tell when someone we trust and love is deceiving us?" I asked.

"I guess there is no way to tell, but it's sad and it hurts," Don said.

"I know! It's sad to lose all of our hard-earned money," I said. "But to lose trust in a loved one is even more painful."

"The way Ron and his family took advantage of us on their meal, I doubt he will ever repay the loan," Don said.

"Well, I am with you there," I said. "I'm afraid we will never see our money again. Thank God they are the ones who will have to live with it and not us."

Later, we learned the second mortgage Ron gave us on his house was useless. The state of California protected people like Ron; he knew he would never have to honor the agreement of the second mortgage. I wondered how many friends, besides us, Ron had given second mortgages to so he could borrow money?

Several hours into the trip, the sky turned dark, and the kids dozed off. Don was trying to turn the music down so it didn't bother them, but he stopped when he heard an announcer interrupt the program.

"We are sorry to interrupt our program, but we have very sad news. We just learned an unknown gunman shot John Lennon in New York this evening. He was pronounced dead a few minutes ago."

"What!" I exclaimed. "I hope there was a mistake."

"I'm afraid not," Don said. "They are usually certain before they make such an announcement." Don sighed. "Another brilliant artist and wonderful human lost their life to a gun. Damn those guns!"

"Sad. It's so sad," I said as tears pooled in my eyes.

That night, we pulled into a campground to get some rest before continuing our journey. It took us four days to get to the South Carolina border.

"Well, at least it was shorter than the trip from Florida to California," I said with a smile.

"You mean the trip that took us almost three months," Don added.

"Nevertheless, it was a wonderful three months," I replied with a smile. "I will never forget that trip; I hope you and the kids feel the same." I turned to look at Don and at the kids and saw them smiling too.

Chapter 11

SOUTHERN CHARM

CHARLESTON WAS BEAUTIFUL, but it was too quiet for me. It was nothing like the exciting city of Los Angeles. The people I met seemed polite and friendly, but I heard that prejudice was still common in the Deep South. I knew it would take time for me to get used to the change.

One day I complained to Don, "I don't like it here, because it's too quiet and boring."

"What are you talking about?" Don exclaimed, defending the city. "There are more than three hundred thousand people living in Charleston!"

"Well, I don't see that many people here," I grumbled, "but I do see a lot of mosquitoes and gnats. I'm sure there are more than three hundred thousand of them."

"Well, I like it here," Don argued. "At least I don't have to drive through a red-light district on the way home from work every night."

"You could have taken a different route."

"Why don't you give Charleston a chance?" Don asked.

"Okay, I will, but I heard there were fewer than three hundred thousand people, not more."

"Whatever!" he snapped.

Although I complained to Don about the South, I agreed it was a better place to live and raise our children, which was more important to me than the excitement of a bigger city.

We rented a three-bedroom, two-bath home from a sweet lady named Mrs. Ravenel. Her son was a South Carolina state senator. She lived just a few blocks from us, and since we were new in Charleston, she helped me find the beach, the park, the school, and the grocery stores. She was like my mentor. She invited me to her house for coffee, and she let our children play on her dock. In return, I invited her to my house for tea and eggrolls. She became my first friend in Charleston.

The children liked their school, and Don loved his job. However, Don often came home drunk. I was afraid he might have an accident and kill himself or someone else. We fought a lot over his drinking, but I loved him, and I never thought of leaving him, even though I was sad and lonely each time he went out drinking and gambling with his friends. And since I was new to Charleston, I had no one to share my feelings and family problems with; that hurt worse.

Now and then, Don took our family to his friends' or coworkers' homes for parties, where he always had too much to drink.

One time, all five of us were in the car, coming home from a pool party, and Don was as drunk as a jellyfish. He was speeding and weaving all over the road. I looked over and noticed he had his hand over one of his eyes again.

"Don! Watch out!" I yelled. "You're going to get all of us killed if you don't open your eyes!"

"Okay."

"What are you doing?" I asked. "Why are you covering your face? Do you have a headache?" I knew why, because he told me before. He was trying to see the road better. I was just trying to make him mad so he wouldn't fall asleep.

"No, I don't have a headache!" he answered with an attitude. "I thought we discussed this issue many times already. Why do you keep bringing it up again and again?"

I thought to myself, *This is good. He's mad, which means he's awake now.*

I didn't bother responding until the car swerved out of control, and I had to yell for him to pay attention again. Don continued to weave back and forth, and I continued to yell at him all the way home. The children were scared but sat quietly in the back seat; they knew nothing about their father's drinking problem, because when he drank, he was nice, and I was angry. They thought I was just being mean to their daddy and often stood up for him.

After that, I decided I would never take the kids with us to a party if it involved drinking; I did not want to put my children at risk again.

Besides drinking, Don also had a gambling problem. Each night after work, he walked from the VA hospital to a nearby private club to drink and play slot machines. Other times, he went to shoot pool, but when drunk, he thought he was a pool shark and bet too much money; he usually lost. He burned up a lot of our savings, but whenever I asked him about it, he never gave me a straight answer. I had to find it out by looking into our accounts myself.

When Don was late, the children often asked, "Where is Daddy? Why is Daddy late for dinner?" I always made excuses for him being late. The children believed Don was perfect, and I didn't want them to know his other side. They were too young to understand their father's addiction problem, and I never intended to explain, because I wanted them to love and respect their daddy.

"Dad works hard to buy you guys what you want and need," I told them. "He wants you guys to have what his family couldn't afford to buy for him when he was young." This seemed to satisfy their curiosity, and they quit worrying about their dad coming home late at night.

Although I didn't have a perfect husband, I wanted my children to believe they had a perfect dad, and in many ways, he was a very good father to them. He seldom raised his voice or disciplined them. I was the disciplinarian, teacher, doctor, mother, and, in a lot of ways, father to them. Sometimes the kids didn't like me, because I was hard on them, but I believed it was my job. I wanted them to know the difference between wrong and right, as my parents and my culture taught me.

Many nights after I put the kids to bed, I sat at the window, looking out to the street, waiting for Don, even though I knew he might not come home until the morning. I sat up all night, praying that he wouldn't kill himself or someone else.

Sometimes I just sat motionless and stared outside, waiting and watching as each headlight came into view, hoping it was Don. My heart went up and down as the headlights appeared and disappeared, until one of the cars pulled into our driveway.

If Don didn't come home all night, the following morning, I would send my children to school and call a taxi to go looking for him. I went from the nightclubs to pool halls and friends' homes to the VA hospital where he worked—anywhere I thought he might have spent the night. If I couldn't find him, I called the police station and the hospitals to see if he had been in an accident, arrested, injured, or even killed. There were even a few times when he seemed to disappear from the face of the earth for days.

One time, in the middle of the cold month of February, Don disappeared into thin air for two days. I went to the VA hospital to look for him. I saw his car in the parking lot; I was so happy and thought he was safe at work. But when I went inside to ask about him, no one knew where he was, not even his boss. I went home and called around, but there was no trace of him in any hospital or police station. I was afraid he might have walked to the Cooper River Bridge, drunk, and jumped to his death. He had told me many times that when he was drunk, the thought of taking his own life occurred to him often. I called the police and reported him missing. I told them Don might have jumped off the bridge. The police promised they would send divers to the Cooper River Bridge to look for his body. The children saw me crying and questioned me, but I could not bring myself to tell them their father might be dead. I just told them their father was out of town on a business trip, and I was crying because I missed him.

I figured Don was dead, and I had to think about planning his funeral. I was scared and beside myself; I didn't know what to do. We were new to South Carolina, and I didn't know who to talk to. I was convinced he was dead, and I had to figure out funeral arrangements.

Before I went to bed, I took a notepad and the telephone book to the table, and with tearful eyes, I looked through the ads for the churches, funeral homes, and cemetery lots. I wrote down as much information as I could and planned to call all of them in the morning to find out the costs and what was involved in a burial. And then I went to bed.

Early in the morning on the third day, the phone ringing woke me, and I ran to answer it, expecting a police call telling me they found Don's corpse.

"Hey, honey. Do you know where I am?" The voice was weak and trembling; at first, I didn't recognize it.

"Who is this?" I asked.

"Linda, it's me," Don responded on the other end. I was shocked, but before I had a chance to answer him, he continued. "I am so sorry to put you through this again," he said.

I was so happy to hear his voice—the voice I thought I would never hear again.

"Where on earth are you?" I asked.

"I'm in Asheville, North Carolina," he replied. "I'm freezing cold; I must have been walking around in the snow for hours without my jacket."

"How did you get there? Asheville is over three hundred miles away. I saw your car in the VA parking lot. How did you get there without a car?"

"I don't know how I got here," he said, "but the most important thing is for me to find a way to get home."

"Do you want me to come up there to get you?" I asked.

"No, Linda. I've put you through enough hell already. I won't ask you to do more, but to try to understand my sickness and forgive me," he said. "When I get home, I must do something about my stupid drinking."

"How will you get home from there?" I asked.

"I'll have to catch a bus or a train, I guess."

"Do you know where the train and bus station are?" I questioned him.

"No, I don't, but I'll find out," he replied. "Honey, I'm on a pay phone, and I'm out of coins. I need to hang up now, but don't worry, I'll find my way home. I love you."

"I love you too, and please be careful," I said.

"I will. And again, I am so sorry." The phone clicked off, and he was gone.

I was so excited and happy at first, but the more I thought about it, the angrier I became; I couldn't wait for him to come home so I could kill him.

He stayed sober for a couple of weeks. Then one night, he didn't come home again. I was at the window waiting and praying for him, as I always did.

In the middle of my prayer, I saw headlights pulling into the driveway. For a minute, I was happy to see him, but then the happiness disappeared and anger took over. I stopped praying for him and started cursing him. "You SOB!" I mumbled. "I can't wait for you to come in here; I'm going to kill you!"

As soon as he parked and the car door sprung open, he staggered out and almost tumbled to the ground; I ran outside to help him. Lucky for him, he was too drunk for me to kill him that night. I guided him into the house, helped change his clothes, and put him to bed. I pulled a cover over him, lay down next to him, and cried. I felt so sad and lonely, but Don couldn't see my pain because of his addiction. I thought of our journey; it was not always smooth or easy, but our love for each other remained constant.

Don's addiction took a toll on both of us, and we suffered together. I learned later that he also suffered from post-traumatic stress disorder, because of his experiences in the Vietnam War. I also learned that one of the symptoms of PTSD was the excessive use of drugs and alcohol. Knowing this, however, didn't make it any easier; the more he drank, the more we fought, and we fought often.

One day, it occurred to me how much Don's drinking was costing us. He was not just paying for his drinks, but he gave tips for each drink as well, and he was a big tipper. I thought if I could convince him to drink at home, it would cost less. With him drinking at home, I could keep an eye on him and control his drinking.

I was happy with my plan and couldn't wait for Don to come home to share my idea with him. He came home early that day and hadn't started drinking yet.

"Hi, baby," Don greeted me as he came to the sink where I was washing dishes. He gave me a kiss on my forehead.

"Hi, yourself. You are home early," I replied with a smile.

"Yep," he grinned. "I had important paperwork to do, but I decided to bring it home to work on it and to see you."

"Thanks, I'm glad you're home early," I said. "I have something important to talk to you about as well."

The kids heard Don's voice, so they stopped watching the television and came running to the kitchen to greet him. He gave them a kiss on their foreheads.

"Okay, let me change clothes, and I'll be right back," he said.

While Don changed his clothes, the kids watched television, and I warmed up the food and set the table.

"Can I help you?" Don asked when he returned to the kitchen.

"Nah, everything's done, but thanks anyway."

"What did you want to talk to me about?" Don asked as he sat down.

"I don't want you to take this wrong, but I have an idea, and I want you to hear me out before you make any comment."

"Okay!" Don said.

I stopped working on the food, walked to the table, and sat next to him. I kept my voice low so the kids wouldn't hear me; they had very keen hearing.

"I know you've been going to the bars quite a bit," I started, "and I know it costs a lot of money for drinks and tips. I think if we buy liquor and you drink at home, it would cost less and you wouldn't have to worry about driving home drunk." I smiled and asked, "What do you think?"

"Are you sure?" he asked. "I thought you didn't want to see me drinking in the house. That's why I don't drink at home."

"Don, I don't want to see you drinking at all, period. But if you must drink, I'd rather see you drink at home."

"Okay, I'll give it a try," he replied.

"The only thing I ask of you is if you drink at home, don't drink more than two drinks a night. That way, you'll never get drunk," I explained.

"I'll give it a try," Don said.

"I'm glad we had this talk," I said as I stood up, excited. My plan seemed to be working.

The next morning, Don went to work, the kids went to their school, and I called a taxi to take me to the liquor store.

"Where are you going?" the driver asked as I entered his cab.

"Please take me to a liquor store."

"Okay," he said as he backed out of my driveway.

A few miles later, he turned into the parking lot of a liquor store and stopped. He waited for me outside while I went into the store. A young, handsome man offered to help me. I told him I just wanted to look around first. He said "Okay! If you need me, please let me know." He smiled and walked away. I grabbed several bottles of different sizes, shapes, and colors and took them to the counter. The young man came toward me.

"Is that all you want?" he asked.

"No, it's not." I smiled. "I'm still looking."

Since I didn't drink, I had no idea what was in the bottles. I just picked the prettiest bottles with the lowest price tags and hoped Don would like them. I made many trips back and forth between the cabinets and the cashier's counter. When I finished, I told the young man to total it up. I was shocked when I saw the bill. It cost so much more than I expected, but I wrote the check anyway.

"You must be having a big party," the good-looking cashier commented. "Can I come to your party?" He flirted and winked at me while putting the bottles into boxes and bags.

"Can't one party by oneself?" I replied with an ornery smile. "Could you help me take these outside to the waiting taxi?"

"I sure can, but I would like to come with you to your party too," he said. I ignored him, grabbed one of the boxes, and started out the door.

The taxi driver saw us, got out of his seat, and helped load multiple bags and boxes into the trunk. The driver took me back home and helped me unload. I paid him and gave him a big tip. He gave me a card and said, "This is my number. You call me whenever you need a taxi, you hear?" I thanked him, he got into his cab, and I carried my liquor inside.

I took a stepladder to the kitchen, cleaned out several top shelves, and stacked all the bottles neatly inside. I organized them by size, height, and color so it would be easy for Don to find them. I felt a little guilty for spending that much money on liquor, but I knew it made sense in the long run.

Satisfied with my bottle decorations, I closed the cabinet. I couldn't wait for Don to come home and see it. I waited and waited, but he didn't come home until after midnight. By then, I was too upset to show him anything. The next day, before he went to work, I followed him to the door and said, "Hey, Don, could you please come home early tonight? I have something I want to show you."

"Okay, I will," Don said with a smile as he gave me a kiss on my forehead and walked away. I returned to my liquor cabinet, opened it, looked at it, and smiled with satisfaction. Don was late again but not as late as the night before. I served dinner to him and the kids. While waiting for all of them to take their showers, I did the dishes. After showers, Don walked into the kitchen in his pajamas.

"What do you want to show me?" Don asked.

"Wait until I finish with the dishes," I said, smiling. Don sat at the table and waited for me. I dried my hands and asked, "Are you ready?"

"Sure!" he said but looked puzzled. I opened the cabinet and showed him all of the liquor bottles. His eyebrows lifted, and his jaw dropped in shock.

"Where in the world did you get all of that?"

"At the liquor store," I said.

"Can I try some?"

"Of course you can. I bought all of them for you. But before you drink it, you have to promise me something."

"Sure, anything," Don answered.

"You must swear on your dead father that you will not drink more than two drinks a night."

"I swear I will not drink more than two drinks a night ever again," he said, and I believed him.

"Good!" I said with a smile. "Since this is your first night, I will celebrate with you." Don seemed happy, and I was so proud of myself for doing the right thing.

The first night, however, we couldn't just taste one; we had too many bottles, so we had to try them all. Needless to say, I was not a drinker, and it didn't take much to make me tipsy. On the other hand, it took more than two drinks to get Don drunk. As could be expected, we celebrated a little too hard, and we both were as drunk as jellyfish.

Don was good after that. He came home early each night and always had a couple of drinks before dinner, but for some reason he always seemed to be dizzy before we went to bed. When I asked him about the amount of liquor he consumed, he always told me he had just two drinks. I asked him why he was drunk from only two drinks; he said it was because the liquor I bought for him was much stronger than those served in bars. I believed him, until I caught him drinking straight from a bottle and then pouring himself two more drinks. I confronted him, and he swore on his father's grave that he would never cheat again. I believed him. But the liquor in the cabinets disappeared way too fast; I often had to renew the supply. When I raised my concern about the disappearance of the liquor, Don told me that it evaporated fast because of the alcohol content; I believed him.

Believing him was one thing, but watching all of the bottles emptying fast was another. I began to have suspicions and watched him like a hawk. Don was drinking faster than I could replace the bottles, and I fought with him each time I caught him cheating. Our fights started verbally and small in the beginning but soon escalated into violence. At first, we waited for the kids to be out playing in the yard or asleep, but soon we fought wherever and whenever because we were too sick to care. I began to throw and break things. Don walked away at first, but soon he joined the fight. We started to break larger things, such as furniture, a television, and even a small piano.

After one of our fights, Don waited for the children to come home from their school and took them away. I had no idea where they went. I was worried at first, but then I became angry; the more I thought about it, the angrier I got. I took all of his clothes outside, piled them up high, poured gasoline on them, and set them on fire. The neighbors called the police. Two of them came to where I was stewing over a pile of burning clothes, and one asked, "What are you doing, ma'am?"

"I'm burning some old clothes," I said.

"Put the fire out, ma'am," he ordered. "It's against the law. You can't burn things around here without a permit."

"Okay!" I said. I strolled back into the house, filled a large bucket with water, and walked back out as slowly as I could. I took my time pouring water over the burning clothes, but by the time the fire was out, all the clothes had burned to ashes, as I intended. The police left, but I was still angry. I went inside and took all of the bottles of liquor out of the cabinet. One by one, I emptied them into the sink.

Later, when Don came home with the kids, I was sitting at a kitchen table full of food. I watched him go to the cabinet to get himself a drink, but it was empty; he said nothing to me. Then he went to the bedroom to change his clothes, but there were none. He realized what I had done. He sent the children to bed and came straight at me. He stood in front of my face, put his fist close to my nose, and snorted, "You! You! No one on this earth can stop me from my drinking! Do you understand me?"

I was angry, but I said nothing. Don took my silence as an insult and shook his fist even closer to my face. He was about to say something, but he had no chance. I went crazy, grabbed his fist, and started a tug-of-war. We were wrestling on top of the table full of food, until the table collapsed on its side, spilling soup, cooked vegetables, and noodles throughout the room. We didn't stop there; we continued to pull and push each other as we screamed and cursed at the top of our lungs. The kids heard the commotion and came out to check on us. We both yelled at them at the same time, "Get back to bed! Go back to bed!" They went back to their rooms, and we continued our tug-of-war until we were exhausted.

We sat on the kitchen floor, trying to catch our breath. Seconds later, I glanced at Don; at the same time, he turned and looked at me. When our eyes met, we immediately turned away from each other. The second time I caught his eyes, I started to giggle, and we both broke out into uncontrolled laughter; I was laughing so hard that my stomach hurt. Between our laughing spells, Don and I tried to talk to each other.

"Do you remember when we did this in Vietnam?" I asked.

"Well!" Don replied, still laughing. "At least this time I didn't put my fist into a concrete wall and have to go to the emergency room with a broken hand."

"Yeah!" I said, laughing. "At least you didn't use the shotgun to blow a hole in the ceiling, like you did the last time, and I had to hire a carpenter to fix it."

"We are lucky; we didn't put each other in the emergency room today."

"And we're also lucky we didn't break any good furniture today," I responded.

"Yep, I agree," he said.

"We may not have broken anything, but we still have to clean up this unholy mess," I declared.

Don stood up first, came to me, and offered his hand to pull me up from the floor, and we gave each other a big hug.

While straightening up the furniture, Don stopped laughing and said, "I think you started this tonight." He grinned.

"No, I don't think so," I responded. "It was your fault for putting your fist to my face. You know better than to do that," I countered, and I could feel the anger returning.

"Should we declare peace?" Don suggested. "Let's quit blaming each other," he said as he reached over and gave me a kiss.

"I agree," I said.

Together, we straightened up the furniture, picked up the dishes, and cleaned off the floor.

WHILE TAKING CARE of my garden one hot afternoon, I went inside to escape the heat. I sat on the couch and turned on the television, which for me was unusual; I seldom watched it in the daytime. I watched one of the soap operas and was surprised to see the actors and actresses talking about alcohol addiction and a program called Alcoholics Anonymous. I watched intently, trying to grasp every word they said, and realized they were describing Don and me. When the show was over, I turned the television off. I couldn't wait for Don to come home so I could share what I learned with him.

As soon as Don walked into the house, I asked him to sit down.

"I have something very important to tell you, and I believe it will help both of us," I said. Before he had a chance to respond, I continued, "I watched a soap opera today where they talked about a program called AA, or Alcoholics Anonymous. This program is supposed to help people who drink too much and have a drinking problem." Before I could say more, Don cut me off.

"It is not for me. I don't drink too much, and I don't have a drinking problem!" he barked. "You are the one who has a problem with my drinking, not me. I can stop any time I want to; I just don't want to right now." Don reacted just as the show predicted; he denied it. But I persisted.

"They also said if someone in the family has a drinking problem, the whole family suffers. I believe you have a drinking problem, and I am suffering because of it!" I exclaimed.

"No way!" he shouted. "That is BS, and it is the most stupid thing I have ever heard."

"Don, why don't you look into it," I said. "What do you have to lose? It's better than fighting with each other all the time." I reasoned with him and was surprised; I didn't even raise my voice. "And besides the fighting, we also have financial problems because of your drinking and gambling."

"What are you talking about now?" Don asked.

"Don't play dumb with me, Don. I went to the bank a couple days ago to cash a check, because I needed the money, but when I saw our bank balance, I was shocked. You not only spent all of our savings, but we now owe the bank twice as much."

"Who told you that?" he demanded.

"The people at the bank!" I cried.

"How much did they say I owed?" he asked with mock concern.

"We owe more than fifteen thousand dollars."

Don was surprised I knew about our money situation. He put his arms around me and said, "I am so sorry, baby. I will try to make it up somehow."

"I don't know how or what you can do," I cried. "We are out of money, and you still drink like a fish; I've tried to save money by using coupons, but when I save ten cents, you spend ten dollars on liquor and two more on the server's tips. It's just not fair," I sobbed.

Don loosened his grip on me, held me at arm's length, and announced, "You're right. It's not fair, and I am so sorry." I will do something about this. What did you say about the AA program?" he asked. "If you think I have a drinking problem, then I'll check it out. Tell me more about Alcoholics Anonymous."

"I don't know more than what I already told you. I don't know where or when the meetings take place. You need to call the AA hotline and find out."

I was so happy; Don finally admitted he might have a problem. He was not only drinking and smoking, but he also had the gambling, and prescription drug addictions as well. Don called the AA program and discovered meetings close to our home. For the next few weeks, he went to some meetings, but he didn't stop drinking entirely. When he was about to stop going to meetings, I offered to go with him to provide support and hoped he was not going to give up on the program. At my first meeting, I met one of the AA members, and she told me about a family support group called ALANON, which she said I should attend. "The support group meets at the same time, in this building," she explained, "but in a separate room."

Soon, these programs were our priority. We made new friends and attended all of their functions, whenever and wherever they had one.

We both benefited and learned so much from the meetings. My group kept me from going crazy, and Don's group helped him stay sober, as long as he attended the meetings.

While the kids were in school, Don was at work, and I stayed home doing chores. The monotonous daily routine was getting to me. I felt trapped and bogged down, and I decided to go look for a job without telling Don.

"What kind of work can I do?" I asked myself. "What can I do with my GED?" I mulled this problem over in my mind until I came up with a solution; there was something I could do. I thought, *I can do nails. I'm sure I can qualify as a manicurist, even though I've never tried to do nails professionally. I've done it for friends and family members, and besides, I've done my own nails for years.* I remembered all of the details from the manicurist, when I had my nails done in Vietnam, and it didn't seem hard. *So, nails it is; I can do nails.*

I was excited about the idea and couldn't sleep. I wanted the night to be over so I could go looking for a job. After breakfast the following morning, I waited for Don and the kids to leave the house, and as soon as they left, I hit the road.

Since I didn't have a car, I had to walk for miles under the hot sun. I stopped at every beauty salon on the road and asked for a manicurist job, but most of the people I talked to didn't even know what a manicurist or a pedicurist was. I guessed there wasn't a demand for those services in Charleston. However, those salon owners and managers I talked to were very nice; some even offered me a job as a hairstylist. Too bad I didn't know how to do hair.

One nice man, who looked about thirty and was not very tall, offered me a job as a receptionist.

"What would I have to do as a receptionist?" I asked.

"Answer the phone and make appointments," he replied.

"I would love to work for you, but I don't speak English well enough to answer the phone; with my accent, I'm afraid no one would understand me." We both laughed.

"I understand you," he said. "I like your personality and your positive attitude. I wish I could hire you," he said as he continued working on an elderly lady. "I'm so sorry I can't help you, but I'll tell you what you can do. Go to a beauty school, get a cosmetology license, and come back here to see me."

"Thank you. I will." I left his salon and said to myself, "I wish I could do hair or speak English better. I could work for that sweet man."

I continued to walk many miles under the hot sun, all the way down to the end of the business section, and then I crossed the street and walked back to where I started. It was hot, and I was tired and disappointed. I was about to give up and return home. But instead, I kept on walking on Savannah Highway. I knew if I kept going, I would end up in downtown Charleston.

Chapter 12

CLOUDY SUMMER

IT WAS AFTER midday when I reached Saint Andrews Shopping Center. I was soaked with sweat from walking under the blazing sun and stopped to wipe my forehead and rest my feet for a few seconds; I looked around at the shopping strip for a beauty salon but saw none. Discouraged, I was just about to return home when I saw a little nail boutique. I walked to the door, stopped to look inside through the glass door for a second, pushed it open, and walked in. I stood there, at the front of the store, just glancing around; a middle-aged woman thought I was a client and came to greet me.

"Hello, how are you?" she asked with a weak smile.

"I am fine, thank you," I answered.

"What can I do for you today?" she asked.

"I'm looking for a job. Do you need a manicurist?"

"I do; what kind of manicures can you do?"

I smiled and replied, "Any kind you want."

"Can you do acrylic?"

"I did something like that in Vietnam, where I came from," I lied, "but if you want me to do it your way, just show me once.

"How long have you been doing nails?" she asked.

"Oh, fourteen to fifteen years," I lied again.

"You must have been doing nails when you were a child," she commented.

"I'm older than I look." I smiled.

"Okay, when can you start?"

"Right now," I said.

"Okay, come with me," she said as she took me to the back of the shop. "Put your purse up here." She pointed to one of the small shelves and said, "And I'll show you what you need to do."

"Yes, ma'am," I answered as I put my purse up and followed her back to the front. "Do you have more people working here besides yourself?" I asked.

"No, I just started a few months ago, and I don't know how things are going to work out, so I've been reluctant to hire anyone, but you seem to be the right one."

"Lucky me!" I grinned.

"No, we're both lucky," she said and gave me a big smile for the first time since I'd walked into her shop. "By the way, my name is Sally."

"I'm so happy to meet you and work for you."

Sally took me to one of the nail tables and said, "This will be yours; it has everything you need to do manicures, nail tips, and acrylic nails."

I glanced at all of the unfamiliar instruments Sally showed me. Except for a few nail files and a cuticle snipper, I had no idea what the rest were used for. Sally recognized my confusion, gave me a sympathetic smile, and said, "Don't worry about all of those things; we'll learn as we work. I'm also new to the job, and all of these instruments were confusing to me at first too." She smiled and winked at me. I had an impression she didn't know much more than I did, and that made me feel better.

"I don't have any clients for you today, unless someone walks in," she said. "Meanwhile, you can sit and watch me, because I want you to do everything my way."

"I'll be happy to do it your way," I grinned. "My way might be a little bit rusty and old-fashioned for your clients." Although, there really was no "my way" because I had never done it before.

Minutes later, while she showed me her tools, one of her regular patrons walked in.

"Hi, Irene!" She greeted her client and tried to introduce me. "I want you to meet . . . ah . . . this is, um, ah, eh . . ."

She couldn't introduce me because she didn't even know my name; I'd forgotten to tell her earlier, so I covered up for her. "Hi, Irene. My name is Linda, and I'm glad to meet you." I offered Irene my hand and a big smile.

"Oh, I am pleased to meet you too, Linda," Irene said. "Sally, where did you find Linda? She is so friendly; I like her already." Sally didn't answer Irene's question and asked her to sit down at her table.

"Thanks, Irene," I said. "Actually, I was lucky and found Sally myself." I smiled as I sat back down at my new table near Sally. I watched and listened to Sally and Irene's conversation; they were talking and laughing as if I didn't even exist.

I watched intently as Sally worked on Irene's nails. Now and then, they looked at me and smiled. Thirty-five or forty minutes later, Sally finished with Irene's manicure. Irene stayed at the same table and dried her nails under a small fan. Sally went to the back room and, minutes later, returned with a pedicure bucket, half-filled with soapy water. She asked Irene to take her shoes off and put her feet in the bucket, and then Sally plugged a long electrical cord into a wall socket.

"Linda," Sally called, "I want you to watch me carefully while I'm doing Irene's pedicure. I want you to do it my way."

"Yes, ma'am," I said. "I'm watching." I paid careful attention to what Sally did and how she did it. It looked easy and similar to the pedicure I received in Vietnam, except for the long foot massage. Right before Sally finished with Irene, a beautiful and cheerful blond lady walked in.

Sally looked up from the floor and said, "Hey, Nancy."

"Hey, Sally," Nancy replied with a cute pout. "I don't have an appointment, but I need my nails done for a special television advertisement. Do you have time for me?"

"I'm sorry, Nancy, after I finish with Irene, I have another manicure and pedicure to do. However, this is my new girl." She pointed to me. "Her name is Linda, and she can do your nails if you don't mind."

"Sure, I don't mind if Linda does my nails," Nancy said. "Do you mind, Linda?"

"Not at all; I'll be more than happy to give you a manicure. Please sit down at my table," I said cheerfully, acting as if I were a professional.

As Nancy prepared to sit down, Sally looked up at me and winked, so I smiled and winked back. I didn't do exactly what Sally had shown me. Instead, I took the time to pamper Nancy, by massaging her hand and arm longer, before I painted her nails. Nancy liked my work and tipped me well.

Sally's next client needed a full set of acrylic nail tips. Again, I sat and watched her perform. Sally was good at it, and the client's extended nails looked natural. The next day, I bit off one of my nails before I went to work. I wanted Sally to extend my nail tip so I could watch her technique closer.

"Hey, Sally," I said as I walked into the shop, "I just broke one of my fingernails while doing dishes this morning," I lied. "Could you please fix it?"

"I sure can," Sally said. "Who wants to go to a manicurist who has a broken nail, right?"

Sally extended my nail with a long plastic tip but cut it down to match the length of the rest of my nails. She filed it and filled it with an acrylic powder mixed in with a strong chemical liquid; it was hard for me to breathe. I was eager to learn and watched her every move. When she was done, I looked at my new nail, admired her work, and complimented her.

"I like the way you did it, Sally. It looks so natural; I can't tell the difference between it and my real nail."

I kept looking at my new nail, admiring it. I was impressed with her technique, but it didn't look hard to do; I was confident I could do it myself.

A few days later, a group of four young teenagers walked into the shop. They all wanted acrylic tips for prom night. Sally took two girls, and I took the other two. It took me much longer to do the clients' nails than Sally, but in the end, they were all happy. Within two months, I became a professional nail technician; I did manicures, pedicures, nail tips, and sculptures. I began having my own repeat clients, including some of Sally's patrons who preferred me to Sally, including Irene and Nancy.

I was happy to work for Sally, but it seemed she had a change of heart about me. She became unfriendly and made me mop the floor and clean the toilet—a job intended for the janitor. Sometimes, she would send me home right before my patrons' appointments. When I asked her about my clients, she told me they all had canceled. I believed her at first, but then the cancellations happened more frequently, and I began to think she wanted me out. She was upset because her clients preferred me, but I was trying to do my job well. I thought highly of her, but what she did bothered me. One day, while I was there, Nancy came in.

"Where have you been, girl?" she asked as we hugged. I looked at her with a sad smile, but before I could utter a word, Nancy said, "I came here every week and asked Sally about you, but she kept telling me you had already gone home. I didn't understand why you kept leaving before my appointment; I began to think you didn't like me anymore."

While I was doing Nancy's manicure, I whispered, "I didn't go home on my own; Sally sent me home."

"Linda, I thought so." She hardened her lips, shook her head from side to side. "I have a friend who owns a beauty salon," she whispered. "She would love to hire you, because I've been telling her about you and how good you are with nails." I looked at Nancy with gratitude.

"I would love to move from here. I have a feeling Sally will let me go soon."

"You don't have to worry about that over there," Nancy whispered. "You will be the only one who does nails."

"That would be perfect!" I was excited and raised my voice, but Nancy put her finger over her lips to signal for me to calm down. Thank God, Sally was doing a pedicure, and with the bucket's motor running, she couldn't hear us.

"Don't talk so loud," Nancy said in a low voice. "I need Sally's advertisements for my job. I do commercials for television, radio, and the newspaper. Who knows, someday I might be doing ads for you too."

"Where is your friend's salon?" I asked.

"Not too far from here," she said. "Maybe two miles."

"I guess I could walk there."

"Walk? Why do you have to walk?" she asked.

"Because I don't have a car yet."

"You need a car," Nancy said.

"I know. Maybe after I work for a while and save the money, I can get myself a used car."

"I understand," she smiled.

"Where and when can I go to your friend's salon?"

"Meet me here after work," she said.

"Here at this place?" I raised my eyebrows.

"No, Linda, meet me at the corner." She tilted her head to the right. I knew exactly where she meant. "I will take you there at one thirty."

"Good. At one thirty, my kids will still be in school, and they won't be home until three o'clock or after. Thanks, Nancy."

"Don't mention it," she said as she bent her head closer to me. "And especially don't mention it to Sally."

"Oh no, I'm not going to," I said.

I met Nancy at our arranged time, and she took me to the salon. She parked her car, and we walked into a tall building, went up a couple stairs, and entered the salon. A middle-aged woman with bleached blond hair greeted us with a big smile.

"Hi, Nancy, and thanks." She gave Nancy a hug and shook my hand.

"Hi. My name is Shula, and I am the owner of this salon," she said with pride. I glanced around and saw three hairstylists working on their clients. Two turned to look at us.

I smiled and said, "Hi, my name is Linda, and I do nails."

"I know," Shula replied. "Nancy told me about you. She said you are a very good nail technician and have been doing nails for a long time. I need a good nail person here."

"Yes, it seems like I've been doing nails since I started to walk and talk," I bragged; I was not about to tell her I had just started a couple of months ago.

"See, Shula, what did I tell you," Nancy said.

"What about her pay?" Nancy asked. "Remember, she is good at what she does." Nancy glanced at me and winked to let me know she was taking care of me. "I pay my hairstylists fifty percent, but I'm willing to pay her eighty percent, providing she furnishes all of her own supplies," Shula offered.

"I'll take it," I jumped in, as if I were afraid she would change her mind.

"Good, very good," Shula said. "When can you start?"

"I can start tomorrow if you want me too." I grinned.

"Okay, how about nine in the morning?" Shula suggested.

"I have to start later than nine o'clock, because I need to go to the supply store to get all of the things I'll need for manicures and pedicures first," I told her. "The day after that, I can come to work from nine until two or two thirty."

"That will be fine," Shula said with a smile. Nancy had been watching us, and she was pleased with herself for the outcome.

I thanked Shula for hiring me and then turned to hug Nancy and thank her for helping me.

"I will see you later," I said and then left her shop to walk the two miles back to my house.

Don came home from work that afternoon, and I told him about my job. "I found a new job, but it's too far for me to walk," I announced. He looked confused. He didn't know I had a job, much less a new one. I thought I had told him, but perhaps I had forgotten. Whatever—it was not a big issue to me. "What would you say if I bought a small used car," I continued, "and went to the DMV to get a South Carolina driver's license?"

"Where are you working, and what do you do?" he asked, surprised.

"I've been working for the last few weeks at Saint Andrews Shopping Center as a manicurist. I always walked home before you and the kids came home, but I'm changing jobs, and it's too far for me to walk," I explained.

"What about the children?" he asked with concern.

"What about the children?" I responded coldly.

"Who will take care of them?"

"Who do you think has been taking care of them for the past few months, or ever since they were born?" I asked sarcastically.

"Fine, you do whatever you want to do. I don't really care," he said.

"I just want to do the right thing to help this family."

"When do you want to look for a car?" he asked.

"As soon as possible, like right now," I exclaimed.

"Don't you think it's a little late for car shopping?"

"No! I don't think it's late," I replied. "It's just six, and I think the car dealers stay open until eight or nine."

"Fine, just tell the kids to stay home, and we'll go," he grumbled.

Don took me to a used car dealer somewhere in North Charleston. After test-driving a few of them, I decided to take a Ford Capri. I bargained with the salesman for a lower price, but Don was embarrassed and whispered for me to stop. I ignored him. The salesman preferred Don, because he didn't bargain.

"I am the one who is buying the car," I told the man. "If you want to sell it, you have to answer my questions." He looked at me with surprise, and in the end, I bought the car for a thousand dollars less than what Don was willing to pay. I took the driving and the written tests the next day and passed both. I was happy with my new life and the way things were turning out.

Shula approached me one day, after I was done with a client, and asked, "Is your cosmetology license up to date?"

"My what?" I asked.

"Your cosmetology license, the license you need to have if you are working in a salon," she said.

I was confused and replied, "No, I don't have one. I've been working in a nail place for months, but the owner never asked me for a license."

"Well! That was a nail shop," she snorted. "In a hair salon, you're required to have a license; even the shampoo girl has to have one."

"Where can I get one?" I asked.

"You'll have to attend a beauty school," she said.

"Where and when?"

"There are several beauty schools around Charleston; you'll have to look them up yourself. You can continue working here, but you will have to get a license as soon as you can."

I went home and explained the situation to Don and asked for his help. We found a beauty school named Farrah's in the phone book and it was located in North Charleston.

Early the next morning, I drove to the address listed in the phone book. Once there, I got out of my car and walked into the school, not knowing what to expect. I asked one of the students where I could go to register, and she pointed me in the right direction. I walked toward a counter, where a heavyset older woman was sitting at her desk, smoking a cigarette.

"Hi," I said, smiling, as I approached her.

She glared at me, took another puff from her cigarette, and asked roughly, "What do you want?"

"I want to sign up for a class," I said.

"What class?" she demanded, expressionless.

"I just want to sign up to get a license."

"There are many kinds of classes here," she snorted. "We offer classes in barbering, massage, skin care, and cosmetology. Which one do you want to sign up for?"

"I want to sign up for the nail manicurist's license," I said with an uneasy feeling.

"Did you hear me? Did I say anything about a nail license?" she growled.

My first thought was *If I go to this school, I'll probably have to deal with this unfriendly old woman, and that is not going to be good.*

"Do you have a class for a nail license only?" I asked.

"For that, you will have to go to a different state," she barked. "Besides, why would you want just a nail license? If you get a full cosmetologist license, you can do everything, including nails," she said with a know-it-all attitude and took another puff of her strong-smelling cigarette.

"The reason I want only a nail license is because I only want to do nails, and besides, I think a nail license would cost less and take less time to obtain," I replied.

"Well, as I said, you can get it in a different state but not in South Carolina," she grumbled.

"No, I want to stay here. Let me sign up for the course in cosmetology," I said.

"Do you have a high school diploma?" she asked.

"No," I replied, "but I have a GED. Is that enough?"

"That's good enough," she answered.

"Can I go to school part-time? Between my job and my three children, I don't have enough time to attend full time."

"We can work something out," she lowered her voice and replied. When she realized that I was signing up as her student, her attitude changed.

She arranged my schedule so I could do it all, and in a short time, I learned to love Mrs. Jeannie; I believed I was her favorite.

I juggled my time between my job, school, our three children, and household chores. It was overwhelming, but I was determined not to give up.

During that time, I received a letter from my brother-in-law saying his large family of twelve people escaped from Vietnam by boat and were stranded on Pulau Bidong, an island near Malaysia. I was happy to hear the news but very disappointed to hear that my sister was not among them. They needed help, but there was very little I could do to help them, especially with our limited finances. That made me feel very bad, and all I could do was pray for their health and safety.

Not long after I received my brother-in-law's letter, I came home from work one day and checked the mail. As I opened the mailbox, I saw a letter from Bay, my beloved brother. I was anxious and tore into the letter straight away. I opened the door with one hand and read the letter with the other. I threw my purse on the table and continued to read.

"My dearest sister," he wrote, "I hope you and your family are safe and happy. It has been a long time since I saw you and heard from you. My life has not been the same since the day you left me. I have been confined in a hard labor camp for almost three years now." I was shocked to hear he was in prison; my hands were shaking, but I read on. "I was in a thirty-five-foot boat, packed with sixty men, women, and children trying to flee the shackles of Communism to find freedom. For me, it was more than that; I wanted to find you and to be with you and your family, because I miss you and love you so much, my big sister." Tears streamed down my face as I read on. "While our boat was sailing out toward the open sea, the Communist police caught us and brought us back to land. The rich people on my boat paid the police, and they went home with their families. The poor people, like myself, ended up in hard labor camps, especially when the police discovered I was one of the leaders who had arranged for the escape attempt. I knew I would be here longer than the rest. Each day, all of the prisoners have to go out to the forest, chop wood, and clear the land, on which we plant vegetables. We work hard but are fed very little; they feed us just enough to keep us alive so we are able to work."

My heart ached for my poor little brother. Tears blinded me, and I had to stop for a second to wipe them away with the back of my hand. I took a deep breath and continued. "I have lost so much weight, and even you, my dearest sister, would not recognize me. I look like a skin-covered skeleton. My eyes are dull and sunken deep into my hollow cheeks. My lips are dried, cracked, and turned purple. My face is wrinkled, and I look ninety instead of twenty-four. I am so weak from hunger, and I don't think I can take it much longer. That's why I'm writing you this letter to say goodbye. I want you to know how much I love you and how much you mean to me. You are always in my mind and in my heart. Please, my dearest beloved sister, hold me in your heart, kiss my tears away; I picture you holding me, drying my tears, and saying to me, as you always did when I was a child and was scared of something or someone, 'Everything will be all right, my little baby brother. I am here with you, and nothing can get you; everything will be fine.' I want to hear your comforting words again; I need your loving arms now more than ever."

I sobbed uncontrollably and let my tears flow down to soak my blouse as I held on to his precious letter. I tried to read on.

"If I die right now, I will die happy, knowing you were with me in my heart and I am in yours. If I never see you again, I want you to remember that I am always with you in spirit. I miss you more now than ever before, and I love you, my big sister; I will forever."

Signed, "Bay, your baby brother."

I felt as though my heart had broken into thousands of pieces. I could not take any more pain. I ran to my bedroom with his letter crushed to my chest; I threw myself onto the pillow and sobbed, knowing that there was nothing I could do.

Don with the manicure table he built for me in 1981

DURING THIS TIME, Don quit drinking for a few months and was like a different person. He realized how hard I was working, felt sorry for me, and decided to custom-build a manicure table for my birthday. His father was a carpenter, and Don inherited some of his dad's skill with wood. It was beautiful, and I loved it. When I opened a little drawer beneath the table, I was surprised to see a hand-painted poem written on the bottom of the drawer. *As long as stars burn in the sky, my love for you will never die.*

He had added below the poem, *For my precious Linda, with all my love forever. Don, 3-8-82*. He had always had a way with words, but this one brought tears to my eyes.

I still struggled with having enough time for school, my job, housework, cooking, shopping, and caring for my three young kids. Every morning after I opened my eyes, I made breakfast for everybody. Then I had to pack lunches for them and send them off to school. I washed dishes, changed my clothes, went to school, and then went to work. After work, I came home and did chores. On the weekend, I went fishing and picnicking with my family, or I worked on my herb garden. I was so busy that sometimes I couldn't see straight.

I came home from work one day and saw a mountain of dirty clothes stacked high in the laundry room, so I decided to wash them. I found Don's light-tan suit mixed in with all the other clothes. Instead of taking it to the dry cleaner, which I didn't have time to do, I decided to wash it myself. I examined the suit before I put it into the washing machine; I saw many dirty spots, along with a dark ring on the neck. After I put it in the wash, I added a lot of the Clorox bleach. *If a little bleach is good*, I thought, *a lot of bleach is better*.

When the washing machine stopped, I opened the lid and was shocked. I remembered putting a tan suit in the washer, but the one that appeared in front of me was a light peachy color. I didn't understand what had happened to Don's suit; I took it out and put it in the dryer, hoping the tan color would return, but instead, it shrank. I was afraid Don would be mad, but I had no choice; I hung it back in his closet. A few days later, Don had an important meeting and was looking for his favorite tan suit but couldn't find it. He came to the kitchen while I was cleaning up after breakfast and asked, "Hey, Linda! Do you know where my tan suit is?"

"What tan suit are you talking about?" I pretended I didn't know.

"The one I wear all the time when I have a big meeting."

"I don't know which one you're talking about," I lied. "I did wash one of your suits, but I think it was peach, not tan."

"I saw it in my closet, but it's not mine."

"What do you mean?" I played dumb. "All of the clothes in your closet are yours." He went back to our bedroom, took out the suit, and showed it to me.

"Who does this one belong to?" he wrinkled his face and asked with suspicion.

"Oh, that one?" I replied nervously. "You don't remember? We went to the store and . . . and . . . we bought it together."

"No, I don't remember buying this one," he said as he examined the suit.

"Why don't you try it on?" I said with a smile.

"I don't like the color," he commented and went back to the bedroom. Later, he walked back to the kitchen with the suit on. When I first saw him, I almost broke out laughing, but I didn't dare. The suit looked so funny on him; it was wrinkled, tight around his waist, and very short on his arms and legs.

"It looks good on you," I lied as I enthusiastically nodded my head and raised my eyebrows.

"I don't know about this," he replied with a frown.

"What do you mean? I think you look sharp, very sharp, in it." I turned away, not letting him see my lying face, as I continued to try to convince him. "You look very stylish in it. It's a new color this year, and you are the first one to wear it."

"Really?" He smiled. "Perhaps I'll give it a try."

"Yes! You should," I said with enthusiasm. I felt bad watching him walk out of the house, but I had no choice.

When he came home from work, he was upset and said, "I am so embarrassed; people at work made fun of my suit. They said I should have donated it to the Museum of Modern Art." He took off the suit and threw it in the garbage. I didn't say another word, nor did I dare take the suit out of the trash can.

I WAS DETERMINED to cut down on my school time by getting just a nail license, so I asked Don to write to the government of South Carolina and ask them to grant me a nail license. After Don wrote the letter to the governor, we sat back and waited; days turned into weeks, but nothing happened. I called them, and they told me there was no such thing as a nail license in South Carolina; if I wanted to work in a beauty salon, I needed the cosmetologist license.

Not long after, I met my friend Mrs. Ravenel's son, Senator Arthur Ravenel Jr., at a party. I decided to ask him if there was anything he could do to convince the state of South Carolina to issue a separate nail license. He promised me he would look into it. After weeks, I didn't hear from him. I asked Don to write him a letter and to write Senator Strom Thurman as well, urging them to change the law regarding the issue of nail licenses in South Carolina. I even asked Mrs. Ravenel to talk to her son about the matter, and she said she would. Months later, I still heard nothing.

One day, in the middle of my cosmetology test, I received an urgent phone call from Shula, the salon owner; she wanted to see me right away. I didn't know what was going on and asked my instructor for permission to leave. She said it was okay for me to go, but I would have to make up the test later. I thanked her and sped back to the salon. I ran upstairs without stopping to catch my breath. When I walked inside, I saw Shula cutting some woman's hair. I went to her and said, "Shula, I came as fast as I could, because you sounded urgent."

Without looking at me, she said, "I need to talk to you." Just like that. I stood there like a dummy for a while, feeling very uncomfortable.

"Do you want to talk to me now?" I asked.

"Yes, but you have to wait," she snorted. "I have to finish cutting my client's hair first."

"Okay, I'll wait for you, but I need to go back to school to finish my test," I said, and she rolled her eyes in irritation.

I walked away and sat in one of the waiting chairs. I had no idea what caused her to have such a bad attitude and act that way. I waited and waited for her to finish with her client, but rather than talk to me, she started with another one. I lost my patience. I came to her and asked, "Do you want to talk to me first, before you take your second client?"

"Well, you'll just have to wait," she said, and she began to work on her client.

Instead of sitting back down, I opened the door and went outside. Right at the door, I saw the janitor mopping the hallway. I spoke to him every day; he was very friendly. I walked up to him and said, "Excuse me."

He stopped mopping, looked at me, smiled, and said, "Yes, ma'am?"

"Could you please come inside and help me carry a small table to my car? I'll pay you for it."

He nodded his head and said, "Okay, ma'am. I will." He put his mop down and followed me. When I returned to the salon with a black man, everyone stopped working and looked at us. I ignored their stares and helped the man move everything that belonged to me, including the manicure table Don made for me, out the door. Shula realized what I was doing and tried to stop me from moving out, but it was too late. I was done with her attitude and her salon. For the next few weeks, Shula called me several times a day, apologizing and asking me to come back to work. Each time she called, I thanked her and told her I would think about it. I never returned to her salon.

After quitting work, I devoted all my time to cosmetology school. I studied hard and took as many patrons as I could. My efforts paid off. I received a first-place trophy every month.

Mrs. Jeannie became my favorite person in the school, and vice versa. I did her hair and nails once a week, and she loved it. She thought I was a good role model and always asked me to help other students who were in need. And of course, I took advantage of the opportunity to show off my talents.

A nice middle-aged African-American lady walked in one day and wanted her hair to be hot-combed, a common hair procedure for very curly hair. Of course, Mrs. Jeannie thought there was no one who could do it better than me, including herself, and she told me to take the job. She ordered all the other students who were not busy at the time to gather around to watch and learn.

I ran around preparing all of the products needed for the job, including wet towels, an iron comb, the Vaseline jar, and a hot portable oven, made especially for heating the metal comb. It took a lot of preparation, and my fellow students helped me prepare.

Everything was ready to go. Over twenty students surrounded me, watching me. I felt like a surgeon preparing to show a bunch of medical students how to conduct their first operation. I was confident, because I had performed the procedure many times before in front of students. Some of them watched me very intently, while others covered their noses with their hands to avoid the strong odor. The first few times it worked out great, and I glanced at some of the students who were too busy talking to each other to pay attention to me.

"Look here, you guys!" I said and acted as if I were their instructor. "You have to watch me if you want to learn." I was satisfied with my authority and returned to my job. Again, I took the hot iron comb from the oven, but because of the distraction, I forgot to cool it on the wet towel first, and when I applied it to the lady's hair, a whole section of her hair burned right off into the palm of my hand. I turned to look at the students and saw horrified faces. The client, however, was not aware of what had happened to her head and kept on yapping. She had been telling me how bad her last hairstylist was since she sat down.

I didn't know what to do with the hair I held in my hand. I looked around at the other students, raised my shoulders, made faces, and handed them the block of hair. I was secretly asking them for help. They all raised their eyebrows, made faces, and shrugged their shoulders, indicating they couldn't help me. I threw the handful of hair to the floor behind me and continued my job. I took another hair strand, pressed it straight, and combed it over to cover the hole in her head. When I finished, she gave me a big tip, and I sent her out the door. After she left, I turned to the class, grinned, and exclaimed, "Now, you all just learned what not to do!" They laughed and then helped me clean up the mess.

Chapter 13

BOAT PEOPLE

IN 1982, DON and I bought a small house with three bedrooms and two baths in West Ashley. Two weeks after we moved into our new home, I received a letter from overseas, this time from my two brothers Kinh and Khai, who escaped from Vietnam by boat. Like my brother-in-law, they too were stranded on Pulau Bidong, an island near Malaysia. Lucky for them, I was able to help. Don and I prepared sponsorship papers and, months later, brought them to the United States. Somebody in Texas sponsored my brother-in-law and brought his huge family of twelve people to the Fort Worth area. My two brothers, who were twenty and thirty, came to Charleston and lived with us in our small home; it was cramped but cozy. They went to school to study English and worked part-time at various jobs.

It was nice to have my two brothers with us; they helped me cook and keep an eye on the kids while they made new friends. A month after they came to live with us, I graduated first in my class from cosmetology school and received the best all-around student award. I received a total of nine awards.

I was given eight first place trophies and a best overall student award, at Farrah's Beauty School in February of 1983.

I found a new job in downtown Charleston near the VA hospital where Don worked, and it was nice for us to meet each other for lunch every day.

Everything was going well with our relationship. Our children loved their schools, and we liked our jobs. I even received congratulations from Senator Strom Thurman, stating the nail license I had requested for South Carolina was approved. Of course, it came too late for me; I had already graduated as a licensed cosmetologist, but I hoped my efforts helped others.

Although I was busy with the new house, new job, and garden, I still made sure we spent a lot of time with our children. We took them to beaches, rivers, and lakes to fish and picnic. Sometimes we took them to Lake Marion or Lake Moultrie for a weekend, but other times we went to different states for longer trips. Instead of the big, comfortable camper, now and then we just took our tents and went to the Chattooga River in the Smokey Mountains, between Georgia and North and South Carolina, to camp out. The campsite at Burrell's Ford was very remote; we had to park our car down the road, and each of us had to carry our own camping gear and hike up through a wild trail to get there. The only modern convenience in the campsite was an old, bug-infested outhouse, which we seldom used. I wanted to teach our children survival skills so they could fend for themselves without modern technology and experience what I did as a child growing up. For two weeks of each year, we stayed free of telephone and television and ate whatever we caught and harvested in the wild.

Twelve-year-old Teresa, me, and eleven-year-old Nicky, at our campsite

Smoking trout over a natural wood-burning fire pit, at our base camp

The children often brought their friends along with us. I encouraged my children and their friends to catch anything that crawled, flew, or swam. They were to cook whatever they caught and eat whatever they cooked, including snakes, turtles, frogs, crawfish, and even grasshoppers. I believed these lessons would teach them how to stay alive, regardless of what might happen to them; besides, it was fun for them to be challenged.

A YEAR AFTER my two brothers came to live with us, I received another call from the Red Cross, letting me know my third brother, Bay, escaped from Vietnam; he was on Palau Bidong Island and needed a sponsor. I was so happy to hear the news, but there was more: My sister and her youngest daughter had also made it to the island, after being left behind for years to care for my family's property. While I prepared the paperwork to sponsor my brother, my sister's husband in Texas sponsored her. I was so happy, knowing all of my siblings would soon be on United States soil. I wanted nothing more than to see all of them happy and safe in the land of the free.

Don and I quickly completed the necessary papers to sponsor Bay, but he was not alone; he had a girlfriend and an eight-month-old daughter with him. We sponsored all of them, and they came to live with us.

My little three-bedroom house was packed tight with ten people of all ages. It was chaotic at times, but there was never a dull moment and always a lot of love and fun. I didn't want to change a thing; in many ways, I wished we could stay together forever.

One day while helping me weed my garden, Bay told me about his life in Vietnam.

"My life was harder after you left," Bay said. "Our father treated me with an iron fist, just as he treated you when you were younger. I believe our father considered you and me to be the two black sheep."

"I am so sorry I was not there for you," I responded.

"You couldn't have helped it," he said, and we both smiled.

Bay and I loved to work in the garden, and when we were together, we often shared our stories. I told Bay what my mother had told me on one of my visits to her in Vung Tau. She said, "Your father just punished Bay a couple of days ago."

"Oh, why?" I asked Mother.

"For doing something your father didn't approve of," she said.

"What did my father do to poor Bay?" I asked her.

"He beat Bay with a cane until Bay turned black and blue," Mother said as tears filled her eyes. "Then he tied Bay's wrists together with a rope, threw one end of the rope over a ceiling beam, and hoisted Bay up until he dangled in midair."

As I spoke, I glanced at Bay and noticed him nodding his head, as if he still felt the pain. I was about to continue what our mother had told me, but Bay chimed in and told me the rest of the story.

"He continued to hit me with the wooden cane," Bay said, "but that was not enough; Father used a pair of pliers and pinched my inner thigh until it almost bled." Bay took a deep breath. "I screamed and called out for help, and Father finally stopped." Bay lowered his voice and took another deep breath. "He left me hanging there and left the house." Bay threw a handful of weeds in the trash. "I don't remember who took me down; I was sixteen back then."

"Wasn't that right before you came to live with me?" I asked.

"Yes, it was,"

When he finished his story, I started to tell him mine. "I remember another time," I said, "when I was about nine years old and our brother Kinh was about three; our family lived in a small town near Nha Trang. Kinh and I were outside chasing the ice cream man, who was on a bicycle with a large box attached to the back seat. He rode slowly on the street as he rang a loud bell and yelled at the top of his lungs, 'Ice cream! Ice cream! Who wants to eat cold ice cream? It's sweet and flavorful!'

"We ran behind him, hoping he would stop to make a sale so we could look inside of the box when the man opened it. Sometimes, I would stick my head closer, to look at the colorful ice cream sticks; I liked to feel the cold air on my face, and the smell of all the fruit flavors made me drool." While I told my story, I glanced over at Bay and saw him looking back at me, smiling. "Kinh and I were in the middle of the chase one day, when Father saw us running out at the street. I was afraid he would punish me, but instead, he stopped the man and bought one yellow stick for our three-year-old brother and told me not to touch it; then he walked away. I had only had ice cream once or twice and was drooling while watching our brother eat his. Temptation got the best of me. I begged Kinh to give me a taste of his, and he did. Father came running out from his hiding place and slapped me so hard that the half-eaten ice cream flew out of my hand.

"When Kinh realized his ice cream was on the sandy ground, he started to scream bloody murder. I was in shock, but before I could react, I heard Father's deep voice, 'How dare you! How dare you disobey me. I told you not to touch the ice cream. If I wanted you to have one, I would have already bought you one!'

"He slapped me again, and from the depth of his throat, he said, 'This will teach you to listen to me the next time.' Father walked away; Kinh was crying, but Father paid no attention to him. I realized he had done it to teach me a lesson; I just wished his lessons had not been so harsh. I rubbed my painful face as I walked toward the melting ice cream. I tried to pick it up and salvage it for our poor brother, but it was too late. The hot sand had melted everything except for the bare stick.

"I apologized to Kinh and promised to buy him another ice cream when I had the money. He nodded his head and hugged my neck; we held each other and cried." I smiled and asked Bay. "Do you want to hear one more story?"

"Of course," Bay said. "We still have more weeds to pull."

"When Kinh and Nho were about four and five, Mother gave birth to you." I pointed my finger at his face in a loving way. "I devoted all my time to the three of you, especially you, because Mother was too busy with her chores, and she needed my help. Our family was so poor; we never had enough to eat. If I wanted a snack, I had to go into the kitchen to steal Mother's onion, garlic, or ginger and salt. I always shared them with you guys. I didn't know how, but Mother always found out what I did; perhaps our onion and garlic breath gave us away." We both laughed out loud. "She never punished me but always told me to stop stealing her stuff, because she needed them for cooking.

"In desperation, I often stole fruit from the neighbor's trees. When the trees were not producing, I would go to Father's medicine cabinets. Since he practiced Chinese medicine, he stored many goodies there, such as dried prunes, plums, cinnamon sticks, and even roasted peanuts. The peanuts were not for medicine, however. He kept them for his own enjoyment while drinking his rice whisky; he never shared his peanuts with us kids. I would wait for him to leave the house and then sneak into his medicine cabinet, if he forgot to lock it. I would take a few peanuts, a dried prune, a salty plum, or sometimes just a small piece of a cinnamon stick. I knew how much trouble I would be in if I got caught." I shook my head, as if I still feared my stepfather. "I shared the stolen goods with you guys at our hiding places. I always told you guys not to tell our secret, but for some reason Father always found out, and he always punished me. If I was lucky, I would receive a few slaps on my face or a few whacks from a bamboo stick on my behind. If he was in a bad mood, he would hit me with whatever he found until I turned black and blue and then tie me to a pole or a tree. That was how our father trained us." I looked at Bay and saw him nodding his head and tightening his lips.

"Yes, I knew," he said. "How could I forget?" I smiled and continued with my story.

"Do you remember one day at the dining table when Father told us about how lucky we were?" I asked, and he nodded his head.

"'You are all lucky,' Father said, 'because I don't take a stick to you guys as much as my father did to me.'" As I talked, Bay kept nodding his head as if he remembered it too. "'When I was younger,'" Father said, "'my father told me to dig a hole in the backyard. When the hole was deep enough, he handed me a banana plant with its leaves chopped off and told me to plant it upside down. I knew it was wrong, but I didn't dare correct my father; I knew better than to ask him why. When I was done, he told me to dig it up and replant it the right way. Before he walked away, he told me it was a good thing I didn't correct him, because he was my father and teacher, and I would always be his son and student, so never attempt to correct him. You guys think you guys have it rough? You didn't have to live with my father; he disciplined me ten times more than I do you kids."

Bay and I were smiling when the story ended. We were happy our rough past was behind us. We believed our stepfather's story, and we have seen most Vietnamese practice the same teaching. It is part of our culture, custom, and tradition, whether we like it or not. By the time I finished my stories, Bay and I had finished our weeding and gathered two baskets full of vegetables and greens.

AFTER A SHORT while, my youngest brother, Khai, found a job and moved in with one of his friends. Kinh moved in with an older couple downtown. He helped them with their chores and went to school to learn English.

Bay found a job making picture frames; he knew nothing about it at first, but he learned fast and was promoted to supervisor in a short time. He was preparing to move his family out of my house, but before he did, he went fishing with my family.

While everyone else was busy running around, Bay and I sat fishing at the riverbank. He turned to me and smiled. "I am so lucky to be sitting here next to you," he said, and I turned to him, smiled, and patted his lap.

"I couldn't be any happier to have all of my brothers and sister here in America with me," I said. "But how did you get out?" I asked, and he began to tell me about his escape out of Vietnam by boat.

"After I was released from jail the second time, I was more determined than ever to leave Vietnam and the shackles of Communism," he explained. "I found many people who wanted to escape from Vietnam like myself, and asked them to give me money to build a boat for our escape. I gathered as many people as I could and collected as much money as possible; then I bought all the equipment I needed and began to build the boat. The more money I gathered from people, the larger the boat became; I hoped to build a much larger boat than the one I had used before. I wanted to build one that would be safe in the rough and turbulent ocean. I knew many people who had tried to get away in small boats and were sunk by huge waves; some of them were from our own family."

"I heard of those family members through Mom's letter. Were their bodies ever recovered?"

"Are you kidding," he said. "Sharks were always there, just waiting for someone to fall overboard."

"How large was your boat this time? And how many people were on it?"

"It was about thirty-five feet long by twelve feet wide and was packed tight with seventy-one people," he said, "including our sister, her baby, Khai's girlfriend, and my girlfriend."

"What about food, water, and a toilet?" I asked.

"We stored enough food and water for a week, and we did have a small private place for a toilet and shower combination," he explained.

"You brought water for the shower too?" I asked.

"We used the salt water from the ocean."

"What about people who became sick or died?"

"If anyone died, we were prepared to throw them overboard. Thank God we didn't have to do that." He shook his head. "But I heard there were many other boats who did. I also heard some sick people were thrown overboard alive, because of the fear of contagious diseases."

"Oh my God! Poor people," I exclaimed. "I also heard the pirates often attacked. Do you know anything about that?" I asked.

"Yes, they robbed, raped, and killed people, and then they destroyed the boats to hide their crimes." My brother looked away to hide his sorrow for those who didn't make it.

"Are you sure?" I asked in disbelief. "How could there be such evil on this earth? They had less empathy than animals. I am so happy you are safe here with me; I love you so much." I smiled and gave him a big hug.

"I thank God for being here with you; there were many times I thought we were not going to make it at all."

"Why?" I asked.

"Because the Communist police patrolled along the shoreline and tried to stop anyone from leaving Vietnam," he explained. "And when we finally escaped out to the open ocean, we were worried about the pirates. There were many times I thought the violent waves from bad weather would swallow us all."

"Wow!" I replied and shook my head.

Bay continued, "We spent five days in the angry ocean, hoping to be picked up by an American ship; if a different country had picked us up, they might have sent us back to Vietnam, which none of us wanted. We were waiting and hoping, but an American ship never came. Finally, we made it to an island, and those who were already there came out to help us onto solid ground."

"How big was the island, and how many people were there before you?" I asked.

"I'm not sure," he remarked. "There were many islands just like ours, with thousands of people who were waiting to be sponsored by their loved ones. Otherwise, they had to wait for some organization to sponsor them and take them to their new home. Some of the unlucky refugees were returned to Vietnam by their rescuers."

"Wow! What a letdown for those who tried so hard to get out, only to be shipped back to where they were so desperate to escape. I'm so lucky to have you here with me."

"No, I am the luckier one," he replied.

"How many times did you try to escape?" I asked.

"Oh, I tried many times, but I only got caught twice. I had to go to a hard labor prison camp for three years the first time. I thought I would die there and never see you again," he said and shook his head. "The second one was not as long," he said.

"I think I am still luckier than many people, some of whom are still in prison as we speak. Our sister, Nho, tried to escape with her infant child many times but could never make it; she always returned home crying." He stopped talking for a few seconds, picked up a pebble, and threw it hard into the water, as if he were trying to get rid of his unpleasant past. "The reason Nho tried so hard was because her husband and her three children had already left Vietnam; she wanted to be with them. One time, Mother told me that when the tide was low, Nho had to return home with her infant baby in her arms. She didn't know what had happened or why her boat had had to return, but when Nho got back to the house, Mother didn't even recognize her own daughter—both Nho and her baby girl were covered in mud. It was sad but also kind of funny." He glanced at me, and I saw a hint of a real smile in his eyes.

"Where were you then?" I asked.

"I don't remember why I wasn't there." He shook his head. "I was probably in prison."

"How and where did you get on the boat, since the Communist police were always on the lookout for those who were trying to escape?" I asked.

"You know our family lives on the river, right?" he asked, and I nodded. "Well! Father secretly let hundreds, if not thousands, of people use our landing behind the house for escape. Father allowed the boat owners to pick up the refugees, but with one condition: The boat owner had to take us kids out of Vietnam whenever we were ready."

"What about Mom and Dad?" I asked. "Why didn't they come with you guys?"

"Mom and Dad wanted to stay behind until the rest of their children had safely escaped to America."

"How and when did you guys know the right time to get together? Who asked who, and how did people know when to come to our dock?"

"At night, when the tide was high," he explained, "Father signaled to the boat owners that it was time to go. The boat owners then signaled to some of the escapees, and the escapees gathered each other. They would round up and get on board, and from our dock, they sailed out to the open sea, if they didn't get caught."

"Is that how you guys got away too?"

"Yes," he said, "but it wasn't always easy. Most of the time, we had to return because of bad weather, boat engine problems, or police patrols at the mouth of the ocean."

"How long did it take you to build a boat, and how did you keep it hidden from the authorities?"

"After I got out of jail the last time, we built the boat right out in the open. When they came to investigate, we told them we were building a fishing boat and gave them a substantial bribe. They left us alone. When we finished with our project, we waited for the right time. Then, one dark night, seventy-one people silently boarded the boat anchored behind our house. As the captain, I guided the boat out to the open ocean, and with a compass, I brought the boat safely to the island."

"Wow!" I said. "I am so sorry you had to go through all of that," I said as I reached over and kissed his cheek.

"The price we pay for our freedom I think is worth it. Thanks to you and your husband, I am now sitting here fishing with you and your family." Tears of happiness ran down our cheeks as we turned to hug each other right before a fish bit.

Chapter 14

LONELY FROG

ONE SUMMER AFTER all of my brothers moved out of our home, we took our three children to North Carolina for a long camping trip. Don drove us to the Cherokee Indian Reservation and found a nice campsite. After we checked in with the office, Don drove around until we found what we thought was a good spot. He maneuvered the camper and parked it under a large tree, right on the edge of a pond. After we all jumped out of the car, we helped each other set up our temporary home. While Don connected the water hose and the sewer line, I fixed dinner and tidied up inside.

I looked out through the window and watched our three kids, aged eleven, twelve, and eighteen, take turns pumping up an inflatable raft. When they were done, Eddie lowered the raft into the water, and all three kids took turns rowing the boat around the beautiful pond. The sound of my children playing and their laughter warmed my heart; I smiled with contentment.

Later, I called all of them in for dinner. After the meal, we showered and went to bed. I twisted and turned for a long time but couldn't sleep because of the noisy bullfrogs.

Since I couldn't sleep, I got out of bed and woke Eddie. "Hey, Eddie," I whispered. "Wake up, son. Wake up." I saw him move, so I said, "Hey, I have something to tell you."

"Yes . . . ma . . . am," he mumbled. "What do you want, mom?"

He was about to go back to sleep when I asked, "How would you like to go frog hunting with me?" When he heard the words *frog hunting*, his eyes sprang open. I told him about my plan to catch those annoying frogs. Although he was half-asleep, he sat straight up and was ready to help me with my plan.

"Eddie! All we need to do is make a gig to spear the frogs," I smiled.

"That sounds like fun, Mom, but what can we make a gig out of? And after we make a gig, where can we go to gig frogs? And how can we see them in this pitch darkness?" He frowned as he waited for my answers.

"Well, we can make gigs from the shish kabob forks we have," I said.

"Then what?" he asked with doubt.

"Well! All we need is a small straight pole; we already have a boat and a flashlight."

"And where can we go to find frogs?"

"Can you hear the frogs croaking in the pond right now? Listen, just listen." After he heard the sound of frogs, he got excited and jumped off the bed.

"Okay! I'll go look for a pole; you get the shish kabob sticks ready, okay?" he said. And just like that, he opened the door and went outside with the machete.

Our camper. I am at the door and Teresa is at the picnic table.
We were preparing breakfast.

As soon as Eddie left, I went to the kitchen to look for the twine, shish kabob sticks, and the flashlight; I took all of them outside to wait for Eddie. A few minutes later, he came back with a long, straight pole; it was perfect. I took three long, sharp shish kabob sticks, and with Eddie's help, we tied them to one end of the pole. I carried the three-pronged gig and the flashlight, while Eddie carried the oar and a bucket out to the pond. We whispered as we climbed into the inflatable raft, and Eddie pushed it off the shoreline. I sat in front with the gig in one hand and the flashlight in the other, while Eddie sat in the back with the oar and rowed us along the edge of the pond.

We listened for the sound of frogs and inched toward them. Using the flashlight, I pointed to the frog and guided Eddie to the exact spot. The bright flashlight's beam shined straight into the frog's eyes, and it froze. I stabbed it with the gig, put it in the bucket, and then we continued along the grassy edge until we found the next victim. One by one, I speared nineteen huge bullfrogs that night. I took them back to the campsite and sat them on the picnic table in front of our camper. While Eddie put the raft away, I prepared the frogs.

I marinated them in ginger, soy sauce, and hot pepper, then put them in the refrigerator. The next morning, I coated them lightly with white flour and deep-fried them for breakfast, and what a breakfast it was.

Teresa and me holding the frog legs. Eddie was fishing behind us.

Eddie and I repeated the same hunt each night; we caught more frogs than we could count. We had fried frogs, curried frogs, sautéed frogs, steamed frogs, broiled frogs, baked frogs, and barbequed frogs. We ate frogs for breakfast, lunch, and dinner, as well as for snacks. Besides frog hunting at night, our family went hiking up into the Blue Ridge Mountains, went down to the river for water tube drifting, and fished for trout in the daytime. Although we caught and ate lots of trout, our main dish was frogs.

After two weeks of camping, we prepared to leave. I was ready to go home. When I finished packing, I went to bed. Instead of going to sleep, I just lay there with my eyes wide open, realizing how quiet it was compared to our first night. I listened for the frogs, but there were not many of them left in the pond. The next morning before we left, I served the rest of the leftover frogs for breakfast, and Don drove us home.

BAY AND HIS family moved to an apartment, not too far from us.

Khai, my youngest brother, moved to Texas and married his girlfriend.

Kinh decided to move back to live with us and help me with the garden, while still going to school to learn more English.

I still worked at the same old building downtown. I liked my job, but I didn't like the parking lot. When there was a high tide on top of the heavy rain, the parking lot became part of the ocean. It was hard for me to dress for work, because I felt like I had to swim to my job after I parked my car.

One day, I went shopping with my friends at the Citadel Mall and bought a nice western skirt along with a plaid shirt. Of course, since they were western clothes, I needed western boots to go with them.

I found a beautiful pair of colorful high-heeled cowboy boots with pointed toes. Lucky for me, they were on sale, but there was one drawback: the boots were two sizes larger than what I wore. But since there were no smaller sizes available, I bought the boots anyway. I knew I would have to put a ton of tissue and toilet paper in the toes before I could wear them, but since the shoes were on sale and for half-price,

I couldn't resist and was determined to make them work. I was happy with my purchase, and I planned to dress up in them the next day.

After breakfast, the kids left for school, but Don still hung around the house. I fixed my hair, put on my makeup, and tried on my new outfit. The skirt and the plaid shirt fit perfectly. I looked at myself in the mirror and nodded my head with approval. I was happy with the way I looked. Next, I rolled up a handful of toilet paper, stuffed it into the cowboy boots, and pushed it all the way down into each of their toes; I tried them on, but they were still loose. I took them off and put more paper in them, and then I tried them on, but again they were still too big. I repeated the technique over and over and tried them on again and again; they were still loose. For some reason, the boots seemed to be much larger than the day before. I emptied out the toilet roll and began with the Kleenex box. I pulled out a handful at a time and stuffed it tightly toward the toes, as far as possible. I had stuffed so much paper in them that the stupid boots began to look pregnant, but when I tried to walk on them, they still felt loose. In desperation, I came up with a great idea. I thought if I cut off the high heels, they would fit me better, since they were too tall anyway. I took the boots to the garage and looked for the machete. When I found it, I gave each of them a few whacks on the heels; I realized there were steel rods underneath the leather instead of wood, as I thought. So I chopped down on them harder, but I still couldn't cut through the steel rods. I realized chopping off the heels was not as easy as I thought. After ten or fifteen minutes of great effort, all I did was work up a good sweat and ruin my hairdo and makeup. The heels, however, began looking like two skinny octopi with countless arms, playing peekaboo with me. I knew then I needed help and was about to call Don. But before I did, Don heard the commotion in the garage and came out to check on me.

I saw him already dressed for work, looking good in his coat and tie. But when he saw me, he was shocked and did a double take. I was fully dressed, holding a machete in one hand and a torn boot in the other. My hairdo was messed up, my makeup was smeared, and sweat ran down my face. He frowned and asked, "What on earth are you doing?"

"I am trying to fix my boots," I said.

He looked at me, then he looked at my boots and asked, "What are you trying to do to them?"

"I was trying to cut the heels down shorter," I replied.

He could tell by the way I looked that I was making fruitless efforts with my boots and offered to help. He took the machete from my hand, and while I held the boot down on the brick step, he began chopping on its heel. After several attempts, he too realized it was going nowhere with the machete. He stopped, looked at me, and shook his head.

"There is no way I can cut this steel rod with the machete," he said. "The only way I can do it is with a hacksaw." I looked at him with hope and excitement, but he looked at me with sympathy. "But I'm late for work already; let me do it for you this evening."

"This evening?" I responded and looked at him as if he had just lost his marbles! I raised my voice and said, "I need these boots to go with my outfit right now. Look at me; I already have my western clothes on, and I must have cowboy boots to go with them. You can't go to work until you've helped me," I demanded, but then I begged, with a pitiful expression. "Can you please do it for me right now?"

He sighed and said, "Well, I guess I'll have to be late for work." He managed to crack a hint of a smile.

"Thanks, honey!" I gave him a big smile.

Don went to his toolbox and turned things upside down but couldn't find a hacksaw. "I can't find my saw," he yelled out to me.

I was watching him from a distance, and to me, he didn't seem to be looking very hard for the saw.

"Don! I don't think you are trying very hard to look for it."

"I'm late for work already," he growled. "This evening, when I come home, I'll have to go to the hardware store and buy a hacksaw before I can help you."

"So! Why can't you do it now?" I pressed.

"I can't do it right now; I must go to work. Can't you please wait?" He sounded mad and looked as if he regretted his offer to help me in the first place. But I wasn't about to let him off the hook that easy, so I made a suggestion.

"Don, the hardware store is only one mile away. It will only take you five minutes to go and come back." I gave him no room for an excuse.

"Yes, five minutes, if there is no traffic; then I may have to wait in line to pay for it," he argued.

"If you hadn't fought with me, you would have already gone and come back," I said.

"Okay, but I'm telling you, I'll be very late for work." He looked at his watch and said, "In fact, I'm already late right now." He didn't look too happy, but I was so desperate I didn't pay attention to his sour face.

With a big smile, I said, "Oh, thanks, honey! I owe you a big dinner tonight."

"You will owe me more than just a dinner." He grinned mischievously and left.

"Whatever!" I said, smiling.

Don was gone for ten minutes and came back with a hacksaw. I helped him hold down the boots as he began sawing them. It was not as easy as we thought; we worked hard and were both soaked in sweat. Finally, the heels were off, and I was happy. I gave him a sweaty kiss on his cheek to thank him for his help.

"You are welcome," he said as he stared at me while I examined my boots.

In our rush, we'd forgotten to measure the heels before we cut them. When I put them together to compare their length, they were lopsided and uneven. I was so disappointed as I looked at the torn boots; there was nothing more I could do about them. I couldn't ask Don to recut them; I feared he would be even more upset. So I thanked him again and gave him another quick kiss on his sweaty forehead.

"You are welcome," Don replied again and was about to walk away, but instead he paused, looked at me, frowned, and asked, "I'm curious about the boots. Why on earth did you want to cut the heels off?"

"They were too high," I replied with a smile.

"Then why did you buy them?" he asked.

"Because they were on sale for more than half off," I said.

"I see. And if a pair of elephants were on sale for half price, would you buy them too?" he asked sarcastically.

"Don't start with me again, Don," I barked.

"I didn't start anything; I just asked a question," he said, smiling.

"Well, I don't like your sarcastic question." I pouted but still smiled with him.

"I just wanted to know if you would buy a pair of elephants if they were on sale," he laughed.

I didn't want to start an argument, because we both were so late for work already, so I ignored his sarcasm. Thank God, he didn't know the boots were also two sizes larger, and I was not about to tell him.

"I'm so late," Don said. "I'll have to work overtime tonight to make up for my lost hours. I'll see you later!" He kissed my sweaty forehead, ran to his car, jumped in, and started the motor.

"Thanks, Don! I'll see you later," I shouted as he drove away.

I took a last look at my boots, and then I put them on. They still felt loose, and they looked old, torn, and ragged, with uneven heels; they looked nothing like the beautiful pair I purchased the day before. They were not only scratched, but they were also discolored from being rubbed on the brick steps. They reminded me of an antique pair I saw in the museum a long time ago. When I walked in them, I noticed the toes were pointing straight up toward the ceiling. Because the heels had been cut shorter, the upturned toes pointed upward even more. I tried to walk in them, but it was hard; I felt like a duck waddling on its uneven legs. I knew I looked weird, but I had no choice but to wear them to work.

That day, there was a heavy rain on top of a high tide. I thought it was not a big deal, since I wore high boots that came up over my knees; I was confident my boots were high enough to keep the water out. I grabbed my Japanese umbrella hanging from the wall; I had received the beautiful umbrella from a friend on my thirty-eighth birthday, just months earlier. For whatever reason, I was determined to look my best that day.

The traffic was bad because of the downpour, but I managed to make it to work. As I expected, the parking lot was flooded, and the heavy rain did not let up. I struggled to get out of the car, opened the umbrella over my head, and waded in the water. My boots were shorter than I thought, and the water level was higher than I expected. By the time I reached the building, water had filled my boots. I opened the door to enter a long hallway, and before I entered the beauty salon, I laid the wet umbrella on the floor, took off my water-filled boots, and turned them upside down to drain out the water. Instead of water, the whole roll of wet toilet paper and all the Kleenex tissue came out with it. I looked at the pile of messy white balls scattered on the wet floor and wondered how on earth I could clean them up before someone else saw them. I bent down and tried to pick up the soggy paper from the floor, but it disintegrated in my hands. I looked around, saw no one, and quickly put my boots back on. I picked up the umbrella, but the stupid thing fell apart at the seams. I was surprised and didn't know what had happened to it. I took a closer look and realized the beautiful Japanese umbrella was made from some kind of waxy paper and not cowhide, as I had thought. I threw it back to the floor, opened the door, and entered the salon, acting as if nothing had happened out in the hallway.

My manager saw me first, and as I expected, she was not too happy to see me. She rolled her eyes as soon as I walked in.

"Linda! Where have you been?" she asked. "You're very late."

"I know, and I am sorry," I said. "I thought I would have to swim to work today," I smiled as I waddled past several hairstylists to get to my station. I noticed a male hairdresser eyeing me as I passed him. I ignored him and walked faster, trying to get to my workstation before anyone else noticed me. As I walked, I could hear gurgling sounds from my over-sized wet boots, and the faster I walked, the noisier they became. It sounded as if I were farting as I walked. Besides the noise from inside the boots, their metal heels clunking on the tile floor caused more ruckus. I ignored everything and continued to walk to my station. Since I did both hair and nails, I had the largest space of all, but it was located all the way back in the corner of the salon. When I reached my station,

I took my boots off and used the hair dryer to dry them out. On the chopped-up leather heels, I saw many tiny octopods appear and come to life. They started curling up and wrapped themselves around the bare metal heels. The dryer the boots, the curlier they became. When I put my boots on, they looked as if I had two small brownish-black roses blossoming on the bottom of my heels. Although the outsides of the boots were partially dry, the insides were still soaking wet and became very heavy. I felt as if I wore ten pounds of lead instead of the boots, and it was very difficult for me to walk in them.

The male hairdresser named Mike, who was eyeing me earlier, watched me with every step I took, and as soon as he was finished with his clients, he motioned for me to come to him. Like a good puppy, I lumbered toward him.

He looked at my boots and frowned. "What in the name of God are you wearing, Linda?" he asked and then laughed in front of a dozen clients and other hairstylists. "Linda! Why are you walking like a duck?" he said.

I was embarrassed and didn't answer him. I was about to turn around and run back to my station to hide. Instead of leaving me alone, he called the other people to look at my boots.

"Leave me alone, Mike! You are a crazy queer," I snapped at him and ran back to my corner.

Mike wouldn't let it go and yelled out loud, "You are a yellow duck," referring to my yellow Asian skin. "And now you are walking like one too!" He laughed as loud as he could, but he didn't stop there. He followed me to my station and continued making fun of me.

"Shut up, Mike, or I'll cut off your head with my shears," I threatened, but it didn't work, and he continued to laugh at me for the rest of the day.

I loved Mike; he was my best buddy in the salon, but at the same time, I wanted to kill him.

I thought I had had enough with those stupid boots and promised myself I would throw them away as soon as I got home, and I did.

Chapter 15

LIFE HAPPENS

I HAD BEEN working for over two years at the salon in downtown Charleston near where Don worked; the job was good and I was very happy, especially when I was able to meet Don and spend a few minutes with him at lunch. That ended, however, when I returned from lunch one day. The owner and manager took me aside and said, "We don't want to see you and your husband having lunch together out by the pond anymore."

"Why?" I asked.

"Because it looks bad and unprofessional."

"Why? I was there just for lunch," I asked, and the other one chimed in.

"Some people might think differently," she said with a smile. "And it would not look good for our salon's image."

"I see," I replied and walked away. I didn't say anything more to them, but when I went home from work, I told Don about it.

"Hey, Don, I have bad news; my bosses told me we can't have lunch together at the pond anymore."

"Why?" Don asked in surprise.

"My bosses said we looked bad out there under a tree; we might give people the wrong impression, and it would not look good for their image."

"What a bunch of crap!" Don exclaimed. "We sat under the tree just to have lunch, for heaven's sake!" He was mad, and I didn't blame him; I was mad too.

"I know it," I said, "but they might have their own reasons; who knows?" I raised my eyebrows.

"They are full of it!" he said in disgust. "You need to look for another job where you will be respected."

"Okay, I'll think about it," I said.

So Don and I stopped having lunch together, and he began going out to eat and drinking with his friends. It made me very worried, and our relationship soon went from good to really bad.

Don drank and spent money we didn't have. He went to bars and clubs almost every night after work, and sometimes he disappeared for days. We fought all the time over everything—money, the kids, and even our intimacy. I couldn't take it anymore, and we agreed to temporarily separate. Don moved to an apartment, and I stayed at the house with our children.

Eddie was nineteen. He was good at art and was on the school soccer team. Teresa was thirteen, Nicky was twelve, and they were both in the school band and straight-A students. Teresa excelled in art as well. I was so proud of my kids. Thanks to my children's love and support, I was able to survive the drama of our marriage and separation.

Teresa was my biggest supporter. One day, she advised me to divorce her father, even though she loved him; she felt sorry for me and didn't want to see me suffer anymore. It was very sad for me since Don left home; I felt as if he took a part of my heart with him when he moved out. His absence did not affect the children too much, because I was always there for them, but I was lost without my soul mate.

During our separation, Don often came back to visit the kids, but he never stayed home for more than a few minutes. Although we were cordial, we seldom spoke to one another. I was always happy to see him, but each time I saw him leave the house, I felt like my heart would split into a hundred pieces. I still loved him very much, but I did not want him to come home until he changed.

Don came back to visit one day and took me aside to talk without the kids listening. "I love you and miss you so much," he said. "I want to move back home and renew our relationship." He looked sincere, and I believed he wanted to come home just as much as I wanted him to.

"I love you and miss you too," I said, "but things have to change first."

"I understand."

"I want nothing more than for you to move back home," I said, "but I cannot take any more of the drinking, gambling, and disappearing for days at a time." My words tore me apart, but I held my ground.

Don accepted the condition and went back to Alcoholics Anonymous. I believed he was trying very hard to overcome his addiction. He quit drinking for a couple of months and then moved back home; I was happy.

I hadn't looked for another job, as Don suggested, but instead I looked for a place to open my own salon. Teresa and I drove around for months but didn't find a suitable place. Even at her young age, she was very beautiful, sweet, and smart; I cherished her and her opinions. When I didn't have time to make my own lunch, she would do it for me, and she always wrote me a loving note and put it in my lunch bag. I kept most of them for souvenirs.

I loved her more than life, and we could not have been any closer. When it was her birthday, she always bought a gift for me and wrote, "This is for you, for giving birth to me." I couldn't have asked for a better daughter. I took a break from looking for the salon and drove Teresa around through a very nice subdivision—the one I'd always loved and admired, even though I knew I could not afford a house there. When we drove into South Pine Bark Lane, I saw a nice two-story home with a for sale sign in the yard. I stopped the car and backed up to take a closer look.

"Teresa, what do you think?" I asked.

"I like the outside," she replied.

"Me too. I like the big yard and the large oak trees. Since we both like the house, why don't we get out of the car and knock on the door?" I asked.

"Why not, Mom? Let's do it," she said and opened the door.

An old, unfriendly woman opened the door, and I told her we were interested in buying her house. For some reason, she didn't seem too eager to sell it. In fact, she didn't want us to see the house and was trying to talk us out of buying it.

The house we looked at

"The house is not really for sale," she said. "We just have the sign up." I thought it was odd to put up a for sale sign and then not want to sell it. I liked the looks of the house, the yard, and the location. I went home and talked to Don about it, but he too tried to dissuade me. He made negative remarks without even seeing it.

"It's too big and too expensive, and we can't afford it," he said.

Because of Don and the owner, I was even more determined to buy the house. I found a realtor, who took me back to the house and showed me the inside, which was a dirty, smelly mess!

"What's wrong with people?" I asked the realtor.

"I don't understand it either," she said. "According to her husband, she doesn't want to sell the house and keeps it dirty so no one will buy it."

I said nothing more as we opened the door and walked out to the beautiful waterfront backyard. "I love this yard," I said, "but I don't like the chaos and the mess inside."

Our kids fishing in the backyard, years after we purchased the house

"Remember," she said, "it has five bedrooms, two and a half baths; although it is dirty and messy, you can have it cleaned up in no time."

"If we bought the house"—I smiled—"it would need a complete makeover. I need to go home and talk to my husband first."

The next day, I took Don to see the house; he didn't like the mess and didn't want to buy it. It wasn't until I threatened to do it by myself that he gave in. We bought the big house, against his wishes, in early 1986.

It took months for us to clean it up. We cut down walls and changed everything inside, including all the filthy toilets and nasty carpet. When we yanked up the disgusting carpet, we found maggots. When we tore down the false kitchen ceiling, we found cockroaches and a cooking pot, placed there to catch the leaking toilet water from the second floor.

Lucky for us, my brother Bay moved back to live with us, and he helped me with the renovation. His common-law wife had left him and their three-year-old daughter for another man. Together, we cleaned out the two homes—the new one to move into and the old one to rent out. It was a lot of work, but we finally finished both of them several months later.

AFTER WE MOVED into our new home, a friend gave me a beautiful black-and-white cat. We named him Cosmo. Nicky loved him, and he followed Nicky everywhere, just like a dog. When Cosmo was about a year old, he followed Nicky across a busy street. Nicky didn't know the cat was right behind him, until he heard a car's wheels' screech; he turned around and witnessed his beloved cat thrown ten feet up into the air and landing right in the middle of the street. He ran to pick up his lifeless pet, cradled it to his chest, and ran home crying.

When I saw my thirteen-year-old son with his dead cat on his chest, I felt sorry for him and promised him I would get him another one. The next day, my brother Kinh and I went to a cat rescue shelter somewhere in North Charleston, to adopt a cat. When we walked in, I saw many cats cooped up inside their small dirty cages without food or water. I felt sorry for them and couldn't wait to take one home. A female worker saw us walk in, and she alerted the other employees; they all seemed nervous when they saw us. They took turns walking in and out of the room, kept their wary eyes on us, and watched our every move. Meanwhile, my brother and I looked into each cage and spoke to each other in Vietnamese. Kinh's English was very limited, and I wanted him to understand what I was saying. I was lucky enough to stand close to one of the workers as she made a phone call. I presumed it was to her boss. She wasn't aware I stood near her; I overheard her whisper, "There are two Asians in the shelter. They both look very suspicious. I am scared; what do you want me to do?" I could not hear the other end, but I thought about the poor girl; she must have been terrified by our presence. After all, we are Asian, and some Asians do eat cats. The rest of the workers acted busy but didn't take their eyes off us. I smiled and thought, *Poor people, they act as if I might sneak around, catch one of their cats, and devour it alive.*

When I asked them about adopting a cat, none of them would give me a straight answer. A few minutes later, I saw another girl make a phone call, and when she came back, she told me all of the cats in the shelter had already been adopted. Their tactics made me feel sad; we went home empty-handed. It was bad for me but more so for the poor cat; it missed the opportunity to have a good home. I hoped that the person who denied my adoption wouldn't end up euthanizing the poor cat.

ONE SATURDAY, MY only day off, I decided to take it easy. I was in my housecoat sitting at the counter in my new kitchen, enjoying a hot cup of morning coffee. I looked around, admiring our finished project. I took another sip of coffee and thought about opening my own salon and what I needed to do to make it happen. As I picked up the coffee cup and was about to put it up to my lips, the phone rang and woke me from my daydream. I reached over and answered it.

"Hey, Linda!" It was the voice of my manager. "Did you forget you're supposed to work today?" she scolded.

"Oh my God!" I exclaimed. "I am so sorry!"

"Bobby is your nine o'clock hair and nail appointment, and she is already here. And right now, it's five minutes after nine."

"I am so sorry; please tell Bobby I will be there in ten or fifteen minutes," I said.

"You better hurry up, you hear! I don't want clients to be waiting long! I hope this will be the last time," she said.

"Yes, ma'am." I hung up the phone, threw down my coffee, and ran to my bedroom to put on my dress. Without putting on makeup or combing my hair, I grabbed my purse and bolted out the door. I flew through the neighborhood like a maniac. I approached an intersection and saw the yellow traffic light, but I flew right through it as it turned red.

In the corner of my eye, I saw a blue light begin flashing behind the first stopped car on my left. When my eyes met the policemen's, I knew I was in trouble, so without waiting for them to pull me over, I pulled over into the median and waited for them to turn around. While waiting for the police, I let my car engine run, unbuckled my seatbelt, and took off my jacket. Minutes later, the police car pulled up right behind mine, and two blue-uniformed men got out. One of them approached my door, but instead of rolling down my window, I opened the door and hit him so hard it almost knocked him down.

"My God, lady! You broke my leg!" he growled as he walked to my open door and bent down to rub his shin.

"Oh no! I'm so sorry, ma'am" I said, shaking like a leaf. The second policeman rushed toward me with his hand on his gun holster. I was afraid he was going to shoot me.

"Do you know you ran a red light?" the first one asked.

"Yes. I know and I am so sorry, ma'am." I started to cry.

"If you knew, then why did you do it?" he barked.

"Because I was going too fast, and I couldn't stop," I explained.

"Too fast?" He frowned. "How fast were you going?"

"I think I was going fifty or more miles an hour," I exaggerated. I wanted to give him a reason as to why I couldn't stop.

"Fifty or more?" he questioned me in surprise. "Then you were going twenty miles or more over the speed limit! The speed limit is only thirty miles an hour."

"Yes! I . . . I . . . I . . . know and I . . . I . . . am so, so sorry, ma'am," I mumbled.

"Do you have a driver's license?" he demanded.

"Oh, yes. I do, ma'am." My tears blinded me as I tried to put my car into park. I had my foot on the brake as I reached over to the passenger side, where I'd left my purse. Unfortunately, the purse had fallen to the floor. As I struggled to reach for my purse, my foot slipped off the brake onto the accelerator, and the car jolted backward. I was terrified and confused. I tried to hit the brake harder, but instead I hit the accelerator again and sent my car flying backward into the police car.

Both of the policemen held on to my car, trying to push it forward, as they both yelled, "Stop the car! Stop the car, lady! Stop the car!"

I tried to stop the car by pressing on the brake again, but my foot was still on the accelerator, and again it jolted backward.

"Stop the car! Hit the brake! Stop the car! Damn it, lady! Hit the brake!" Both of the policemen were screaming at the same time. I was confused, but they thought I was crazy, drunk, or on drugs and was trying to flee the scene. I was overwhelmed and couldn't understand why my car kept rolling backward. I was frightened. They realized my confusion, and one of them stuck his head into my car as he continued to scream at me. "Put your car in park! Damn it, lady. Put it in park!" But I still didn't understand him.

I glanced at the second policeman, who was pointing his gun at my head, so I immediately held both of my arms up in the air to surrender. The first one realized I didn't understand him. He had had enough of my stupidity, so he crawled over on top of me and tried to reach the gearshift knob while still yelling something about the park. I was confused and yelled back, "Park! Park! What park? I don't know what park you want!" I glanced down at my lap and watched the policeman grab hold of the gearshift and slip it up one more notch, from reverse into park position. Still confused, I kept my hands up in the air and let him do whatever he needed to do. When the car was in park, he reached for the key, turned off the engine, and crawled back out. I felt relieved when his heavy body and his gun were completely out of my lap.

How and why I had my car in reverse instead of park, I will never know. As soon as he was out of the car, he raised his voice and began questioning me again, "Lady, do you know how to drive?"

Frightened, I answered him nervously, "Yes! I do."

"It's okay for you to put your hands down now," he said.

I was glad he gave me permission to put my arms down so I could wipe my running nose and tears with the back of my hands.

"Let me see your driver's license and your insurance card, and be very careful this time!" he demanded.

"Oh, yes, ma'am," I said as I reached down to the passenger side floor, retrieved my purse, took out my insurance card and driver's license, and gave them to him.

He looked at my name, my picture, and me and then asked, "Well, Mrs. Baer, how long have you been driving?"

I thought about it for a couple seconds but couldn't remember exactly how many years. So I said, "How long have I been driving?" I asked the policeman, but I was actually questioning myself to see if I could come up with an answer.

"That's what I just asked you, Mrs. Baer," he said.

"I know! I know!" I wondered why he kept calling me by my name and how he knew my name in the first place; he must have known it made me more nervous. At home, Don called me by my name only when he was mad, and I guess the policeman was mad too. I looked up at him and tried hard to come up with a reasonable answer.

"Oh, maybe sixteen or seventeen years, somewhere around there. I can't remember exactly right now; I'm so sorry, ma'am," I said.

"Have you ever been stopped by the police before?" he asked.

"Oh no, ma'am. I have never been stopped by the American police before." I was being honest.

"Are you sure?" He raised his eyebrows.

"I am very sure," I replied.

He took my card and driver's license and walked to the other policeman, who had just put his gun back into the holster. I could see them whispering to each other, but I couldn't hear what they were saying; I just hoped they wouldn't put me in jail. A minute later, the first one came back to my car.

"You are very lucky today," he said. "We're going to let you go, but you have to promise me you will always wear your seatbelt, and you must never ever let me catch you speeding or running a red light again." He continued to preach, and I continued to listen. "Do you understand me? Never ever again."

"Yes, I promise," I replied. "I will not speed or run a red light ever again, and I will always wear my seatbelt." As soon as I finished my words, he handed me my driver's license and the insurance card.

"Thank you so much, ma'am, so very much," I said as I stuck them back into my purse.

I put on my seatbelt, started the engine, and inched out into the busy traffic. In the rearview mirror, I saw one of the policemen rubbing his leg where I'd hit him with the car door, while the other looked at the front of the patrol car. I was sure I'd done some damage when I'd hit it, because I'd heard the sound of glass breaking when I'd backed into the headlight. I felt bad for them. They were just trying to do their jobs. However, the worst feeling came when I realized I had called both of the policemen *ma'am* the entire time.

Of course, I was very late for work, but when I told the manager the reason I was late, she thought I was making up an excuse. Bobby, my client, on the other hand, laughed. "It's only you, Linda, only you," she said as she shook her head.

I HAD TO postpone searching for my own salon, because I was busy working on the houses and editing my book, *Red Blood, Yellow Skin*. But the hunting resumed after the police incident. I found a possible spot in an old concrete block duplex close to our home, but it was for lease and not for sale. I was looking for something to buy, but I took down the phone number and called to make an appointment to see the place anyway. A few days later, an old gentleman met me at the location. It looked good outside, but the inside needed a lot of work to turn it into a salon. When I asked to buy the building, he said it was not for sale.

"I know, but what would happen if I wanted to buy it?" I asked.

"I don't know," he smiled. "You have to talk to the owner, Mr. Long; his office is right there across the street," he said as he pointed to a red brick building.

After I left, I went home and told Don about buying it rather than leasing it. Don objected to the idea, as he did the house. He said we couldn't afford it, and he didn't want us to go deeper into debt. I didn't blame him; we had just purchased a house against his will.

Again, I had to figure this one out by myself. I called my sister in Texas, told her about my plans, and asked her to help me with the money. After listening to me, she agreed to lend me what I needed, even though she did not have it herself. She agreed to borrow it from a loan shark for me.

The money part was no longer a problem, but convincing the owner to sell instead of leasing was my next obstacle. The next day, I went to see the owner without an appointment. Mr. Long looked to be about eighty-five to ninety years old.

"Hi, how are you?" I said with a big smile as I walked toward him. He looked surprised when he saw me.

"Hey there," he greeted me. "What can I do for you today?"

"Oh, you can do a lot for me, if you want to, Mr. Long," I gave him a big grin.

"Oh! Okay," he said, and he seemed to be a little confused, but he asked me to come in and told me to have a seat. He was in a two-story building with a big office. Every few minutes, people were coming in to ask him questions or get him to sign papers. He apologized to me for the interruptions.

"Can I ask you for a big favor?" I cocked my head like a child and tried to look sweet.

"What is it you want?" he asked.

"You see, I like the building you have across the street," I said.

"Yes, and it's for lease," he said.

"Well, I know it is, but I don't want to lease it; I want to buy it," I said, and he looked even more surprised.

"The building is not for sale, ma'am," he said, shaking his head. "It is for lease only."

"I know! I saw the sign," I said, "but I still want to buy it; I hate the thought of renting or leasing anything."

"Oh no, it's not for sale. I don't want to sell it." He was adamant about it.

"I know, but I want to buy it; please sell it to me," I begged.

"How are you going to buy it if it's not for sale?" he asked.

"But I know you will sell it to me," I said. I was determined.

"Let me ask you this," he said. "What would you do with it if I sold it to you?"

"I will open a hair salon so I can take care of my big family: my three children, three brothers who just barely made it out of Vietnam by boat. None of them can speak English." I continued to exaggerate my story. "One of my brothers, whose wife left him for another man, has a three-year-old baby." I stopped a few seconds for effect and to catch my breath. "And I also take care of my old, disabled veteran husband, who served our country for years. All of them are dependent on me to bring food home for them. Besides, I will cut your hair, your wife's hair, and do her nails for free for the rest of my life," I said with a big smile. "Oh, and I will take care of all the people who work here too."

"Wow! What a big commitment you just made, but why that building?" he asked.

"Because I can live in one side and do hair and nails on the other," I answered.

"It makes sense, but can you afford to buy it?" he asked with sympathy.

"With your help, I can," I answered with a pitiful expression.

"How can I help?" he asked. And then he realized he was about to sell me the building. "Wait a minute here, young lady! The building is not for sale. I'm keeping it as an investment."

"Oh, but you really want me to have it, because I am just like one of your children, and at your age, you don't need any more investments. What you need is a relaxing vacation."

"Hey, John! Come in here," he called to one of his partners or employees. While waiting for John, he looked at me and shook his head in confusion. He probably had never met anyone as crazy as me and had to call for reinforcements. John came in; he was the same man who showed me the building the day before.

"What's going on?" John asked the owner.

"This lady wants to buy the duplex," the owner said.

"Oh? I didn't know it was for sale," John replied.

"It isn't, but she wants to buy it, and she's not taking no for an answer," he said with a crooked smile.

"Well, you're the owner. You deal with her." John smiled and walked out of the office.

"Mr. Long, can I ask you one thing?" I said.

"If it doesn't hurt me, go right ahead," he joked.

"What is the duplex zoned for?" I asked.

"It's zoned commercial," he replied.

"Good! And how much do you want for it?" I asked.

"One hundred thousand dollars and not a penny less," he said.

"What!" I exclaimed, "That is too much for an old building that is about to fall apart."

"Look here, young lady, I'm not selling it unless you pay me one hundred thousand," he replied sternly.

"Why do you want so much money from a poor person like me, who just wants to survive and help her family?" I said. "Besides, I don't think you need it as much as I do. I promise you, I will take care of the building and put it to good use. You'll be proud of me." I continued pressuring him, "Please sell it to me, and use the money for your retirement."

"Let me think about this." A few seconds later, he said, "I'll take ninety thousand and not a cent less."

We bargained back and forth for a while, but in the end, he sold the duplex to me for eighty-five thousand.

Chapter 16

LEGAL DILEMMA

SOON AFTER I bought the building, and before I quit my job, I handed out my business cards to let all of my clients know about the new salon. I didn't have the money to hire workers, so Don and my brother Bay helped me. While Don tore down the walls, my brother and I painted. Don built shelves and tables and installed shampoo sinks and mirrors. I looked for secondhand furniture, while Bay finished painting and put up all the window mini blinds. The salon looked and felt much larger after we tore down all the walls and changed the carpet.

When we finished with the inside, we went outside and painted the whole building a soft shade of pink; I didn't like pink, but I thought it would be an eye-catching color. I hired a professional to install inscribed black awnings around the building. Next, I designed the sign: It said, "Linda B. Hair, Nail, and Skin Care," and Don made it.

Days later, I rented a large neon sign and hung a long welcome banner across the front porch. They both said, "Grand Opening." The morning after the signs were up, the salon was operational. All my elegant and sophisticated clients who followed me from downtown started pouring in, as I expected.

A week later, my excitement and happiness were cut short, however, when I received a letter from the county zoning board, ordering me to shut down my business immediately. The property was zoned for office business, not for a hair salon. In order to continue to operate as a salon, I had to rezone my property. I was scared and hurt, and I didn't know what to do. I hired a lawyer and asked him to help me. He explained the difference between the two business zoning laws and told me I had the wrong one. I asked him to write a rezoning request for me, and together, we took it to the county zoning board. A board member took our papers and told us to come back in thirty days; they needed time to analyze my zoning request. I was disappointed, but there was nothing more I could do; I left with my lawyer and went home to wait.

Meanwhile, I let my clients know what was happening with the zoning problem; they understood and willingly came to see me through the back door, and I continued to operate my salon without a zoning permit. A month later, I met with my lawyer, and we returned to the zoning board. The board consisted of one woman and five men. There were a few people ahead of us. When it was our turn, they read my proposal and immediately turned down my rezoning request. They stated my building was located right in front of a subdivision, and they were concerned that those who lived behind my shop would object to having a hair salon so close to them.

I listened as my lawyer tried to explain why my salon wouldn't be a burden to those who lived there and why my building needed to be rezoned. He also said he knew the neighborhood well and they didn't mind, because his law office was just a block away from them. I watched them going back and forth for a long time and saw the members of the board shaking their heads, as if they had already made up their minds. I didn't like what I saw and heard, and I told my lawyer to sit down and let me take over. He was surprised at my request and reluctantly sat down.

I stood up and began my argument, "Good evening, lady and gentlemen of the board. My name is Linda Baer, and I am here to beg the board for mercy. I am the wife of a disabled Vietnam veteran and the mother of three young children. My three brothers recently escaped from Vietnam with their families by boat. None of them speak English. They all live with me and depend on me for food," I lied and paused for effect. "I am trying to help all of them by opening a salon to make money and feed them. Since the board closed my business, I can do nothing for my family." Tears started pooling in my eyes. "If I can't reopen my salon, we will all end up on welfare and food stamps." I stopped to catch my breath. "I don't think you all would want to see that happen. It would not be good for my family or for our government. They would have to feed all ten of us, provide our medical care, and pay for our medicine. I don't want to leech on our government, and I don't want to teach my siblings or my children to depend on welfare and food stamps. What is stopping you from helping me?"

"Well, ma'am," one of the male board members replied, "we are here to listen to you, but we don't think the neighborhood near you wants your building to be rezoned."

"Sir, what gave you that impression?" I asked.

"I live right behind your property, and I know my neighbors well; I doubt they would want your property rezoned."

"Sir, I already bought the property and invested every single dime I have in it. What would you do if you were in my situation? What would you suggest for me to do with it, if I can't rezone it? All I want is to have a chance to work hard and to feed my hungry family." Tears streamed down my face as I pleaded.

The lady on the panel took pity on me and gave me advice.

"Why don't you rent your building to the right kind of business and open your salon somewhere else?" she asked.

"Ma'am, I would love to, but I can't. I already used all of my savings, and I'm too deep in debt with the bank to borrow any more. I don't have another choice."

"Too bad," she said. "There is nothing more we can do for you."

"With all due respect," I said firmly, "since you all seem concerned about the neighborhood objecting to having a beauty salon at my location, what would happen if I surveyed all of the neighbors and asked them to sign a petition stating they had no objections? Would you still have a reason to keep me from opening my salon?"

None of them answered my question, and they began to talk among themselves. A few seconds later, one of the members asked, "Can you give us a few minutes? We need to talk in private." Then they left the room. My lawyer sat watching me in silence, and when we were alone, he said to me, "Linda, you should be a lawyer yourself."

"No, Stan," I said. "I'm bad enough already," I smiled and winked at him. "I don't need to be a lawyer to go to hell." We both laughed out loud.

Five or ten minutes later, the board members returned to their seats, except for one, who remained standing and made an announcement.

"The zoning board," he declared, "after considering your case, has decided that if a significant number of property owners in the neighborhood around you, especially people who live behind you, sign a petition stating they would not object to having a beauty salon on the corner of Crull Avenue and Ashley River Road, we will reconsider your request for rezoning." He sat down and gathered up all his papers.

"I think that is fair, sir," I replied. "Thank you all very much." My lawyer and I left the zoning board and walked outside.

"Wow! You are something else, Linda B. I didn't even think of that," he said, and asked, "Can you write a proposal, or do you want me to do it?"

"No, I can't do it by myself," I answered, "but I'll ask my husband to help me."

My lawyer took me back to my house and dropped me off. After we hugged, I told him to send me the bill.

As soon as I stepped in the door, I called out to Don; when he answered, I told him what happened and asked him to help me write a petition. After I gave him an idea of what I wanted to say and how I wanted to say it, he had soon prepared a sad and moving appeal letter. I smiled after I read it, and thought, *No one on earth could refuse signing this.*

The next day, I took Thuy, my almost three-year-old niece, and walked to all of the businesses around the area and then to all of the homes in the neighborhood behind my building. I showed each of them the letter, explained my zoning problem, and of course, told them my sad story to encourage them to sign. After listening to me and reading my petition, they all signed without question, except for one lady who lived a couple of houses behind my salon. She said, "My husband is one of the zoning board members. He is the one who was against the rezoning."

"Oh! I see. But why?" I asked.

"I don't know why he didn't want your beauty salon there," she said "but I do know he was the one who reported you to the zoning board, when he saw your sign go up. He was mad because your grand opening sign was too big and was blocking his view of oncoming traffic."

"Oh, I am so sorry. I'll do something about it," I said. "Thank you for sharing the information."

"You are welcome," she replied. "Would you like to come inside for a cup of coffee?"

"No thanks, I need to be going home, because my niece is hungry," I smiled, "but I do want you to come to my salon for a cup of coffee and a free haircut."

"I will," she said.

That afternoon, I came home with a piece of paper full of signatures.

Weeks later, I brought the petition with all the signatures back to the zoning board without my lawyer, and they approved it.

My beauty salon legally reopened on April 13, 1987. I started out with two stylists; we did everything for our clients, including hair, nails, skin care, body massage, body waxing, manicures, and pedicures. I worked ten hours or more a day, six days a week, hoping to make enough for food and mortgage payments.

My new salon

As my reputation grew, I became so busy that Teresa, my beautiful fourteen-year-old daughter, had to come help me answer the phone after school. My clients loved her and encouraged her to become a hairdresser; she took their advice, and after she finished high school, she went to cosmetology school and graduated with honors. I sent her to the high-end salon downtown for more practice; she was involved in many competitions and won numerous first place trophies for color and cut. When I felt she was a good enough hairstylist, I let her return to my salon. We worked side by side, and my duplex next door became her home. She lived and worked in the same building while attending the College of Charleston. At first, she studied biology and then changed to environmental law, hoping to become a lawyer.

At one point, Tulane University in New Orleans accepted her and offered her a scholarship, but after visiting the campus, she turned it down, came back home, and decided to study art. She became a talented artist and began working with her friend at the Gibbs Museum of Art in downtown Charleston; still, she continued to help me in my salon and was excellent with hair and nails.

I was busy at home doing my chores, cooking, gardening, and working on book, but at work, I was even busier. I reached a point where I couldn't take on new clients, unless they were referred by my own clients or friends. My appointment book was full, ten hours a day, six days a week. I needed help, so I hired another hairstylist named Anne. She was sweet and eager to help, but she was a little bit absentminded; instead of helping, she made a mess out of my appointment schedules.

For example, on her very first day of work, she told all of my clients who called for an appointment to come at twelve noon. When twelve o'clock came, all five or more of them showed up at once. After my initial shock, I apologized to everyone, and after we had a good laugh, I rescheduled them. After that day, Anne became well known and was loved by everybody. Anne also had a problem with spelling patrons' names correctly, and it was very difficult for me to know who was coming. At first, I tried to correct them, but soon I gave up and just looked at the appointment book to see if the space was filled. Then I just did whoever showed up.

One day, Caroline Fisher came to get her manicure, and afterward, she wanted to reschedule her appointment; all of the stylists were busy, so she tried to help by looking at my appointment book and rescheduling herself. When she couldn't find her name, she turned to me and said, "I can't find my name in the book." She looked confused. "You don't have me down, but you have somebody by the name of Calin Fish in my space."

"It's your new name," I explained. "Our Anne here decided to change the spelling a little." We all laughed, including Anne.

I WAS CONCENTRATING on painting Marian's nails one day when the phone rang. I looked around and saw everyone was busy, so I asked Marian to excuse me, and I answered the phone while still painting her nails.

"This is Linda B. May I help you?" I said.

"Hey Linda B. This is Bob," the man on the phone said.

I knew several Bobs and had no idea which Bob it was, so I asked, "I'm sorry, Bob, but I don't know exactly who you are."

"This is Bob from the AA group," he reminded me.

"Oh yes, Bob! How are you?" I asked.

"I am fine, thanks." Bob said excitedly, "I just caught a twenty-pound catfish and can't wait to give it to a sweet lady like you," he flirted.

"Can I pick up the fish later?"

"No, I won't be home tonight."

"I see. Hey, Bob," I asked, "could you give me your phone number, and I'll have Don call you."

"That's fine," he said. Then he gave me his number and hung up.

As soon as I finished Marian's nails, I made a quick call to Don.

"Hey, honey, do you remember Bob, the fat guy in our AA group? He wants to give us a big fish." I talked without catching my breath, because I had another client waiting for me.

"But why are you calling me?" he replied.

"Well, I called you because I'm with many clients and don't have time to go pee, much less go pick up a stupid fish." I was irritated.

"Yes, I know," he said. "But why are you calling me?" He sounded unwilling, which upset me even more, so I raised my voice.

"Why do you keep saying that?" I was loud, and all of my curious clients turned their head to look at me.

"I am so sorry, but you are talking to me, Linda," his voice sounded sad, but I had no time to feel sorry for him.

"Don, you need to call Bob and go pick up that stupid fish. You remember the big fat guy, whose humongous stomach hangs all the way down to his knees?" I barked.

"Yes, I do know, but I don't know why you are calling me."

"Don, I'm in a hurry and don't have time to play games right now. Here is his number," I said as I started to read the numbers from the note pad.

"Linda! Linda! Linda!" He kept interrupting me, but I ignored him and continued to read out loud, until his last word shocked me into silence.

"Sorry, Linda, but this is Bob, and that is my number, and I just gave that to you." My jaw dropped, and I was about to crawl under the table.

"Oh, my goodness!" I exclaimed. "I'm so sorry, Bob. I called the wrong number."

I could hear the whole salon roaring with laughter as I hung up the phone. Marian was laughing so hard she fell backward. Her wet nail polish, smeared all over my pink wall.

I helped her up and repainted her nails. "That was the funniest thing I ever heard in my entire life," she said. I glanced around and saw others wiping their tears from laughing.

I felt bad for calling him a fat man with humongous stomach. Poor Bob.

Don did go pick up the fish, and soon the fat Bob story spread, and I was the brunt of the joke. Weeks later, I saw Bob at one of the meetings. I smiled as I walked toward him. "Hello, big fat Bob." He frowned as he shook his finger at me, in front of everybody watching and waiting for him to kill me. But instead, he gave me a big bear hug. I didn't apologize to him, because the word sorry could never make up for what I'd said about him.

A NEW CLIENT walked into my salon on one of our busiest days and asked for a waxing job. I looked around for help but saw that everyone was busy with their clients. I didn't have time to ask her what kind of a waxing job she wanted. I just assumed she wanted a bikini wax and sent her to go to the waxing room. I told her to take off her pants, lie on the waxing bed, and wait for me. When I finished with my client, I went to the waxing room. I saw her lying there half-naked; I smiled and said hi again as I put on a pair of rubber gloves. I dipped a cotton puff in the baby powder dish and was about to apply it to her bikini area, to protect her skin from the hot wax.

"Would you please spread your legs wider?" I asked.

She looked up at me in confusion and asked, "Do I have to go through all of this just to get my eyebrows waxed?"

"Oh no!" I uttered in shocked surprise. "I thought you wanted a bikini wax."

"Oh no, ma'am!" she said and looked embarrassed.

"Then why on earth did you take off your pants?" I asked.

"I'm new to this," she said. "I thought this is what you wanted me to do to get my eyebrows waxed."

"Oh no," I said, laughing. "This is the wrong end. Please, turn around; I need to work on your other end." By then, she had loosened up and started laughing with me. She turned around, and I did her eyebrow wax with her pants off; she never returned to my salon after that day.

Chapter 17

HURRICANE HUGO

IN 1988, I gave Teresa my Capri and bought a used silver Nissan 300ZX sports car. It was the first valuable car I'd ever owned. Although it was a year old, the car still looked new, and I treated it as if it were my baby. I liked to drive fast with an open sunroof to show it off. I couldn't stand to see a fingerprint or even a little dirt on it—I'd spit on it and use my shirttail to wipe it clean. There was one drawback about the car though; it was built low to the ground. When Charleston had a heavy rain, which happened often, the car would submerge in a deep puddle, and sometimes the engine would die. Even with this problem, all three of my kids loved the car, and they all jokingly said they wanted me to will it to them when I died.

A few months after I bought the car, the weather forecasters warned that a category-five hurricane, Hurricane Hugo, was heading for Charleston. The governor of South Carolina urged an evacuation for anyone living within the expected path of the storm. Since we lived in a two-story brick home, I felt safe and was secretly excited. My family didn't share my feelings, however, especially my sweet daughter. She was so afraid of the hurricane and pressured us to leave town. I didn't want to go and made up all kinds of excuses.

"We can't leave our home, cars, animals and pets, and a garden in full bloom, which needs water every day," I said without catching my breath.

"Linda! Nothing is worth more than your life," Don argued.

"Oh, Mom, can we please go now?" Teresa begged. Eddie and Nicky didn't care whether we left or stayed.

"Why don't you two leave, and I'll stay behind and keep an eye on the house and the animals," I suggested.

"Mom! You are not staying here by yourself," Teresa demanded.

"No, I will be home with Uncle Kinh, Eddie, and Nicky" I said.

"Kinh has to stay at the hospital where he works to help out when there is an emergency. He is not coming home," Don said.

"You can't stay home, Mom," Teresa said.

"Why not?" I asked. "If it gets too bad, I'll leave." Teresa wouldn't take no for an answer and started to cry.

I felt bad for being selfish and started to pack. I also called my friend Kim and asked her to join us. Kim had a broken foot and had to wear a hard cast, from her thigh down to her toes. I knew it would take too long for her and her family to get ready, and we didn't have time to wait. We took off first and told her to catch up with us in a hotel in Atlanta, Georgia, where we made reservations.

"Teresa, why don't you leave your car home and ride with me?"

"No, Mom, I don't want to leave my poor car at home by itself," she said and began pouting. She had wrecked her Capri the very first day I'd handed it to her. She was fine, but the car wasn't. We had bought her a cheap used car. We didn't know how reliable the car was, and I didn't want her to drive it for such a long distance, but she refused to leave her car home.

"Okay, then," I said, "but you'll have to keep up with us."

"I will, Mom. I promise," she said.

When we were ready, I was the first one to pull out of the driveway. Eddie followed in his black, sporty Camaro, and Nicky rode with him. Don lumbered along in his Ram Charger SUV, with Teresa following behind him in her small car. No one wanted to leave their vehicle behind, even though all of us could fit comfortably into Don's SUV.

The traffic was horrendous on Interstate 26; it seemed like everyone in Charleston was on the road. It took us two hours to go the first ten miles, but it improved after we were out of town.

We had just driven past the Interstate 95 cut off when I looked into the rearview mirror and saw white smoke coming from Teresa's car. I pulled to the shoulder first and waited for her to catch up. Eddie stopped after me, and Don was right behind Eddie. When Teresa pulled in behind us, we all walked back to her.

"What happened?" I asked.

"I don't know, Mom," she said. Don and I decided we couldn't let Teresa drive her car all the way to Atlanta; we had to find a gas station, where she could park it until the hurricane passed.

Moments after reaching a gas station, Teresa's car died; we rented a space to park it, and she rode with Don. She didn't want to ride with me; she said I drove way too fast for her.

After Teresa was safe with Don and the freeway was opened up to traffic, I was able to drive faster. I took advantage of the situation and tried out my car. I drove an average of between eighty-five and ninety-five miles per hour. Eddie was right behind me in his Camaro, with a dozen more cars following us; they must have thought I had a police radar detector.

After seven hours, Eddie and I slowed down as we approached Atlanta and found our way to our hotel. We were lucky we didn't get a speeding ticket. The police probably ignored it because of the hurricane. I promised myself never to drive that fast again. An hour later, Don, Teresa, and Kim's family showed up.

The first night after we ate our dinner, we glued our eyes on the television to watch the hurricane and its path. After midnight, the kids and Don were tired and they fell asleep. I stayed up to watch Hurricane Hugo as it headed straight for Charleston and the low country area. I was shocked to see so much damage caused by the storm after it went through. It knocked down countless aging oak trees, messed up several major bridges, and destroyed a thousand homes. The wind and ocean surges moved boats from their docks and lifted homes from their foundations and deposited them in the middle of streets. The television also showed the West Ashley area where we lived, but I didn't recognize any landmarks. After seeing all the damage, I was glad Teresa and Don forced me to leave Charleston, but after watching the news, I began to worry about my animals at home. I twisted and turned all night, worried about them. I hoped they all survived, and I couldn't wait to get home to check on everything. The next morning, I talked to Don about going home early.

"Hey, Don! Are you awake?" I asked.

"I am now," he grumbled.

"I want to go home early to check on the animals and our property. What do you think?"

"I don't think it's a good idea," Don said and went back to sleep.

"Why? The hurricane already passed," I said loudly, trying to wake him.

"It's going to take some time for the cleaning crews to get the roads cleared enough for us to drive home," he explained.

"How long?"

"Maybe two to three more days."

"Two to three more days!" I exclaimed, "There's no way I can stay here that long and let all my animals die."

Half asleep, he replied, "It would be better them than you."

I had already made up my mind to go home as soon as the sun came out. I asked Don for his approval, but regardless of what he said, I was going home.

"Are you sure you don't want to go home this morning?" I asked him again.

"No way, Linda! I do not; it's a bad idea," he repeated.

"If you don't want to go home this morning, do you mind if I do? I need to go home and check on my animals, my salon, and our home. I am too worried about them to stay here any longer."

"I don't want you to drive home by yourself," he said.

"Oh no, I won't. I already called Kim this morning and asked her if she wanted to go home with me. She said she would; she wants to go home to check on her restaurant too," I explained.

"Okay, if that's what you two want to do, go ahead, but don't expect me to go home with you," he said with some irritation.

"No, I don't. Kim told me her husband and her two kids wanted to go home with her too."

Don shrugged his shoulder; I could tell he was a little upset, but he said nothing more to me and turned to watch news of the storm's damage on TV.

After I packed my suitcases and was prepared to leave, Eddie and Nicky asked if they could come too.

"If it's okay with Dad, I say you can," I smiled with him. By then, Don and Teresa were the only two staying behind; they ended up changing their minds and decided they would go home too.

As everyone was preparing to leave, I started to have second thoughts about pressuring everyone to go home early. What if we went home and something bad happened or someone got hurt? I knew I would be blamed for it, because this was my idea. However, I was too worried about my beloved pets and couldn't wait to get back home to check on them.

I'd started out with just a few pets, but I hadn't stopped there. I let the ducks, chickens, and geese lay eggs, and then I hatched them in an incubator. Soon, I had over three hundred animals running and swimming in our backyard. The more they hatched, the bigger the coop I built.

I did the same thing with the koi; I let the koi mate and lay eggs, and then I took their eggs from the big pond to a small pool, where I hatched them. When the koi hatched, I fed them with ground up fish food. I cared for them until they grew larger. I selected the ones I wanted to keep and gave away the rest. I started out with a small plastic pond, but each year the koi numbers increased, and I had to build a bigger pond, until I couldn't build it any larger.

Forty-one-year-old me, talking to and feeding watermelon to some of my two-legged children

One time, a bunch of my baby ducks fell into a small bucket, half-full of water. They panicked and stepped on each other trying to get out. By the time I realized what happened, three of them had drowned. I felt so bad and decided to administer CPR to their limp bodies. I pressed on their little chests and blew into their tiny beaks. I rotated between all three, and to my surprise, they all revived. I took them inside and dried them with my hair dryer. They not only came back to life, but they also grew big and later laid eggs to make more babies.

I told my duck-reviving story to my dear friend Mary Ellen Braun while I was cutting her hair; she laughed so hard it brought tears to her eyes. "Baby, you should have been a veterinarian," she said as she wiped her tears. "You would be very good at it, darling."

"Oh yeah! I guess I'm in the wrong profession now," I said laughing.

"No, baby, you are good at cutting hair too," she said. "I don't know what I'd do without you; no one could cut my hair as good as you do, baby."

"Hey, Mary Ellen," I smiled, "in many ways, I have been a doctor to my own animals."

"I know you have, sweetie, I know. I thank God for bringing you here, to America; you are a good person and the best hair dresser too," she said as she reached up and gave me a kiss on my cheek. "You are something else, Linda B. God bless you, baby. God bless you."

"Thanks, Mary Ellen," I said.

"No, thank you, Linda B. God sent you to us. You are so sweet and positive; there is no one else like you, baby."

"Oh wow! With all of those nice compliments, your haircut will be free today," I said and gave her a big kiss on her cheek as we both smiled.

I glanced in the mirror and saw where she left her deep-purple lipstick on my cheek. I always felt good each day when I came home and looked in the mirror, before I washed my face, and saw the collection of lipstick left there from clients.

"Hey, Linda!" Don called and awoke me from my daydreaming. "Do you want to go first?"

"Yes, I would." I replied.

The two families of nine people and four cars lined up in the parking lot and were ready to go.

Before I took off, Kim came to me and asked, "Is it okay for me to ride with you? I'd like to have someone to talk with on the way home. My husband seldom talks to me while he's driving."

"Sure, you can ride with me and keep me from falling asleep," I said with a smile. We all loaded up and left.

The closer we were to Charleston, the more damages I saw. There was a lot of debris and fallen trees on the freeway, but not many people traveling on it. I had to slow down to avoid all of the obstacles. It was almost dark when we approached Summerville. I turned to Kim and said, "We have only forty more miles to go, but at twenty miles per hour it could take us two more hours to get home."

I was too anxious to crawl along the freeway full of debris and decided to take a shortcut through Summerville. As I drove through the small town, it looked dead and dreary, without electricity and not a person to be seen. The shortcut I took was messier and had more fallen trees and debris than the freeway. I saw no traffic lights or street signs. I couldn't recognize the place, and after a few more turns, I was completely lost.

I drove around in circles and could barely see beyond my headlights. I was hoping and praying to see someone alive so I could ask for directions, but there was nothing for miles and miles. I wasn't sure if I was even going in the right direction. I was afraid.

Meanwhile, Kim constantly complained; she let me know she had made a mistake by going home in my car. I was already scared and frustrated, and then I had to listen to her. I felt like throwing her out of the window, but instead, I kept apologizing to her and concentrated on my driving. Soon, I came to a familiar road.

"Hey, Kim, look! We are at Highway 61. If nothing goes wrong," I said, "we will be home within thirty minutes." We both felt relieved and laughed at our little irritable outbursts earlier.

Finally, after many miles, I saw headlights coming toward us. The vehicle slowed down as it inched beside me, and we both stopped. I rolled my window down and saw a couple in a pickup truck.

"How is the road ahead?" I asked the driver.

"Not good," the man said.

"Why, what happened?"

"A huge oak tree fell and blocked the road; it's impossible to get through," he replied.

"Well, maybe your big truck can't make it, but do you think my small car could?"

"I doubt it," he said and shook his head. "The ditch is full of water, and it was too deep; I tried, but didn't make it. I'm afraid your car is even lower than mine, and I don't think you can get through." The man tried to explain, but the woman in the passenger seat chimed in.

"Whether she can or cannot make it, it is none of your business," she growled. "You need to concentrate and get me off of this road," she demanded.

"Well, thank you. I think I'll give it a try," I said.

"Good luck!" he said and drove away.

I shifted my car back into drive and continued to crawl along in the darkness, fighting my way through fallen trees and garbage. About ten minutes later, and a mile farther, I came to a large oak tree; it must have been the one the stranger described. Just as he said, it was huge and it blocked the whole road. I stopped the car, got out, and stepped down on a wet, messy road to investigate; I squinted and peered into the blackness but saw nothing and heard nothing. I looked down near my feet and saw a ditch full of water, just as he mentioned. I wondered if I could just drive into it and come out on the other side of the fallen oak; if I could, I would be home free. I got back in the car and decided to go for it. My car didn't make it far, however; it sank right away. The ditch was deeper than I thought. I panicked and pushed on the gas pedal; the car sunk more, and the exhaust pipe shot muddy water all over itself. The more I pushed on the accelerator, the more mud shot up and the more the car sank.

We both screamed for help, but no one heard us. I looked out of my left windshield and saw water up almost halfway to my hood. I glanced to the right side, where Kim sat. It was submerged; I was afraid she was going to drown. I struggled to open the door, and as soon as the door cracked open, the water poured in as I tried to get out. I stepped down into waist-deep mud and yelled to Kim to crawl to me over the center console. She tried, but she couldn't. The heavy cast on her leg was too long and heavy; she couldn't move inside the tight car, much less over the center divider. I tried to reach her but couldn't. I was so desperate to get her out. I climbed back up on the doorframe and anchored one foot on the water-soaked seat. I grabbed hold of both her hands, stood straight up, and tried hard to pull her over the center console. It was very difficult. For whatever reason, she started to giggle while I was trying to pull her, and from the giggle, she started to laugh out loud; I couldn't help but laugh with her.

When I finally pulled her to the driver's seat, I stepped back into the ditch and turned my back to her. I told her to hop on so I could carry her to dry land; I didn't want her cast to get any wetter. After I put her down, I went back to the car to get her wooden crutches. My car engine gave out, but thank God, the car's headlights stayed on, even though they were submerged under water. I was very upset and wondered what I could do next. Suddenly, I saw four headlights inching toward us from the Summerville direction.

"Look, Kim!" I said with a smile as I pointed to the two cars, "We're being rescued." Kim leaned on her wooden crutches, stared at the oncoming cars, and said nothing.

I waved as I walked in front of them and signaled for them to stop. The two men and two women got out of their cars, left their engines running, and walked toward me. They were dressed poorly, in shorts, ragged tee shirts, and flip-flops, and they all had cigarettes.

"Hi, there!" I greeted.

"Hi," they all said.

"What do we have here?" one man asked.

"I got stuck in a ditch," I said, "and I need help getting my car out."

"Say what?" They didn't understand my accent.

"I need help," I said slowly as I tried to emphasize my words. "My car is stuck in the ditch." They nodded their heads, and I knew they understood me.

"I think we can help you," the other man said.

"Do you really think you can help me?"

"Of course, . . . hon," said one of the toothless women.

"Do you have a rope or something to tie to my car and pull it back to the road?" I asked.

"What???" one of them asked with a frown.

"What did she say?" the other one chimed in. I smiled, shook my head, and repeated myself again.

"Excuse us," she said, and instead of answering me, they all walked away from me and grouped together behind their cars. I couldn't hear them, but I could tell they were whispering about something.

When they returned, the man with two missing front teeth said, "We have ropes and can help you, but we want to be paid for it."

I took a closer look at him; he looked creepy. In fact, they all looked creepy. They moved closer to me, and I could smell their cigarette breath and unwashed bodies. As they talked, I realized three out of four were missing their teeth, and when they smiled, my hair stood on end.

"How much do you want?" I asked.

One of the women said, "Five hundred dollars."

"Wow! That is a lot of money," I responded, "but I don't have the money with me. Can you follow me to Charleston, where I can pay you by check?" I lied. I had more than five hundred dollars in my purse, but I wasn't about to let them know.

"Sure!" one man said. "We wanted to go into town ourselves."

"Okay, after my car is out of the ditch, I'll take you there," I said.

"That will be good!" a woman said. "That's exactly what we wanted to do."

One of the men found some rope, but it was not heavy enough. He tied the wimpy rope on to the back of my bumper and connected it to the front of his car. Then he started his engine and tried to pull my car out of the ditch, but the flimsy rope kept breaking. We tried to tie them back together again and again. All five of us were in and out of the ditch. We pushed and pulled, trying to get my car back on the road. An hour later, we were all soaked in mud, except for Kim, who stood leaning on her crutches and watching us.

I was sitting on a water-soaked seat, turning the engine on and off as the men instructed. The stronger the engine roared, the more the mud bellowed out from underneath the car. But the stubborn car did not budge an inch. I took a break, got out of the car, and took a good look at it; my once beautiful sports car was now a big wet mud ball. I held out my hand and signaled for them to stop torturing it.

"Could someone take me back to Summerville, where I can find a tow truck?" I asked. One of the men agreed to take me to Summerville for fifty dollars. I agreed on the price and told Kim to come with me. Before I left, I went back to lock up my car; I opened the stranger's car door and told Kim to get in, and then I hopped in behind her. As soon as I got into the car, I had to roll down the windows to let fresh air in, because of the strong smell of tobacco.

The driver's wife sat in front with him, and we headed for Summerville. It took us a while, but we found a fire station. We got out, I paid the man, and they drove off. The place was already crowded with needy people. I fought my way to the desk and talked to a fireman, who was looking at a pile of papers.

"Hello, my name is Linda Baer, and I need help," I said. "Can you please call a tow truck for me?" He wrote my name down and, without looking up, said, "You'll have to wait in line, miss."

"Thank you, sir," I said and squeezed myself next to Kim on a wooden bench. I was worried about my car but happy we were safe inside the fire station.

An hour later, I saw a tow truck arrive; I hoped it was mine, and it was. The fireman called my name and told me my help had arrived. I got up and signaled for Kim to follow me as I rushed towards the tow truck. The driver came to me and asked, "Are you the one who needs a tow truck?"

I smiled and said, "Yes sir, I am, and thank you for coming."

"I'm sorry you had to wait so long, but many others also needed help," he said.

"It's okay; I understand. I'm just happy you came to help me." I turned to Kim, who was hopping behind me, and I waved for her to hurry up.

The truck driver helped Kim into his truck, and I climbed up to the passenger seat and sat next to Kim.

The driver started his motor and asked me where to go as he drove out of the parking lot. I gave him the general location of my car, and he headed toward it.

The driver struggled through the debris until he found my car in the ditch. As we approached it, I was surprised to see those same four people still at the scene. They had pried open my car door and were still trying to pull it out of the ditch. When they saw us, they looked embarrassed, as if they were caught with their hands in the cookie jar. They stopped what they were doing and moved out of the way to let the tow truck get closer to my car. We all got down, and I walked toward those four.

"What were you guys doing with my car?" I asked.

"We were trying to help you to get your car out of the ditch," one of the men answered.

"Thank you, but I've found help," I said, "so could you please move your car out of the way and let the tow man do his work."

I could tell my tow man listened to my conversation, but he said nothing.

After they all moved, the tow man got into his truck and positioned closer to the back of my car. He hooked up the towing rig, and in one easy pull, my mud ball was out of the ditch and back on the road again. I was so happy and ran to thank him.

He whispered to me without the four strangers hearing it. "Do you know those people?"

"No, I don't," I replied. "They're just strangers who offered to help me earlier."

"If you don't know them, just be very careful!" he said again as he unhooked his chain and then put it away. I didn't understand why he warned me, but I soon forgot all about it.

"How much do I owe you?" I asked.

"I will send you a bill," he said. "Just give me your address."

"Yes, sir, I will, and thank you again," I said as I handed him my address.

"You are very welcome," he said. "I'll guide you out of here and make sure you're back on the freeway."

"Thanks again."

He hopped up into his truck and turned it around. Kim and I got in my muddy car, and I turned the engine on; thank God, it started! I rolled down the window and stuck my head out. "Thank you all so much for helping me," I said to the four strangers and was just about to put my car in gear. When they realized I was about to leave, all four of them panicked, ran out in front of my car, and held on to the hood to prevent me from moving. I was confused and didn't know what they were doing.

"You told us you would take us to Charleston," one man said. "Now can we follow you?"

"Why?" I asked. "Don't you know your way home?"

"No, we don't live here," the other man said. "We came to help an old lady friend, whose house was badly damaged, and her phone line is down. She needs our help."

"Oh, I see," I replied.

"Since the hurricane," a woman added, "the police won't let us enter town unless we live there." She showed a sad face. "We tried several times already, but the police kept stopping us. Our friend really needs help, but we can't get into town to help her."

I felt bad for them. "Okay, you guys," I said. "Follow me!"

Before they moved out of my way, one man instructed, "If the police ask, tell them we are your relatives; it's the only way we can get through the checkpoints." I didn't answer him and put my car in gear.

I was confused and didn't understand why they wanted me to lie for them, but since they helped me, I thought it was fair to help them back.

The tow man was waiting for me with his truck's engine running; he didn't move until he saw me moving. I followed him, and the four got back into their cars and followed me and my mud ball.

As soon as we neared the freeway entrance, the tow truck driver honked his horn, and I honked back; he veered to the left, and I continued toward the freeway on the right. At the freeway entrance, there were a lot of police vehicles scattered about, blocking my path, and I slowed down. Two officers walked out to the middle of the road and held up their hands. I stopped my car. I rolled down my window as they approached me, and one of them asked, "Where are you headed, miss?"

"I am trying to get home, officer," I replied.

"Where do you live?"

"In West Ashley."

"Do you have identification to prove you live there?" he questioned.

"Yes, officer," I replied and gave him my driver's license, but it was not enough. So I gave him my business card; he looked at it for a few seconds, and he let me go. Before I had a chance to move, the two men who were following me rushed over to my car.

"Hey, cousin," one said.

"Please tell the officer that we are with you."

"Oh yeah! I forgot," I said.

"Are they with you?" the police asked me.

"Yes, officer, they are with me," I answered. The police told the two men to get back into their cars, and he talked to me alone.

"Well, ma'am, how do you know those people? And you have to tell me the truth."

"I met them earlier, when I was stuck in the ditch; they were there and tried to help me," I explained.

"Do you think they were there to help you?"

"Yes, I think they were."

"Do you really know who they are?" he asked.

"No, I don't know them personally," I said. "But they seem like nice people."

"No! They are not! They are looters! They were here earlier, but we didn't let them through," he explained. "They are using you to try it again. I'm glad you told me the truth, or you could be in trouble."

"What did you call them?" I was confused.

"Looters!" the policeman replied.

"What is a looter?"

"They are thieves, dishonest people, and will do anything to get their hands on your possessions and money," he explained.

"But they seem so nice."

"Do you know why they're here? They are here to rob and steal. They know most people are out of town, and they are trying to take advantage of a bad situation. They are up to no good."

"Now I understand," I told him. "But could I just pay them for helping me earlier?"

"Are you sure they were helping you?"

"Since you explained it to me, I'm not so sure," I said. "They did pry my car door open while I was away looking for help."

"Ah hah! You see what I was trying to tell you?" He rolled his eyes and nodded his head.

One of the impatient men approached us; the policeman immediately put his right hand on his revolver and held up his left hand, to stop the man from coming any closer.

"Can we go now?" the man asked the policeman.

"You sure can!" the policeman said. "Just go back to where you came from."

"Cousin! Didn't you tell the police we are your family?" he barked at me.

"She did." The police covered up for me.

"Can I give him some money?" I asked the officer.

"If you must," the policeman said as he backed away and motioned for the man to come to my car. I opened my purse, took out sixty dollars, and handed it to the man.

"Thanks for helping me," I said. "I'm sorry I couldn't bring you into town."

Just then, he grabbed the sixty dollars from my hand. As I was about to drive away, he yelled, "Lady! You broke your promise; you didn't tell the police we are your cousins. You are no-good!"

I was shocked and confused to see the man turn from good to bad in an instant. I wished then I hadn't given him the sixty dollars.

"Well, at least I'm not a thief!" I yelled back as I entered the freeway and headed back to Charleston.

The closer we came to the city, the more damage we saw. I drove carefully toward West Ashley to avoid the debris.

Once I was inside my subdivision, I didn't recognize it. I peered around into the twilight and saw trees on top of trees; a huge one had fallen on my neighbor's house and crushed the roof. I drove past my own house, which was unrecognizable. Most of the trees were down and the brown paint was chipped off, showing the old yellow underneath. I backed up my car and parked on the street, behind Don and Eddie; I told Kim to stay put, and I got out. I looked down at my watch and saw it was five in the morning. I looked up at our roof and saw a part of it was gone. I fought my way through fallen trees to get to the front door. Since Don and the kids were already home, I assumed they were probably asleep. I knocked on the door, and Don opened it almost immediately.

"Where on earth have you been?" he asked. "I've been worried sick about you."

"It's a long story, but right now, I don't have time to explain," I said. "Will you please call Kim's husband and tell him to come over to pick up his wife? I am really tired, and I don't feel like taking her home."

"I can't call anybody," Don replied. "The telephone lines are down."

"Oh no! I'll have to take her home," I grumbled.

"Where is she?"

"Out there in my car," I said.

"Where is your car?" he asked again.

"Out on the street. I parked right behind you," I said as I pointed to it.

"No! I'm talking about your 300ZX."

"That's my car; it's just a little dirty right now. I'll be right back; I have to take Kim to her house," I said as I started to walk away.

"Do you know what time it is?" Don asked.

"I'm fully aware of what time it is," I snapped, "but there's nothing I can do about it, except take her home. See ya."

"No, you can't take her home," Don said. "Your car isn't built for it. I'll take her home in the Ram Charger. I'm just happy to see you home safe."

"Thanks. So am I!" I cracked a hint of a smile, and it was my first true smile since the day before.

"If you take her home, can I go with you? I want to check on my salon after you drop her off."

"Okay, if that's what you want."

It took us almost one hour to travel five miles to her house and back. After we dropped her off, I was too tired to go to my shop; I asked Don to drive me home instead.

I planned to change my clothes and lay down for a while, until I had enough energy to check out the animals. But I fell sound asleep.

When I awoke, I got up and went outside. I went to check on the animals first, and they looked fine; I fed them, gave them water, and went back inside.

Everything inside the house was intact, but the outside needed a lot of work. I turned the sink faucet on to wash my hands, but nothing came out. I turned on the light switch, but there was no electricity. I realized we had more problems than just the telephone.

While everybody still slept, I went to my salon. I parked the car, got out, and looked at the roof; I saw part of it was blown away. I opened the door and went inside to check out the utilities, and to my surprise, they all still worked. I went home and let my family know the good news, and for days, we took turns going to the shop to use the phone, bathroom, and shower. My salon opened not only for my family but also for friends and clients. During this time, most of the grocery stores were also closed, and those that were open were pretty much empty. Although I did have running water in my salon, the government warned that it was contaminated. They said the storm broke the sewage pipes, and the sewage might be mixed in with the drinking water. So, our family took turns lining up in front of the Red Cross trucks every morning for bottled drinking water.

Our two freezers full of food started to thaw out, and I was afraid the meat and fish would turn bad before we would have our electricity back. I decided I needed to cook it all. I made Don and the kids drag firewood from the backyard to the house and pile it up high. Next, I asked them to help me build a fire pit with concrete blocks. I filled the pit with wood and showed the kids how to light it. First, I burned the wood to make charcoal, and then I used it to cook up all of the thawed-out food.

I cooked far more than my family could eat, and since there was no refrigeration, I contacted my friends and the kids contacted theirs. Soon, our friends and neighbors all joined us and shared our food.

I felt bad for most of our friends, who were lost without their modern conveniences. We were very comfortable without electricity and phone service. It was like camping in our own backyard.

Hurricane Hugo did a lot of damage. We had to replace two roofs, one on our home and one on the shop, and repaint both of them.

We lost most of our fruit-bearing trees and many huge oaks around our yard. The storm destroyed my garden.

Sadly, my koi pond was destroyed, and all of the koi were out to the sea; luckily, most of my two-legged animals survived.

We had water and phone service after two weeks, but it was six or seven weeks before we had electricity. For my family, it was not a big deal, but I knew it would take a long time for Charleston, and the state of South Carolina, to get back to normal.

Chapter 18

WELCOME HOME, DAUGHTER

IT HAD BEEN almost fifteen years since I last saw my parents; I loved them and missed them so much. After the Vietnam War, refugees could not return to their own country, and I lost communication with my family; I didn't know what happened to any of them or whether they were alive or dead.

I hoped and prayed every day that I could see or hear from them again. My prayer was answered while we lived in California, before we moved to Charleston. One day, I went to the mailbox and found an odd letter addressed to me. I opened it, and inside there was another unopened envelope from Vietnam. It was from my parents. I was so excited; my hands were shaking as I began to read it.

"Loan, our dearest daughter," the letter began, "we hope you, your husband, and your children are alive and well. We wanted to let you know we are all alive, but very thin." This meant they didn't have enough to eat. Tears welled in my eyes, and I continued. "The land you left behind for us to use is being cared for by our government, but we do get some fruit from it." They were letting me know the government taxed my fruit farm with a heavy hand, and they didn't get much out of it.

"How are you, our son-in-law, and our grandchildren doing? We hope and pray you and all are fine and healthy. We miss you and love all of you so much. I cry each time we talk about you," Mother said. "Write to us as soon as you receive this letter. May God, Mother Maria, and Saint Joseph always protect you and your family." My tears flowed like a river; I wiped them as I folded the letter and tucked it into my pocket.

My parents knew my husband's and my children's American names but were afraid to mention them. They worried that if the Government knew their daughter was married to an American, they might be considered traitors and punished.

While I was in Vietnam years ago, I heard many horror stories about the torturing of women who were married to or lived with an American near Viet-Cong territory. A friend of mine told Mother and me about a woman who lived with her American boyfriend. The Viet Cong kidnapped and tortured her to get information about her American boyfriend's military activity, but she didn't know anything about it. They dipped her face into a pot of boiling grease; her skin peeled off, and the grease blinded her.

I was sure a story such as that one would scare my parents enough to conceal our American names. I wrote back to them, but I chose my words very carefully to avoid endangering them. We began to write to each other often, but we just asked each other about our health and well-being, and that was it—not much about anything else. When we read the letters, we had to fill in the blanks to understand the hidden meanings. We had to avoid writing anything negative about the Vietnam government, and we were afraid we might never see each other again.

I sent money and gifts to my family often, but they never got them. What they received were leftovers from airline workers, government authorities, mailmen, and thieves. I was so frustrated each time I received a letter from my parents saying they didn't receive my gifts, so I stopped, even though I knew my family needed them. After my brothers and my sister came to America, the mail system improved, and we found different ways to send our parents money.

It was hard for us to return to our country, because the American government declared an embargo against Vietnam after the war. Right before Hurricane Hugo, I learned that some Vietnamese people found a way to return to visit Vietnam, even though the government would not issue exit visas for American citizens, like me, to go there. The yearning to see my old parents was strong, and it overcame my fear. I took the chance and planned to make a trip back there to see them, at all costs.

I used a Vietnamese travel agency to get my visa through Mexico and had to pay a great deal for it. I have no idea how they did it, but they issued me a visa permit to Vietnam and back to America. I didn't like to travel alone and asked a couple of friends to come with me. Before the trip, I bought everything I thought my family and relatives could use or need, including medicine, clothes, whisky, cigarettes, perfume, lotions, deodorant, soap, candy, and chocolates. I packed everything into three large suitcases and a couple of small bags. After so many years of separation, I couldn't wait to see my parents and give them a big hug.

Finally, my wait was over. Don took me to the Orlando Airport in Florida, where I met up with Kim and her daughter, who had decided to join us; after a quick breakfast, we were ready to board the plane. I was excited about seeing my parents, but at the same time, I was nervous about going back to Vietnam against our government's embargo.

The flight was long; we went through Hawaii, the Philippines, Korea, and Thailand, and we had to fill out a lot of forms on the way. We had to take an indirect route, because the Vietnamese government forbade Americans to enter their country, just as America forbade them to come to the US. I believed they were afraid of spies, and I don't blame them. It was a dangerous journey, but I couldn't help myself; I missed my parents so much, so I took the chance.

More than forty hours later, we landed on an old, bumpy runway at Tan Son Nhut airport, near Saigon city. The pilot turned off the engines; I unbuckled my seatbelt and followed a large group of international passengers toward the door.

As soon as my foot touched the doorstep, the humid heat, mixed with the familiar smell of gasoline and kerosene, hit me in my face to welcome me home.

I took a moment to look around and recognized many old, empty American buildings scattered throughout the airport. They were once so busy with military people on the move. Now they looked sad, torn, and falling apart.

I walked down the steps onto the neglected, uneven cement ground; I heard a familiar language spoken around me. It had been so long since

I stepped foot on Vietnamese soil, but I felt as if I had never left. We marched like soldiers toward a large building, lined up, and waited to enter.

Once we were inside the hot building, we lined up again and waited to be processed. Suddenly, I had the urge to go to the bathroom. I looked around and saw the word *toilet* hand-scribbled on a wall at the end of the long building. I told my friends to keep an eye on my things and walked toward it. I could smell human waste before I even opened the door. I gagged and almost walked away, but the need was urgent. What I saw was not a toilet but a pile of human waste, mixed with torn newspapers, filling up a small square room. I thought there must be a toilet underneath somewhere, but because there was no running water, the toilet must have stopped up. I didn't see any toilet paper and assumed people used newspapers to wipe themselves. I closed the door behind me and gagged all the way back to the processing room. Time passed, and I couldn't hold it any longer. I decided to go back to the toilet with a pack of napkins in my hand.

The toilet was even fuller than before, but I had no choice, unless I chose to wet my pants; I tiptoed over the mountain of waste to relieve myself. When I finished, I ran out in a hurry.

The wait to be checked in took longer than expected. The airport workers delivered all the suitcases by hand and stacked them high in the middle of the building. I picked out mine, lined them up together, and then stood back to stare at them. I realized there was no way I could carry everything by myself, and there was no cart to use. I needed help. I looked around, saw a skinny young Vietnamese worker in the distance, and waved to him. When he came within earshot, I asked, "Can you please help me move my suitcases to the check-in booth? I'll pay you for your help," I said.

"Oh yes! I sure can," he answered cheerfully, as if he really needed the tip. It took him two trips to carry all of them, but before I paid him, I told him to wait for me because I would need him again. After my passport and visa were stamped, I asked him to carry my luggage to the customs checkpoint.

"Anywhere you want, ma'am," he said as he took my suitcases and lined them up on the floor at the checkpoint. I paid my helper, thanked him, and he left with a big grin.

Just then, a middle-aged man came over to me with a sour face and demanded I open my purse. After he thoroughly searched my purse, he ordered me to open all of my luggage; I did what I was told. He looked through everything. I stood in silence, staring in amazement as he took some of the gifts out. I saw him stack two cartons of cigarettes on the floor, three bottles of medicine, one bottle of Jack Daniels Whiskey, and several bottles of rubbing ailment to the side. I was confused by what he was doing with my things, until he looked up at me from the floor and asked, "You don't mind me keeping these, do you?" His question was a hidden demand.

"Why are you taking my family's gifts?" I asked.

"I need the medicine for my sick mother," he said, "and the cigarettes are for me and my bosses."

His demands stunned me, and I didn't know how to react. I replied in confusion, "I bought those for my old, sick parents too; why are you taking them?"

"I'm not taking them," he growled. "I asked you for them."

"What if I say no?"

"If you say no," he threatened, "I'll have to take you to the private room, where you will have to deal with a more thorough search and pay tax collectors."

I raised my voice and said, "Tax? I bought these gifts for my family; I'm not selling them!"

Kim and her daughter came to me, and one of them whispered in my ear, "Let him have it; we already went through this with the other agents."

"If you don't pay the bribe," Kim whispered, "I know he will put you through hell on earth before you can get out of this airport; it's not worth the fight."

"Welcome back to Vietnam," I said to them. I gave the man what he wanted. He took my possessions and disappeared into the crowd. My friends went back to their possessions, and I looked down at the big mess on the floor.

Instead of repacking everything neatly, I just threw my stuff together and tried to close the suitcases, but I couldn't. I took part of the things out and stuffed them back several times. I pushed and pressed them as I tried to close down the top, but it was impossible. It seemed as though everything in my suitcases had gotten ten times bigger. It wouldn't close. I was frustrated, hot, and sweaty; I was about to cry, when I heard someone call my name.

"Loan oi! Loan oi!" I looked up and recognized Hen and Bao, my stepbrother and my cousin. I was so excited to see them, and for a minute, I forgot my suitcase problems. When the excitement calmed down, I told them about the search and why I couldn't close my suitcases. "It's normal at this airport," he said. I looked at him and frowned. "Especially for those coming back from America," they both explained. I looked at them in disbelief.

"Can you guys help me push everything back inside and close the lids?" I asked Bao and Hen.

"All of those?" my stepbrother exclaimed.

"Yes, all five of them," I smiled.

"What are you trying to do, bring America home with you?" cousin Bao asked.

"Looks like I was trying to, doesn't it?" I said, laughing. We talked and laughed as I helped them stuff things back into my suitcases. As hard as we tried, we still couldn't close all of them, so we just let them stay ajar and dragged them behind us. I followed Hen and Bao outside, where they said the rest of my family members were waiting.

Under the hot, burning sun, I saw hundreds of people standing outside of a three- or four-foot rusted iron fence. In the middle of the crowd, I spotted my mother! She could barely stand because of her recent stroke. She had one hand over her head to protect her from the blazing sun, and she waved to me with the other; her big smile caused her eyes to disappear under her eyelids. I dropped what I had in my hands and rushed toward her. As I came within reach, she held out her arms over the fence, and we both grabbed each other's necks, trying to pull each other closer as we cried.

"Mother, oh. Mother," I mumbled, "it has been so long; I thought I would never have the chance to see you again," I cried out loud.

"Thank God you are home," Mother sobbed. "I thought I would die without seeing you." We hung on to each other's heads over the fence and let tears of joy flow down our faces. With my eyes closed, I could hear my relatives talking to me and touching me, but I didn't want to let go of my mother.

"We need to get out of this hot sun and go home," I heard someone suggest. I knew Mother must have stood in the sun all day on her bad legs waiting for me; I couldn't stand to see her suffer any longer and reluctantly let go of her. Then I turned to each of my relatives and hugged them and introduced my friends to my family. We talked and laughed, while tears flowed down our faces, as we followed each other out to the parking lot.

Before I climbed into the waiting van, I said farewell to Kim and her daughter; we planned to meet up later. Mother and I entered a six-seat van: I sat next to her, holding on to her boney hands. The van moved through Saigon, which was busy and crowded with people coming and going. I was surprised to see the rundown buildings and messy streets. There were many bicycles, pedicabs, and motorcycles, but no cars. I found the city sad and somber. My mother and I didn't say a lot to each other, but we held hands. Now and then, we turned to look at each other and smile.

"Where are all the cars?" I asked Mother. Before she could answer, Cousin Bao, who sat in front with my nephew, answered me.

"The Russians and Chinese took them all."

"What do you mean?" I asked.

"It's a long story; you'll find out later," he said.

"Why doesn't the government make people clean up the street and paint their houses?" I asked. But before Cousin Bao had a chance to answer, my nephew, who was driving the van, took over.

"Because we don't have any money or time," he said, and then my cousin chimed in.

"We did have money at one time," he continued, "but our government took our hard-earned money to pay the Russians and the Chinese. Now we live in poverty and still owe everything to China and Russia." I could tell he was not too happy with the economy or the government.

"Why?" I asked.

"Did you forget about the Russians and Chinese helping the North take over the South and kick the Americans out of our country?" He was very sarcastic.

"I know they did, but why should we owe them anything?" I asked both my cousin and the driver.

"Do you think they would just help us because of their good hearts? Think again," my cousin said and then continued, "After the Americans left, Russia and China came to Vietnam and stripped us down to nothing, but it's not enough for them; they still want more." He gritted his teeth.

"Everything we do now goes to them," my nephew said. "They are blood suckers; they took our money, cars, trucks, boats, and all other four-wheeled vehicles. When there was nothing else to take, they started taking our furniture, appliances, and everything not nailed down."

"Wow! I didn't know they were so bad," I said.

"Yes, they are very bad!" my cousin said. "They didn't just take the material things; they took our daughters and our women too."

"Wow!" I exclaimed.

"And don't forget," my cousin added, "they also took our food, our life, our self-respect, and our pride. The price we paid for their so-called help has nearly destroyed us." My cousin ground his teeth in bitterness. I was heartbroken for my people, and I felt my country's pain.

I turned around, looked behind me, and saw three young teenagers sound asleep. I glanced over my right shoulder and saw Mother. With her eyes half-closed, she quietly mumbled her rosary. I squeezed her hand to let her know I loved her, and I let her go on with her prayers.

I turned back to my cousin and my nephew to continue our conversation about the conditions in our country and about their life and their family. It took us almost three hours to go sixty miles, because of the bad roads and traffic jams.

Finally, the van stopped in front of my parents' two-story home that I helped build many years earlier. But when I saw it again, it looked worn down, old, and sad. Tears pooled in my eyes as I followed Mother from the van.

My parents' home in Cat lo, near Vung Tau

I saw my stepfather rush toward me with a big smile; I ran to him and held out my arms to hug him, but he stopped and stepped back to avoid my hug. I remembered he didn't like hugs. Most people in Vietnam don't hug, and my stepfather was one of them. I put my arms down and smiled. He then stepped closer to me and patted me on my head and shoulders to welcome his long-lost daughter home. I patted him on his arms and let him know I loved him and missed him too. "How are you, Father?" I asked with a big grin as we walked toward the front door.

"I am good, daughter. How about you and your family?" he asked with a smile.

"Thanks, Father. We are all doing fine," I responded. "You still look young and strong, Father." I complimented him.

"Thanks, daughter. I am happy you are home. It has been fifteen years," he said.

I glanced around at the huge room full of furniture, which I bought right after the house was built; it was still there but was old, torn, and discolored from age.

"Come, sit down with me, daughter. Have some tea and relax from your long trip."

"Thanks, Father. I think I will," I replied and sat down on one of the old lounge chairs. I talked to my stepfather about my family as more relatives showed up. They patted my shoulder to welcome me home. In turn, I reached up to pat their arms to thank them and tell them I was happy to be home.

My stepfather looked at the luggage, smiled, and said, "Do you think you brought enough clothes with you?"

"No, Father, those are not all my clothes," I replied. "They are mostly gifts for you and everybody."

"Aww, I am happy you brought me gifts." He smiled big. "But you shouldn't have brought so much."

I smiled as I stood up and opened the largest suitcase; I knew it had many different kinds of gifts in it. I began taking the presents out; first I handed my stepfather two bottles of Johnnie Walker Scotch, two bottles of Jack Daniels Black Bourbon, four cartons of cigarettes, and a stack of money. After I was done with his presents, I started to give presents out to everyone. I glanced at my stepfather and saw him checking out his gifts with a satisfied grin on his face.

Everyone was so excited. I smiled as I watched them trying out their perfume, deodorant, makeup, and hand lotions. Some of them received clothes or tee shirts; I was laughing when I saw them put on their new clothes over their old ones. I was very happy to see they were enjoying my gifts.

When Mother walked into the room, I handed her a small stack of money, clothes, medicine, and a couple dozen bottles of her favorite Tiger Balm oil. She thanked me and took her gift to her bedroom with a grin.

My stepfather decided to share his cigarettes; he opened one carton and took out several packs. He removed the wraps and began lighting each cigarette himself; then he gave them to everyone, including me.

My relatives, with my stepfather's cigarettes in their hands, in 1989

Mother came back into the room and asked me to help her prepare dinner. I excused myself and followed Mother to the kitchen, built outside behind the house. It was an elongated building, separated into three sections. The toilet and shower were on one end; a wood-burning kitchen was on the other. In the middle, there was a large room holding a huge pig. I stopped in front of the giant sleeping animal.

"Oh, my goodness," I exclaimed. "How big is she?"

"I think the sow weighs over four hundred kilograms," Mother answered.

"Wow, that's close to nine hundred pounds," I commented. "She is big; what did you feed her? And what are you going to do with her?"

"I feed her a lot." Mother smiled. "She is my pet and is a big provider," Mother said. "The sow brings in a lot of money for our family."

"How does she do so?" I asked.

"Each time she has a litter, there is anywhere from ten to thirteen babies," she explained. "I raise them until they are big enough to sell to someone, who raises them as I do. Because I have an unusually large momma, my baby pigs are very desirable and bring in a lot of money; that's how I can afford to buy food for us."

"It sounds like something I would do if I lived here," I grinned. "Mother, I'm very happy for you," I said.

We walked into the kitchen, where I saw four large wood-burning stoves sitting on the cement floor and a large pile of wood in the corner. One of the stoves had a huge black pot sitting on top.

"What on earth are you cooking in that black pot, Mother?" I asked as I pointed to the huge pot.

"Oh, it's for the pig," she said, smiling. "I cook for her, give her a bath, and rub her belly."

Mother and me on my first visit in 1989

"When I die, I'd like to be reincarnated as your pig," I joked and was about to say something else to her but stopped when I saw a tall, skinny woman, about thirty-five years old, walk toward us. She dropped a bunch of grocery bags full of vegetables and food down to the cement floor, came in front of me, folded her arms together, and bowed deeply.

"*Con xin chao di* Loan," which means "I respectfully greet you, Aunt Loan." She said, "I am so happy to see you. I've heard so many good things about you; now I am glad to finally meet you."

"*Chao*," I replied, confused, but I didn't bow to her because of the way she addressed me. I knew she was on a lower rung in the family, and it would be inappropriate. I looked to Mother for help, and she smiled as she explained.

"Oh! This is Lan, your father's granddaughter-in-law," Mother explained. "She lives here with her husband and their four young children, three girls and a boy; they all help us with chores and run errands."

"Yes, yes, yes." Lan repeated herself as if she agreed with mother.

"My parents mentioned you and your family in their letters to me," I said, smiling. "I'm happy you are here to help them."

"Thanks to you and your good heart, I now live in the house you built," she said.

"No, I did not build this house," I said. "I just helped." I looked at my mother and winked at her.

"Excuse me," she said as she bowed to me once more. I nodded my head slightly, granting her leave.

After Lan left, Mother asked, "What do you want to eat this evening?" She smiled.

"Oh, Mother, you know I will eat anything you cook, because I know everything you cook will be delicious," I said.

"How about lemon blanched fileted fish on roasted rice powder, wrapped in fresh herbs with hot sauce dip?" she asked.

"Oh! You remembered my favorite food. Thank you, Mother."

In the afternoon, with help from Lan and our other relatives, Mother fed over twenty people for dinner, and everyone loved her food. After dinner, Father gave out more of his cigarettes.

It was an intolerably hot summer, and my parents didn't have an air conditioner; I felt like I was about to be roasted. I sent Lan to the store to purchase a large block of ice and placed it in a bucket filled with water; I soaked a towel in the cold water and applied it to my burning face and neck to cool off.

I stayed with my family for three weeks, and I couldn't remember one day without a visitor. I had more relatives than I knew I had and more friends than I could remember. They each came and expected small gifts from me. I gave away all the presents I brought with me and started giving away money, until my parents stopped me. My mother came to me first.

"You could give away an ocean, and it would still not be enough," Mother said.

"Yes, your mother is right." Father added, "Even if you gave away a mountain of money, it would not be enough, never enough, so you should save some for yourself."

"And save some for me too," Mother joked.

I thanked them both for looking out for me, but I saw so many poor people who were in need, and I couldn't help but give them all I had. I just wished I had more to give. Most Vietnamese people believed all Americans were rich, and by their standards, we were. An old friend of mine, who was a teacher, came to see me and told me he made two hundred dollars a year. I told him American waiters, waitresses, maids, janitors, and garbage collectors made ten times more in a month than he did in one whole year. I couldn't help feeling deep sympathy for my friend, and I felt sad for my poor people.

While living with my parents, I redid their kitchen and bought them new cooking equipment, including a gas-burning stove for cooking their meals, but Mother still used her wooden one to cook for her pig. I also remodeled their toilet to the more modern style.

After three weeks with my parents, I decided to visit other parts of Vietnam that I couldn't while the war was still on. I talked to my parents at the dinner table one day and asked them to take a trip around the country with me. Mother wanted to go, but my stepfather turned it down, saying he was too old to take such a long trip. Since he couldn't go, I asked him for permission to go by myself, and he was okay with it. Mother still wanted to go, so we asked my stepfather if she could go too.

Although my stepfather mellowed somewhat over the years, he was still in charge of the family, and none of us dared try to overrule him. He was very reasonable compared to the past, when we couldn't discuss anything with him. We all just did what we were told. I remember once, my stepfather had several guests from out of town, who were at our home for medicine. They wanted to go to the south side of Vung Tau but were confused about the directions and asked my stepfather how to get there. My stepfather seemed lost and couldn't tell them where to go. I was sweeping the floor nearby, and I overheard the conversation. Without being asked, I chimed in and told them how to get there. Out of the corner of my eye, I could see my stepfather glaring at me; I knew I was in trouble. The guests thanked me and left. As soon as they left, he rushed to me and slapped me so hard I felt my teeth rattle.

"Who asked you?" he growled, and before I could say I was sorry, he slapped me again with the backside of his hand and left the room, leaving me standing there in tears, holding a broomstick in one hand and rubbing my face with the other. I could feel the imprints of his fingers crisscrossing my face. I was fifteen.

THE NEXT DAY, a large white van, with a driver, parked in front of our driveway, waiting for us to get in. Twelve of us, mostly girls, squeezed into a van that was only supposed to seat eight. Sadly, my mother decided not to go, or my father might not have allowed her to. After saying goodbye to my parents, we started our trip.

We went as far south as the border of Cambodia, and from there we traveled up through the center of the country, to Nha Trang and Dalat. We spent time at beaches, parks, zoos, aquariums, and museums. It was nice to see my country without war for a change. Everywhere I went, people were so nice to me. I don't know how they knew I was a visitor, but the street vendors and salespeople were especially sharp at knowing who I was. They took one look at me and jacked up their merchandise price. They called people like me *Viet Kieu*, Vietnamese who lived abroad; they also thought we were easy targets. When I asked the salespeople why they charged the *Viet Kieu* more than they charged the people who lived in Vietnam, their answer was, "*Viet Kieu* are rich and they can afford it."

I tried to disguise myself, because I didn't want to pay extra for everything, but somehow, they knew; they always knew.

I remembered, when I was younger and lived in Saigon, I did the same thing as the vendors. I jacked up the price of my black-market merchandise and charged more to foreigners, including the poor GIs. Now I understood how it felt to be a foreigner.

I didn't blame the poor people who tried to make money from me. If I could, I would help them more. However, I could only do so much.

As I traveled around the countryside, I saw thousands upon thousands of poor people living with their families in tiny shacks, built right on the edge of the busy highway. Some of the shacks had coconut leaf or king grass stalk for roofs, while others were covered with cardboard boxes or rusty corrugated tin, and they all looked as though they were coming apart. From the moving van, I wondered how these people could survive and where their food came from.

Children playing dangerously close to a busy road

In the western part, near Nha Trang, six people, plus a newborn, lived in this shack.

I was surprised to see those poor children playing happily together. I saw them running around, chasing each other right on the road. I smiled as I watched them, but at the same time, I held my breath, hoping they wouldn't run out in front of our van. I thought of those children and their future, as the van passed, and wondered what they would be when they grew up. Could they become somebody important, like a president or ambassador? Would their lives be better than their parents'? Would they remember their hard life? Seeing their poverty made me feel guilty for having all the food I could eat and all the clothes I could wear. I closed my eyes, sending my best wishes to them; I hoped and prayed that their life would be better than their parents', or as least as lucky as mine. I was glad to see so much of my country, that I'd never had the chance to see because of the war. But seeing the tragic conditions most people had to endure saddened me, and I wished I could do something to help them.

I RETURNED TO my family in Vung Tau, after two weeks of sightseeing. I asked my stepfather for his permission to take Mother to Saigon to meet up with my two friends for a weekend; it was granted, and we all had a great time. Six weeks later my visit was over, and I was packing to get ready to return to America. As I knelt on the floor, folding my clothes, I heard, "Loan oi!" Mother called me from behind as she walked into the room, crying.

"It's over," Mother sobbed. "Six weeks came and went so fast. I feel like you just came home yesterday." I stood up from the floor and hugged her.

"I know, Mother. I feel the same way." Tears pooled in my eyes. "I promise you, I will come home to see you again soon; next time, I will bring your son-in-law with me."

"That is more than I could ask for," she replied. "Oh, I almost forgot," she said and left the room in a hurry. A few minutes later, she returned with an armful of dried food and souvenirs. "Wait! I have more," she said and left the room again. It took her several trips. "I want you to take all of these with you and give them to everybody as a gift from me." She smiled.

"Mother, you want me to take all of that back to America?" I questioned.

"Yes, please," she replied.

"No, I can't," I said.

"Why not? Take them for your husband, children, brothers, and your sister too," she instructed.

"No, Mother, I cannot take all of them. They are too heavy." I raised my voice, "You take them back to the store where you bought them, and get your money back. We don't need all of these things; we can buy them in America." I tried to convince her.

"I want you to take my gifts, not just for you but for others too," she said.

"Mother, I know you spent a lot of money on these things," I said. "I want you to keep your money for a rainy day." I lectured her. "Did you use all of the money I gave you for these, or did you already give it all away, like you always do?" I asked roughly.

"Daughter!" she replied sternly. "If you gave money to me, it is mine; I can do whatever I want with it.

Her words reminded me that I was her daughter and shouldn't have talked to her that way. I felt bad for questioning her; I had been gone for far too long, and I forgot my manners. "Mother, I am very sorry for using my loud voice, but I just want you to save what is yours," I said softly.

She looked straight at me with her stern but loving eyes. "My daughter," she lectured, "if I give things away, I still have it, but if I used it, it would be gone."

"But how, Mother? I don't understand," I said.

"It's like this, daughter," she explained. "If I give my gift to someone else, each time they use it, they will remember me and my gift, which means I still have it. But if I use it on myself, it will be gone, and I won't even remember what I did with it or when and where I used it or what I used it for."

"I see now, Mother," I said as I touched her boney hands, raised them up, and pressed them against my cheek. "Please forgive me and my bad manners." She just smiled and said nothing. I was so thankful for her lessons.

Hours later, I was done packing and was ready for the next day's trip home. I put the suitcases in a corner along with a dozen palm coolie hats and many handwoven bamboo baskets, which I planned to carry on the flight.

The whole family stayed up talking all night; Mother shared her feelings about her children being so far away. And although she was sad, she was happy we lived in the United States and had happy lives.

For years, we tried to bring my parents to America to live with us; Don and I prepared the sponsorship papers, and the American Government had already accepted them, along with my stepbrother Hen and his family, but they all turned the offer down. My parents told me the reason they changed their minds was because they were too old to come to America and burden us. They made the decision to stay behind with my stepbrother and their relatives. I was sad and disappointed, but I understood. All of us siblings got together and sent money to help my parents with their food and their caretakers. Who knows what they would have done if they didn't have us.

The next morning, a van arrived to take me to the airport. I was in tears as I hugged everybody goodbye, except for my stepfather. I just stood in front of him to let him pat me on my head and say farewell.

"Don't forget to come home soon and bring your husband and children too," he said with red eyes.

"Yes, Father. I will," I said through my tears.

The driver helped me with my suitcases, but before I got on board, I turned to Mother and hugged her again for the last time; I could feel her body tremble from sobbing.

"Everything will be fine, Mother," I cried. "I promise you, I will be home again soon. Please don't cry anymore." I murmured, "I love you and will continue to pray for you every day."

"I pray for you all day, seven days a week," she cried.

I kissed her cheek and continued through my tears, "Thank you for your love and your prayers. I love you and will miss you every day."

I let go of her and ran to the van. As it pulled away, I turned back to look at Mother. I saw her bending down, with her hands cradling her face. Lan was standing beside her, holding her up. I felt so sorry for my mother; she gave birth to all five of her children and had twenty grandkids. But as she grew older and needed our help, we were a world away and not there to help her. I cried all the way to the airport and thought of the sacrifices my parents had made so that their children could have a better life.

I went through the checkpoints, had my passport stamped, sent my suitcases ahead, and sat on one of the benches with a pair of red eyes, waiting for my friends to show up. When my two friends arrived, I saw their eyes were just as red as mine. The speaker made an announcement, and we stood up and got on board. I dragged my body toward the plane, but my heart and soul were still back at home with my parents.

After we finally landed at Charleston Airport, I felt relieved as soon as I stepped out of the plane. Although I missed my parents in Vietnam, the American soil never felt so good under my feet; this was the land that gave me so much opportunity, freedom, security, love, and happiness.

Don was at the entrance, waiting for me as I stepped through the door. Smiling, he ran to me, lifted me up off my feet, gave me a bear hug, and whispered in my ear, "From now on, you are not going anywhere without me, period." He put me down and gave me a kiss on my lips.

"From now on," I replied with a big smile. "I don't want to go anywhere without you, period."

Chapter 19

SALON HUMOR

IT WAS GOOD to be home in my adopted country, which I am so proud to call mine. My worst day in America is still better than my best day anywhere else. This country provides me so many opportunities, made me who I am today, and has given me everything I have, and I will never take it for granted.

I was happy to be home and anxious to get back to my salon, to see everyone I loved. After my first visit with my parents, in 1989, Don and I went back to Vietnam to see them often and stayed in the country for six weeks each time.

In September 1993, Don and I celebrated our twenty-fifth anniversary and had a signing party for my first book, *Edge of Survival*, at the same time. We rented a huge National Guard armory building and invited eight hundred guests. Unfortunately, it was on the night that Hurricane Emily hit, and many guests didn't show up, but in the end, we had about five hundred guests.

Our twenty-fifth wedding anniversary party

I had finished *Edge of Survival*, but after unsuccessfully seeking a traditional publisher for two years, Don obtained a business license and became a publisher. He named it Ashley Publishing Company. I designed the book cover, and together we released my first book in 1993.

I brought a copy of my book back to Vietnam, and I asked my stepbrother to translate it to Vietnamese for my parents; they liked it and told me they were proud of me.

Each time I came back to work after being gone for six weeks, I was very busy and overwhelmed. Most of the clients didn't really need me, because my daughter and the other stylists were there while I was gone. However, the clients preferred to wait for me, not because my service was better, but because they wanted to chitchat, and I talked more than the other stylists.

I was forty-five, Don was fifty-six, and our beautiful daughter, Teresa, was twenty-one.

Maria was one of my hairstylists and a good friend. She was from Russia and had worked with me for almost twenty years. When she first came to work at my shop, her English was limited, but somehow, we understood each other perfectly. A funny thing was, whenever there was a client who didn't understand us, we would try to translate for each other. Maria always took over and explained to them what I was trying to say, and vice versa; that always made clients laugh, and our salon never lacked laughter.

Ruth was a client and a friend that had been coming to me for hair and nails more than twenty-five years. Ruth was about my age. She was very daring and always wanted to try out new things.

Ruth had an interesting habit: Whenever she came into the salon, she always lowered the chair before she sat down for a manicure, and as soon as her hands hit my table, she fell asleep.

One day I asked her, "How can you fall asleep so easily; do you have a sleeping problem?"

"No, I don't have a sleeping problem," she explained. "Your salon is warm, cozy, and comfortable, and besides, you are very gentle with my hands, which relaxes me. I don't go to sleep so easy anywhere else, even in my own home."

I smiled and said, "Are you sure I'm gentle? Or perhaps I'm too boring and cause you to fall asleep."

"Whatever!" she said and went to sleep

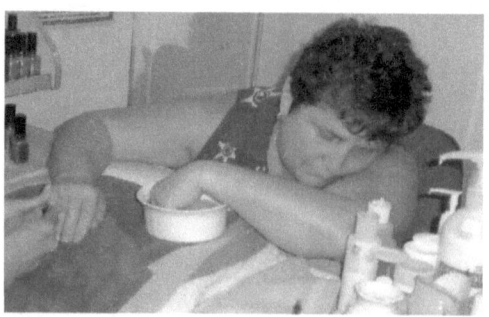

Ruth Oser, a sleeping beauty, was at my manicure table.

Ruth even slept through her haircut, coloring, or facial waxing. When I cut her hair, however, her sleep movements sometimes caused me to cut my own fingers with scissors, and I often needed a bandage. If Maria wasn't busy with her client, I would ask her to help me hold Ruth's head upright so I could cut her hair instead of cutting her ears or my finger.

Maria and I were joking with Ruth one day. "If you don't stay awake," I told her, "we're going to charge you double." Ruth didn't say a thing.

"Yes! Ruth," Maria chimed in, "it takes two of us to cut your hair, and the price has to be doubled." We both laughed, but Ruth ignored us and continued sleeping.

"Hey, Ruth!" I called to wake her up. "I'm serious; I'm definitely going to charge you twice as much."

"Whatever!" she said. "You charge whatever you want." And then she went right back to sleep. Ruth was not a quiet sleeper either; her snoring drew the attention of others in the salon, but they just looked at each other and smiled. All of my clients knew Ruth, and they loved her just as much as I did.

Once, Ruth watched us doing a manicure and pedicure service at the same time for a tall, slim tennis player, who didn't have time to have them done separately. Ruth thought it was a good idea and asked us to do the same for her. Unfortunately, Ruth was neither tall nor slim, but we decided to do what she asked.

While Maria was preparing to do Ruth's pedicure near my table, I was getting ready to do her manicure. When everything was set up for the double service, we asked Ruth to sit at my manicure table and turn sideways so Maria could do her pedicure. While Maria had Ruth's feet soaking in the pedicure bucket on the floor, I had her arm stretched over my manicure table. We both tried to work on her at the same time, but Ruth had a difficult time reaching both of us. If I held on to Ruth's short arms, Maria lost hold of her short legs, and vice versa. We couldn't help but to pull and push her arms and legs like a twisted pretzel. Each time I glanced at Ruth, I saw a pained expression on her face.

Her silence didn't last long, and she began complaining about the double procedure. Maria and I ignored her and kept on pulling and pushing on her hands and feet.

Ruth couldn't handle it anymore, and in frustration, she yelled for us to stop. "Hey, you guys! Listen!" She said, "You guys are killing me!" I looked at Ruth for a second and went back to my manicure.

Maria, on the other hand, was too busy doing Ruth's feet; she paid no attention to Ruth's complaints, nor did she look at the expression on Ruth's face. I overheard Ruth ask Maria to stop the pedicure, because it was uncomfortable for her, but instead of stopping the pedicure, Maria replied, "You are so spoiled. Just sit back, relax, and let us pamper you."

"Relax? I can't relax. You two are torturing me!" Ruth exclaimed.

"We're not torturing you," Maria said, without looking up at Ruth's face. "We're working hard to make you feel good."

"Please, Ruth! Sit back and enjoy yourself," I said.

"This is the most stupid thing I have ever done," Ruth complained. "I don't believe I have to pay to be tortured. I don't see how anybody could enjoy this."

By then, I had listened to Ruth long enough and glanced over my manicure table while still holding on to Ruth's left arm. I saw Maria holding on to Ruth's right foot, pointing it toward the ceiling.

"Hey, Maria!" I called out. "Stop what you are doing and take a good look at poor Ruth's twisted body." When Maria looked up and realized what we had done to Ruth, she immediately put the foot down and began laughing.

"Oh, I'm so sorry, Ruth," Maria said. Ruth looked disappointed but said nothing. I laughed as I chimed in.

"Hey, Ruth, if you were only a foot taller, we wouldn't have this problem," I said to her as we continued to try to finish with her double services.

"Whatever you say, Linda," she snorted. "But you know, I am not going to pay for this torture." Ruth looked mad, but Maria and I were both laughing. The more Ruth complained, the harder Maria and I laughed.

"Linda!" Ruth growled again. "You know I am not going to pay for this stupid service, right?"

"Ruth, you don't have to pay us with your money today," I said giggling. "We've already been paid with laughter." Ruth kept a straight face and wasn't amused by us, but she did pay us in full that day.

NOT TOO LONG after the manicure-pedicure incident, Ruth came in to get her hair highlighted. I always did her hair with combinations of a golden-bronze tone. She loved it and received many compliments. But for some reason, that day Ruth wanted to change her hair color. She wanted platinum highlights to replace her golden ones. I advised her against it.

"Your hair is beautiful the way it is now, Ruth," I said. "Why do you want platinum? Your hair base is jet-black," I explained. "It is hard for me to make it platinum; I would have to bleach your hair out for a long time to get it close to platinum, but it would never be platinum. I thought you liked the golden highlights."

"I like my hair the way it is now," she replied, "but I just want a change. I want to be different. I want platinum highlights," she insisted.

I was reluctant, but I did what she asked. Of course, Ruth went to sleep the moment I touched her hair. It took me a long time to get her jet-black hair as light as she wanted it, but I had to stop the process before her hair fell out. After I shampooed her hair, the highlights looked lighter against her black hair, but not quite white. I blow-dried her hair, and when it was done, her hair looked almost silver. I woke her up.

"Oh, thanks, Linda!" Ruth said, before she opened her eyes.

"You're welcome," I replied, smiling, as I turned her toward the huge mirror.

She opened her eyes wider and screamed, "Oh, good grief, Linda! What have you done to my hair?"

"I just did what you asked me to do, Ruth," I replied. "I gave your hair platinum highlights. I am sorry. It might not be as white as you wanted, but I'll try to make it whiter the next time."

"Whiter?" she exclaimed. "I didn't want my highlights to be whiter; I just wanted them to be platinum." She said, "This is silver! And this color makes me look older!" She was very upset.

"Ruth, I thought this is what you wanted," I said. "This is as close to platinum as I could get. Platinum is silver, and this is the best I could do."

"I don't want this white," she said. "I thought platinum was a golden blond. I didn't know it was white."

"Your hair had golden-blond highlights before," I explained. "I tried to give you platinum, as you asked."

"I look old!" she said sadly. "It looks like I have grey hair."

"That's how platinum, looks against black hair. I thought that is what you wanted, Ruth." I pointed at her diamond ring and explained, "Look at your diamond ring; it's either in silver, platinum, or white gold."

"Sorry, Linda, I didn't realize," she said. "I hate this color. Please, change my hair back to my old color for me!" An hour later, her hair was back to her previous color, and she was happy again.

"From now on, Linda," she said with a grin, "you do my hair the way you think is best for me." I smiled.

I COULDN'T REMEMBER if it was Wednesday or Thursday when Kelly came to get her regular monthly bikini wax. As usual, she stripped naked from the waist down and lay on my waxing bed. I prepared her with baby powder around her bikini area for protection from the heat, and then I applied the hot wax; I had to work fast before the wax cooled and hardened. After I applied the wax, I turned around to get waxing papers to remove it from her skin. There were none. Someone had used the last one and forgot to refill them. I panicked and ran to the stock room to get more wax strips. I had to hurry before the wax hardened.

When I finally found the waxing paper, it was still on a big roll and not in strips. So I had to find scissors to cut it into strips. We had many scissors in the salon, but they were all for cutting hair and nothing else; they were delicate and very expensive. Some of them cost hundreds if not thousands of dollars. I couldn't use them for cutting waxing paper. I ran around like a chicken with its head cut off, looking for the regular scissors. I asked the other stylists, but they were all busy with their clients, and no one could help me. Finally, I found an old pair and started cutting smaller strips from a big roll. With a handful of waxing paper strips, I rushed back to the waxing room.

Kelly still lay on her back, but instead of her legs spread, as I'd left her, she'd grown tired from waiting and put her knees together. The wax had cooled and hardened between her legs, gluing them together. I tried to pull her legs apart, but it was useless. In desperation, I ran back to my styling station and grabbed a hair dryer. I plugged it into the wall socket and turned it on low heat. I held the hair dryer several inches from her pubic area to warm up the wax and hoped it would melt.

"Kelly, I am so sorry," I said.

"It's okay, Linda. It's not your fault," she replied, smiling.

"Don't worry," I comforted her. "I think the hair dryer is working."

Kelly slowly opened her legs, inch by inch. When her legs were open, I saw her pubic hair all tangled up in one big knot! "Oh, my goodness!" I mumbled to myself. "This is a big mess!" I tried again to melt the wax between her legs and untangle her pubic hair. Holding the hair dryer in my right hand I picked off the wax slowly with my left, one hair at a time. It took me much longer to do my waxing job than normal, and I could hear my next client's voice in the waiting room. I was panicking and tried to work on Kelly even faster. Becky, my next client, was a very impatient lady. Instead of waiting for me outside, she went back to the waxing room to look for me. Earlier, when I was running around looking for the scissors, I'd come back to the waxing room and forgotten to lock the door. Becky saw the door was ajar and walked in, right in the middle of me bending down between Kelly's spread legs. I looked up, just in time to see Becky with both of her hands over her mouth, trying to prevent her from screaming, as she ran out of the waxing room.

"Becky! Becky!" I yelled. "It's not what you think."

Chapter 20

MOTHER'S DEPTH

IN 2001, DON and I took our vows in church for the first time, after thirty-two years of marriage. We exchanged vows not so much for Don and me but mostly for my parents' peace of mind. My mother believed that even though our marriage was legal, it would not be accepted in the Catholic Church. She said she could never rest until we were married by a Catholic priest. My mother was growing older, and I just wanted her to be happy and not worry about me going to hell.

Don and I renewed our wedding vows after thirty-two years of marriage. Betty Long was next to me, witnessing our vows.

After the church ceremony, we all went to a restaurant to celebrate. We invited fifty guests to our party but ended up with about seventy-five.

*Minh Nguyen standing next to Don, witnessing our vows.
Mary Allen Brawn and Professor John are in the background*

Some of our friends heard of our party and came to celebrate. We loved them for it and wouldn't have changed a thing. We were blessed and fortunate to have such family and friends in our life.

Not long after our celebration, Don and I planned to take a trip back to Vietnam so we could show my mother pictures and video to prove we were married in the church. I knew it would make her very happy to know her wish had come true.

It was still a long trip, but it was much better than a few years earlier, especially since President Clinton removed sanctions against Vietnam.

When we arrived at Mother's house, I could tell she was not feeling well by the way she looked and acted. Her stroke had paralyzed half of her body, and my stepfather had passed away. They were married for over fifty years. She'd also fallen and broken her arm and hip one month after his passing.

At the age of eighty-five, Mother was confined to a bed most of the time. And to make matters worse, all of her children lived a world away, including me. We siblings tried to visit her as often as we could, but the distance and the cost of traveling from America to Vietnam prevented us from going often. I still managed to visit her every other year and stay with her for at least six weeks each time. Although she had relatives who lived near her and visited her often, I was sure she would love to have her own children with her.

Since we couldn't be there to take care of her, we sent money for whatever she needed and for those who helped take care of her. Physically, she was comfortable, but emotionally, I don't know how she handled it. She gave birth to and raised all five of us, but when she was old and needed us, we were not there to help her. Those who were taking care of her told me she often called for her absent children when she was feeling sad or sick. She would cry out loud and call for all of us by name, starting with me, down to my youngest brother. It broke my heart, and I cried whenever I heard those stories.

I wished my mother had come to America to live with us years earlier. The United States already accepted all of them and sent them a welcome pass to America, but my stepfather and his son changed their minds. After my stepfather made the decision to stay back in Vietnam, my mother had no choice but to stay behind with her husband. I understood her situation, but when her husband passed away, she was left by herself.

One night, Don and I were at the dinner table surrounded by relatives, who came because they heard we were back from America; they not only came to see us, but they also expected gifts. Mother always warned me before they arrived, "Remember, don't give all of your money and gifts away, because there will be more of them coming, and you'll need to save some for the latecomers." She repeated herself each time I visited her. I listened to her and stopped giving out too much in one day, but I wished I could afford to give more.

Since my stepfather died, my mother's health had worsened, but this time, something was different. As we sat there at dinner, I suddenly felt as if that would be the last time I would sit next to her. I don't know why I felt that way, but I did. The thought of losing my mother brought tears to my eyes; I left the dinner table and ran outside, crying. Some of the guests were concerned and came after me.

"What happened?" my cousin asked.

"Nothing," I told her. "It was too hot inside without an air conditioner, and I just needed some fresh air." I smiled, with tears running down my face.

In the daytime, I stayed with my mother at her house in Cat Lo, but at night, Don and I caught a bus or a taxi to a hotel in Vung Tau, where they had an air conditioner. It was about five or six miles from Mother's house, but due to the congestion, it often took thirty to forty-five minutes or more to get there. Sometimes, even in the daytime, we didn't come back to Mother's house and hung around in the city to sightsee instead.

Vietnam had changed a lot; each time we went back to visit, we saw more changes, from people's attitudes to economics and from the run-down Tan Son Nhut Airport to a modern one. Even the bathroom was transformed from a single, filthy, squat-down, plugged-up toilet to a multistall European-style restroom, with running water and toilet paper rolls, and the hot, stuffy, unfurnished waiting area turned into a nice, furnished, air-conditioned room with a bar and restaurant.

Don pedaling me on a pedicab, our last visit in Vung Tau

There were more stores, restaurants, and imported cars, and more foreigners on the streets. I also saw more skyscrapers pop up everywhere, especially in Saigon, and the price of everything went up as well. When I first visited Vietnam in 1989, a large bowl of any kind of soup was about ten cents. That ten-cent bowl of soup inflated to five and then ten dollars in 2002. Houses went from ten thousand to more than a million, according to some of my friends. Before, when I gave my parents a thousand dollars, they acted as if I gave them the whole world. I was sure a thousand dollars wouldn't go that far on this trip. The fruit farm Don and I bought for our investment before our evacuation in 1975 was worth hundreds of times what it had been; we decided to divide it among my relatives, including Cousin Bao, Lan, my stepsister, and my mom. Although Don and I could have used the money, we figured they needed it more than we did.

One good thing about Vietnam was the peace. We felt safe walking around on the streets without worrying about getting shot, bombed, or shattered by explosions. Unlike Vietnam, America had daily shootings on the streets, in schools, and in shopping malls.

Soon, we had to prepare to leave Vietnam again. A van waited in front of my mother's home to take us to the airport once again. It killed me to watch Don and my mother holding on to each other, crying. When Don let go of her, he ran to the van and slumped inside. I gave my mother a last hug. *This is it*, I thought. *The way my mother looks, I don't think I'll have another chance to hug her or see her again.* The thought of her dying kept going through my head as I squeezed her boney body and inhaled her scent for the last time. Tears blinded me as I let go of her. I stumbled to the van's door, and one of my relatives had to guide me to my seat. Before the door closed, I could hear my mother's last words.

"I love you and will pray for you both to get home safely." I was too choked up to answer her. I just bowed my head onto the palms of my hands to avoid looking back at her. I couldn't handle any more pain. It was never easy for me to leave my mother, but it was especially hard this time. After I returned to America, I kept in touch with her as often as I could, but I never had a dry eye when I hung up the phone.

Then, in the Lunar New Year of 2003, I received bad news: My mother had fallen ill and might not live. My sister and my youngest brother rushed back to Vietnam to be with her. I couldn't go. Don was having kidney stone problems, and he was in and out of the hospital. I decided to stay home and take care of him. That's what I told myself, but the truth was that even if Don had not been having kidney stone problems, I probably would not have gone; I didn't think I could handle the pain of watching my mother take her last breath.

The phone rang one afternoon, and I ran to answer it.

"Hello! Hello! Hello!" The static was bad, and I couldn't hear who was on the other end.

"This is Mom," she murmured. "How are you?" My mother was on the other end!

"I am fine, Mother. I am so sorry I'm not there with you. Don is having kidney stone problems," I cried.

"I understand," Mother mumbled. "I wish I could see you one more time before I close my eyes forever." She choked up.

"I know, Mother. I know," I cried. "Please, Mother, listen to me. If God calls you, please go with him, and I will see you later in heaven." I could barely get all of my words out.

"Are you sure you're not coming back?" she asked.

"I will later, Mother, but not right now," I said. "Mother, I love you with all my heart."

"I know you love me, and I love you too, daughter," she said and the phone clicked off.

Two hours later, I had another phone call from Vietnam; I thought Mother had forgotten to tell me something. But it was my sister calling to tell me my mother had just taken her last breath. After my sister's phone call, I cried a river, and I couldn't eat or sleep that night. The next day, I had another phone call from Vietnam; Khai, my brother, called to ask me something about Mother's funeral arrangements. While we were on the phone, I heard repeated loud banging. I asked, "What is all that noise?"

"Oh, that is the hammer hitting the nails to seal our mother's coffin," he replied.

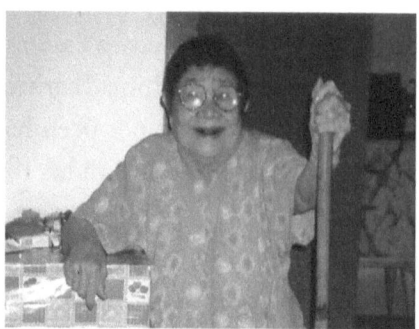

*Mother passed away on March 11, 2003,
soon after this picture was taken.*

After that phone call, I blacked out for three days. On the fourth day, I came to, and Don told me I'd had a blackout and acted as if I were in another world. He might have been right; I could have been with my mother in another world to make sure she was where she is supposed to be, and then I returned to Don, three days later.

Chapter 21

MY LIFE'S JOURNEY

IN OCTOBER OF 2006, Don and I went to Hawaii to celebrate his seventieth birthday. We packed everything we needed into two large suitcases and two carry-ons. Don saw me packing too many snacks and complained about the food; I didn't pay any attention to him and continued packing. Then he started laughing at me.

Family get-together at Don's 70th birthday celebration, before we went to Hawaii;
Nicky was 33, Teresa was 34, and Eddie was 40.

"Honey, we're only going for two weeks, for heaven's sake," he said. "Besides, everything we have here, they will have there as well; Hawaii is part of the United States, you know."

"Well, I know that, but I just want to make sure we have everything we need. I want us to have enough food to eat, just in case the plane crashes in the middle of the jungle," I explained, and Don laughed again. I ignored him. "Remember the one that crashed in the snow somewhere, and people had to eat dead people to survive; they made a movie out of it," I reminded him.

"Okay, honey, take what you want," he said. "I think it's ridiculous to bring the whole grocery store with you, but if you think we'll need it, go ahead." He gave up and walked away.

"I plan to," I said, smiling, and kept stuffing my suitcase tight with nuts, chips, all sorts of candy bars, and crackers. After packing, I went to bed.

We woke early and had a light breakfast with my brother Kinh, who was going to take us to the airport. Everything went well until we were inside the airplane; the engine had a malfunction and needed to be fixed. We sat and waited for what seem like forever before it took off. When we arrived in Houston, we were behind schedule and had to wait for a second plane.

The second flight, however, was canceled, due to mechanical problems, and we had to wait hours for the next one. By the time we arrived in Honolulu, it was late at night, and all we could do was walk around the Marriott hotel, looking for something to eat.

After a light sushi dinner, we walked to a store nearby to purchase two gallons of water to take back to the hotel with us; we always used filtered water for taking medicine when traveling. I put the water in the refrigerator, cleaned off my makeup, took a shower after Don, and went to bed. We were tired and both fell fast asleep.

In the middle of the night, a violent vibration shook the bed and woke me. I sat straight up and looked at Don; in the dim light, I could see he was sound asleep.

"Hey, Don! Wake up!" I yelled, "I just felt an earthquake." He didn't respond, so I tugged at him again.

"What, honey?" he said as he pushed himself up and rested on his elbow.

I repeated, "I just felt an earthquake, and I'm scared." I jumped out of bed and changed my clothes.

Don took his time sitting up in bed and said, "There are no earthquakes in Hawaii. You must have felt someone in the next room having sex," he joked and was about to lie back down.

"Don! Put your clothes on, just in case," I said. "I experienced enough earthquakes in Iran and California to know what it feels like; please get off the bed and put your clothes on!"

Right after my words, the room started shaking violently again; the bed moved back and forth and banged into the wall. All the doors and doorknobs were rattling, as if someone were trying to open them. At the same time, all the lights went off. Don was holding on to the baseboard, and I was holding on to him.

"Oh my God! Oh my God!" I yelled, "We are going to die, Don! The building's going to collapse, and a tsunami will take us out to sea." I shook like a leaf.

"Please be quiet, Linda. We'll be fine. Everything will be okay," Don said. "But you are right; that was an earthquake and a large one too." He sounded worried but tried to keep cool because he didn't want me to be any more hysterical.

"What are we going to do? Did you make out a new will before we left Charleston?" I asked, but before he had a chance to answer, the intercom began broadcasting, "We had an earthquake; everybody please do not panic, and go down to the lobby." It went on to say, "Everyone must be careful and use the stairs only; do not use the elevators. We will provide light from our generator in the stairwells, so just follow the light; it will take you down to the lobby."

Don found his clothes and put them over his pajamas while the intercom repeated the message over and over, urging guests to leave their rooms. It was dark, and we couldn't see our way to the door. I crawled on the floor, found my suitcase, opened it, and felt around for the flashlight. I knew I'd packed a small one earlier, but I couldn't remember where. When I found it, I turned it on, grabbed Don's hand, opened the door, and ran out. The hallway was already packed with frightened people, who were also searching for the stairway to flee to the lobby. In the dim light, I could see people of all ages and genders. Some were in their pajamas and nightgowns, while others wrapped themselves with only towels. Many women had smeared makeup, and their dark eyeliner ran down their cheeks. Thanks to strong hair spray, their hair stood straight up on end. It didn't matter how we looked, we were scared and tried to find our way down the steps. A few minutes later, we reached the lobby. Thank God we were staying on the fifth floor and not higher; I felt bad for those who were staying near the top of the hotel.

It was in the middle of October, but if you looked around in the lobby, you would think we were all dressed up for a Halloween party, especially those women who wore towels, with smeared makeup and messy hairdos. Too bad those women didn't have a martini in their hands; it would make a perfect picture.

The chaos went on for hours, but soon we all were tired, and one by one, went back to our rooms. Instead of going to sleep, Don and I went out to the balcony to investigate. It was dark, and all we saw were ghostly silhouettes of tall buildings.

"I wonder what else can go wrong with our vacation," I said as I stood next to Don.

"Well, at least we're alive," he said, smiling. "And remember, our vacation is not over yet."

"I guess you're right," I said as I tightened my lips in a hard line.

I looked down at the street and saw cars' headlights and panicking people running up and down, as if they were trying to compete with the cars. I felt sorry for all of the drivers, who had to use their horns to avoid hitting the pedestrians, trying to cross the chaotic streets without traffic lights. They all seemed to be rushing to get to somewhere, or perhaps they were like me, afraid of a tsunami. "Hey, honey," Don said. "I wanted to stay out here with you, but I'm really tired and can't keep my eyes open any longer; I guess I'll go to bed." He gave me a light kiss on my forehead and went back inside; I went to bed soon after him.

For two days, most of Honolulu was out of electricity and running water. Everything was closed, including all stores and restaurants. We couldn't go anywhere far or do anything except for walking around, looking through closed shop windows. When we were tired, we went back to our hotel room and dined on the snacks I packed.

From our hotel balcony, I watched people line up on the street, waiting to get into a small pantry store to get water bottles and snacks. The flow of customers was slow because the store clerk had to use a small handheld calculator to process each purchase. I could see and hear some impatient customers yelling and cursing at the slow-moving line. In spite of Don's wishes, we had snacks of all kinds to eat and plenty of water to drink. I felt bad for those people who lined up under the hot sun for a long time just for a bag of snacks. I felt like throwing them some of mine, but instead, I just watched them as I fed my crackers to the sea birds, which came right onto our balcony.

After three days of snacks for breakfast, lunch, and dinner, we were tired of it and wished for a hot meal. Our wish came true; the island came back to life, and we finally had a real, authentic Hawaiian dinner of Spam sandwiches and poi from taro roots. The Spam came from the can.

"This is the same kind of food we eat in America," I told Don while we ate lunch. "I thought we would eat Hawaiian food."

"Well, what do you think, Linda?" He smiled. "This is America."

"But I thought the food would be different," I said.

"Different cooks, perhaps," he said, grinning. "Well, there is a difference; instead of ham, you get spam." He laughed.

"Never mind," I replied as I rolled my eyes.

That was the only hot meal we had before we boarded the cruise ship on October 18, 2006; Don turned seventy years old that day.

*Don and me boarding the MS Norwegian Wind
October 18, 2006, on his seventieth birthday*

We were supposed to travel from island to island for ten days, but after a few days, the old ship lost one of its engines, and the giant could hardly move. It was too slow to visit all of the intended islands; instead, it just floated around in the ocean until the ten-day voyage was over. We all felt cheated, but none of us could do anything about it, except complain among each other. According to rumors, the old ship was to be sold to China after our trip. The poor Chinese people; I wondered if they knew what they were getting themselves into. Don and I spent a few more days in Honolulu after the ship landed. We visited factories, watched native shows, went to Mount Kilauea volcano, and ate a few real native dishes. In the end, the trip was great.

When we returned to Charleston, our family and friends were happy to see us, but they jokingly said they would never travel with us, because we were jinxes.

IT HAS BEEN thirty years since I opened my beauty salon. Many stylists and clients have come and gone, but many are still with me. They have become my family, and I still work on their hair and nails to make them more beautiful; Don has come to know most of them and loves them as well. He is very flattered by their love and attention and jokingly claims some of them as his girlfriends or wives; he's numbered as many as six wives and countless girlfriends.

Years ago, I formed a group of thirteen or more friends and called it *The Seasonal Women's Group*. I chose the name because, as I explained to them, "We are not too old but not too young either, and some of us have no intimacy, or if we do, we do it once in a while, similar to female animals, who come into estrus only once a season." The group had a good laugh, but they loved the name; the Seasonal Women's Group was born. We got together once a month, to go to restaurants or to each other's homes, to drink, cook, and eat.

One day, they all came to my house for a Vietnamese eggroll lesson from me. Since the party was in my house and since I was their cooking instructor, I had the authority to make the rules. My rules were simple:

1. You must try your best to make perfect eggrolls but must keep them separate from the others.

2. You must take your eggrolls home to your family after they are cooked, regardless of how ugly they look—no exception. They argued at first, but in the end, they agreed.

About ten or twelve amateur eggroll chefs were in my house. Some helped me clean vegetables, chop meat, and peel shrimp, while others just sat on their buns at my kitchen island, drank wine, and chitchatted. It was okay though, because I didn't have enough room in my kitchen for all of them anyway. When all the ingredients were prepared and ready to use, I divided them into equal portions for each chef. I gave each of them a bowl full of stuffing, a stack of eggroll wraps, and two large plates each; one plate was for rolling the eggrolls and the other for holding the finished ones. I showed them how much stuffing they needed in each roll, where to put it in the wrapping sheet, how to roll it, and how to seal it with egg white. But for one reason or another, they still asked questions about how, what, and where, even though I had demonstrated for them many times. Those who didn't ask questions were too busy talking, drinking, or fighting with each other over whose eggroll looked better.

When they became too rowdy and didn't listen to my instructions, I yelled, "Children! Stop the fighting and concentrate on how to make a perfect eggroll. If you don't stop arguing, I'll put you all in a corner for a time-out." They all laughed.

"Yes, chef! We will," Betty Long replied, and Ruth Oser gave me a dirty look. Linda Estee gave me a half peace sign, while others stuck their tongues out at me. Keep in mind, the youngest student in the group was forty-five, and the oldest was seventy-five. They were all well-educated, glamorous, and sophisticated, but not on my eggroll lesson day. They were obnoxious, unmanageable, and misbehaved.

"That's better," I said, smiling, as I walked around, checking to make sure they did it my way; then I went back to my own designated spot to work on mine. At the same time, I kept an eye on them, to make sure they did it the right way. Some of my students drank a little bit too much, and it showed on their rolls. Fifteen minutes later, I was done with my thirty roll, and let my students finish theirs. I went to the pantry and took out a large, deep frying pan. I put the pan on the stove, filled it with cooking oil, and turned it on. While I was waiting for the oil to heat up, some of my unmanageable students began fighting with each other again. This time, they all wanted to have their own eggrolls fry first.

"Come on, chefs, you have to wait your turn or I will put you all in time-out." They all laughed, including me. Again, Linda Estee gave me a half peace sign and a dirty look.

Seventy-five-year-old Betty tried to say something to me, but fifty-year-old Sally kept interrupting her; Sally wanted to know how long it would take for her eggrolls to cook; she was hungry and wondered if she could eat them right after they were done. Betty couldn't take it anymore and yelled, "Shut up, Sally." We all burst out laughing at those two and the words "Shut up, Sally" were born. Each time someone in the group talked too much, we shouted, "Shut up, Sally," and we all laughed again.

In the end, they all lined up to bring me their plates full of ugly rolls and waited for me to fry them. I smiled when I saw their deformed work; some looked pregnant from overstuffing, while others were long and skinny. Sally's were rectangular and flat; Linda's were large at one end and small at the other. I guessed I was not a good teacher after all.

"Hey, you guys!" I laughed, as I held up the biggest roll. "I'm afraid to take this one out to a public place." They all turned to look at the overstuffed eggroll in my hand and roared.

Right after I finished frying, some of my impatient student chefs could not wait for their eggrolls to cool off; they devoured them while they were still sizzling hot. Those who burned their mouths made awful moans, which made us all laugh again.

After I'd had a couple of glasses of wine, I couldn't tell the difference between the eggrolls. Although they appeared different on the outside, it didn't mean they tasted different; they all had the same ingredients. It reminded me of human beings: We come in a variety of shapes, sizes, and colors, but we all have red blood inside. The thought reminded me that I'd had three drinks instead of two.

BETTY WAS THE oldest one in our group, and we called her the elder. She was my favorite, and she was the funniest. She always had dirty jokes to share. Betty was Catholic and had eight children. She called me her "number nine." She was my client for over twenty-five years and never missed an appointment unless she was sick or went out of town. She never complained about my care of her hair or nails, nor did I hear her say anything negative about anybody. She was my angel. Each year the group celebrated her birthday by taking her out for dinner. Sometimes, I would give her a party in my house and invite the group to join me. I always gave her an orchid for her birthday, and in turn, she would always give me one on mine.

When Don and I renewed our wedding vows in the Catholic Church, Betty was there to take the place of my mother and was our witness at the altar. After the church ceremony, I rented a small restaurant for our party, at which Betty made a very moving toast to Don and me.

Betty, me, the priest, Don, and Minh at our vow renewals in 2001

When my brother Kinh needed an annulment, Betty was there trying to help him. His wife left him for another man while he was serving in the Vietnamese military years earlier, and he couldn't marry in the church unless he had an annulment. Betty took him from church to church and from priest to priest, trying to help him, but was not successful; this upset her very much.

"Don't worry about it, Betty," I told her. "My brother will be fine without one; do you remember what one of the priests told my brother while we were in his office?" I reminded her. "He told my brother not to worry about the annulment paper and to just go ahead and shack up with the girl of his choice, remember that?" We both laughed.

"I remember," she said. "I never heard of such language coming from our own priest's mouth; what a disappointment. But I won't stop now. I am determined to get his annulment before I die; it is now a matter of principle and not just a piece of paper anymore."

I went to her ninetieth birthday in one of the nicest restaurants on Kiawah Island. Instead of giving her an orchid, I brought her a huge three-foot blue hydrangea bouquet from my own backyard. Don and my brother had to help me carry it into the restaurant. When we entered the room, I could see all eyes were on the flowers as we placed it on one of the tables. The restaurant was large, but her family and friends were larger. I asked around and found Betty sitting with her ninety-two-year-old sister. We came to her and gave her and her sister a big hug.

"Linda B. this is it," she whispered in my ear. "I made it to ninety, and I am ready to go to heaven. I don't want to live any longer."

"Stop it, Betty!" I said. "Do you know how sad and lost I would be without you?"

"I know you will," she said. "But I'll be waiting for you in heaven."

"Today is your birthday," I said as tears started in my eyes. "You shouldn't talk like that; I don't want to hear it."

"I know today is my birthday, and I am happy to make it to ninety," she said with a smile. "But I just want you to know I am ready to go home to see our father, before I get too sick and have to depend on others."

"I don't agree with you, but I understand," I said as I gave her a kiss on her forehead. We walked away to mingle with her other guests. She sat back down to continue talking to her sister.

After her birthday, she was in and out of the hospital. Still, she drove to my salon to get her hair and nails done every week, and when she wasn't able to drive, she had someone else drive her.

"Coming to Linda B.'s salon," she said one day, "is not just for hair and nails but for friendship and counseling too."

"I heard that before, from the other clients," I said. "I feel honored, but I don't know who is counseling who." We both smiled.

Betty never forgot my birthday and always remembered to bring me a gift, until she was hospitalized; she sent one of her own sons to bring me a huge yellow cymbidium orchid to my house. It must have been three feet tall. It was beautiful.

As time went by, her condition worsened. I went to the hospital to see her and brought her three small orchids. At first, she was too sick to know I was there. I saw many people surrounding her hospital bed; most of them I didn't even know. I believed they were there because they thought Betty was not going to make it through the night. One of her sons, the same one who brought the orchid to my house, was standing next to her bed. He recognized me, and as soon as I came near him, he said, "Mother has not eaten, talked, or opened her eyes for days."

"Could I talk to her?" I asked him.

"Sure, you can," he said and then moved out of the way. As I came closer, I saw Betty with her eyes closed. She was barely breathing under an oxygen mask. Tears streamed down my face as I whispered to my friend.

"Hey, Betty, this is Linda B.," I said. "Please open your eyes and get out of this bed." When she didn't respond, I raised my voice, "We are going to a party, and you can't stay in bed like this." I raised my voice again, this time even higher. "Please get your butt out of this bed, Betty!" My loud voiced surprised her family, and they all turned to look at me. I'm sure they thought I was crazy and kept a wary eye on me. But they were even more surprised when they saw Betty open her eyes and smile at me.

"Hey, Betty, let's get out of here. What do you think?" Betty started to say something but nobody understood, until someone took her breathing mask off, and we started having a conversation. My voice was loud, and hers was soft and tired, but I understood what my dear friend tried to say to me.

"Hi, my dearest and precious friend, Linda B.," she murmured between her breaths.

"Hey, Betty. I love you and miss you so much. My salon is not the same without you."

"I know," she said. "But remember what I told you at my birthday party?"

"I remember it, but I don't want to accept it," I said through my tears.

Betty's family thought it was a miracle she came back to life. A few minutes later, one of them asked me to let Betty rest. I gave her a kiss on the backside of her hand, said brief goodbyes to everyone, and ran out of the room crying. I kept in touch with her family to find out about her condition. When I heard Betty was back at her house, I made a pot of chicken and dumplings and brought it to her doorstep. I had been invited to her house many times before, but this time, I didn't go inside. I just handed the soup to one of her daughters, told her the soup was for Betty, and left.

The next day, the same daughter called me and asked if I would come to Betty's house to give her a manicure. She told me Betty's nails were in bad shape.

"I will," I told her, "but it has to be after my work." She was okay with it.

As soon as I finished with my last client, I gathered all of Betty's personal belongings from my salon, put them in a plastic bag, and drove back to my house to pick up Don. He wanted to see Betty too; he claimed she was one of his girlfriends. I parked, and we went up to the third floor. When we entered her room, I saw Betty lying motionless in the middle of the huge blue bed, surrounded by her daughters and granddaughters. When they saw us, they all jumped off the bed and gave us hugs. Before I had a chance to ask about Betty, one of her daughters turned to me and said, "Mom hasn't talked or opened her eyes since the last time you saw her in the hospital."

"Oh! I thought she was getting better," I said as I glanced at Betty.

"No, she is getting worse," the other daughter said, and everyone nodded their heads.

"She's not getting any better, and we think this is it," one of them replied.

I took out the plastic bag containing Betty's nail stuff and prepared to do her manicure.

Don looked around, found a chair, and sat down near the bed.

I climbed on the bed with a bag full of instruments and sat next to Betty with a bottle of peachy nail polish, which I mixed just for her.

While I was doing Betty's nails, I talked to all of the women who surrounded her. We talked and laughed, as if we were in a fun party. Now and then, we mentioned Betty's name in the conversation. Don was sitting near, watching me. Suddenly, Betty mumbled something in her very weak voice. We all looked at each other in shock.

"Hi, Linda," Betty said with her eyes closed. "How are you, my sweetheart?"

"Oh, you are awake," I said. "I had to come to see you and to do your nails, since you are so spoiled and won't come to see me." Everybody laughed, including Betty. After we recovered from our initial shock, we joked and laughed with Betty.

"Hey, Betty," Don chimed in, "if I am your boyfriend and married to Linda, who is your daughter? Isn't that confusing?" Don finished his joke, and the whole room laughed, including Betty. Once again, I saw Betty awaken from her deathbed. Although Betty was awake, her eyes were not open; I think she was just buying time.

When I finished with her nails, I reached up, gave her a kiss on her cheek, and said through my tears, "I love you so much, Betty."

"I love you more," she responded. I climbed down from her huge bed with tears streaming down my face. Don kissed her hand to say goodbye.

I gave all of the nail files and nail polish to one of her daughters and said, "Here, you can have it. I know I won't need them for Betty anymore."

"Thanks, Linda, for everything," she said.

"You are welcome," I replied.

Don and I said goodbye to everyone and left with red eyes.

The next day, I had a call from Betty's family, telling me that Betty had just passed away. I thanked the caller and cried a river. When I calmed down, I called everyone in The Seasonal Women's Group to give them the bad news. The day of Betty's funeral, I believe I cried the most.

As the years have passed, I've lost many of my longtime clients and friends to old age and illness. It is to be expected, after nearly forty years. To this day, I still find myself waking in the middle of the night, crying over them. I miss their voices, their wisdom, their love, and their laughter. The pain of losing someone I love is never easy for me.

After Sally, Betty, and Carrie in our Seasonal Women's Group passed away, it was too sad for most of us to continue, and the group faded away. Now and then, a few of us in the group still go out for dinner, but it's nothing like those crazy days when our group was larger.

AS CHRISTMAS, HANUKKAH, and New Year of 2012 approached, I was running around preparing for two big parties, as I'd done every year for over three decades: one at my salon for all of my clients and the other at my home for family and friends. The coming year, however, was crazier. Besides making a thousand homemade eggrolls for the two parties, I was right in the middle of working with the publisher, preparing to release one of my books, *Red Blood, Yellow Skin*, while Don and I were trying to edit another. Together, we worked hard almost every day for years with each book. At the same time, I was working and managing my salon for the holidays. Those who run any kind of business during the holidays will know what I am talking about; it's crazy, especially in the beauty salon business, because almost everyone wants their hair and nails to be perfect during those days.

I was overwhelmed with a ton of things to do. I had to ask Don to go with me to stores to shop for more food and drinks. While at a traffic light, I turned to him and asked, "What do you want for Christmas?"

"Do you really want to know what I want for Christmas?" I smiled and expected sex for the answer, but that was not it. "I want you to slow down, before you kill yourself," he said.

I looked at him and asked, "Why? Do you think I work too hard?" I grinned, but he looked serious.

"Yes! You do," he said. "I would like to see you take a break from your busy, hectic schedule and spend more time with me; we are older and don't have much time left on this earth," he explained. "At your age, many people have already retired, and although you are still going strong, I think you do need to slow down."

"You're right," I replied. "I promise you, I'll cut down with all my activities."

"I'll hold you to it," Don said with a smile.

"I will do it, after the New Year," I said. "It will be my New Year's resolution."

We went shopping, but throughout the shopping trip, I couldn't help thinking about Don's request. I realized that I was old and he was right; I needed to slow down. I thought of selling my salon and taking it easy.

I kept my promise to Don, and after the New Year, I placed an advertisement to sell my business of thirty years.

Within days, many prospective buyers were interested, but I decided to sell it to people who had never owned a salon before. They were so excited about buying my salon. They seemed interesting, and I thought it would be nice for me to work with them until I retired.

After some time and a great deal of negotiating, we finally agreed on a price.

Right after the new owners took over the salon, they changed everything around, including the name. I wondered why they bought an established, successful business of thirty years and changed its name. Months later, they asked me to let them break the lease so they could move to a new location. I agreed to break the lease and let them take everything out of my salon. All the girls who used to work for me and I also agreed to go with them to the new place.

The new salon, however, was not larger than the previous one, and it was still in the remodeling process. The working area was like a construction site; the unfinished ceiling still had many holes, and electrical wires hung down in every direction. Below were narrow individual countertops and black styling chairs, all covered in white dust. I had more than my share of allergies from the dust, paint, and glue from the unfinished floor. Many times, while walking over the sticky floor, my sandals stuck to it, causing my friends to laugh at me. The whole salon was in various stages of chaos and disarray. Its conditions and atmosphere could not have been worse. Besides the mess, I had no place to offer my clients waxing jobs. There was a small room that I could use for waxing, but it was full of garbage, loose pipes, and empty boxes, which crowded up the space.

The conditions were not appropriate for my clientele, and they started to complain. I assured them that the salon would be fixed soon. One day, I squeezed Tracy in for a facial wax. After we fought through all of the debris to get into the waxing area, I asked her to sit down on a low small chair in the corner. Tracy was very tall, and it was hard for her to sit down on such a low chair, in such a tiny space. Somehow, we managed it. After she sat down on the dusty chair, I tried to figure out how to get her down even lower so I could reach her face. Tracy was over six feet tall; I was only five feet flat, and for me to work on Tracy's face, she had to lie down.

Suddenly, I had an idea. I took some empty boxes nearby and stacked them side by side to make a train. I asked her to lie back, and I pushed and tugged all the boxes under her legs to form a foot holder and asked her to put her feet up on those boxes. It worked! I was able to start her facial hair removal procedure. A few minutes later, the empty boxes began to sag and were about to collapse under her leg weight. Tracy was about to slide out of the chair, but I rushed to finish her waxing. I helped her up to her feet, and she followed me out to the cashier's counter, where she paid her bill.

Before she left, she said, "Linda, you know I love you and never want to leave you, but I'm sorry. I don't want to come back to this awful place again." She bent down and hugged me.

"I understand," I replied. "I'm very sorry too. You've been with me for twenty-five years. It's too bad we have to end our relationship this way." We hugged each other again and said goodbye as tears pooled in my eyes.

My next waxing client was Nathlyn, a beautiful African-American lady. She was one of my regulars and was back for her appointment. After I did her manicure, I took her into the same waxing room where I'd just finished with Tracy. Unlike Tracy, Nathlyn was not tall; she was older, had a bad knee, and had to use a cane to support herself. It was hard enough for her to walk, much less climb over all of the loose water pipes and garbage. At one point, I thought she was going to slip and ski on those loose pipes, which made both of us laugh out loud. Somehow, I managed to get her to lie down, stacked the boxes underneath her legs, as I'd done with Tracy, and began her facial waxing.

"This is the messiest salon ever," she complained. "I thought we were supposed to move to a bigger and a better place, but this is not it." She rolled her eyes. "Why don't they clean this place up?"

That was the longest and the wordiest statement Nathlyn had uttered to me in the twenty-five years since I'd known her.

When I was done with her face, I helped her up to her feet. She brushed off the white dust from her dark clothes and said, "This place is so dusty! I came in here as a black woman, and now look at me! I'm going out as a white one." I laughed and apologized to her for the inconvenience.

"If this place has not improved by my next appointment," she continued, "I'm not coming back here again; you hear?" I just smiled with her and helped her walk out toward the cashier's counter.

At first only Tracy and Nathlyn told me they were not coming back, but soon many other clients, one after another, told me the exact same thing. I thought they were just talking and not serious about leaving me; I believed when the salon was cleaned up, everything would be fine. Months after the move, the salon was still a big mess. My loyal clients and friends began to cancel their appointments. I called them and asked why they canceled their appointments. Even though I already knew the answer, I just wanted to hear it from them. I apologized to each of them and told them that the mess would be cleaned up soon.

Besides losing my clients, my allergies worsened, and I came home every day with red eyes and a running nose.

In desperation, I shared my feelings with other stylists and friends. I found out that most of them had the same problems, and some had already quit. One of my friends and I decided to take a day off and look for another salon to work at. We found out that most of the salons didn't hire part-time employees, and the booth rentals were way too expensive.

I had no choice but to make some quick decisions, whether to retire early or to work full time for another salon; neither one was to my liking. I was worried and lost a lot of sleep over my problems. I talked to Don about my concerns, and he advised me to go back to our old building, where the original salon stood for thirty years, and reopen it.

"Why do you want me to go back to reopen my salon?" I asked. "I thought you wanted me to slow down, and that is why I sold my salon in the first place."

"Well," he said, "after seeing you come home with swollen eyes and asthma attacks every day, I think it's worth it for you to go back to your place."

"Let me think about it," I said.

"What is there to think about?" he responded roughly. "They still owe you money, all your clients are leaving you, the place is filthy, and it's making you sick with allergies. What is there to think about?"

"You are right, Don," I said. "I don't mind moving back to my own place, but I hate to leave them. I just wish circumstances were different."

"Do you have any choice?" Don asked.

"I guess not," I replied.

After several months of remodeling the old shop, I changed the name to Elegance by Linda B. and reopened it. Don and I threw a big party to welcome all of our friends and clients back to my new, old salon.

Stylists at elegance by Linda B. Salon. Clockwise from top left: Brittany, Maria, Rubina, Linda B., and Sarah

Me, Linda B.

Stylists at Elegance by Linda B. Salon. Clockwise from top left: Mira, Cathy, Rubina, Maria, Jackie, Linda B., and Penny.

Me and my friend, Bonnie Koontz

Back to cozy Linda B. Salon, where elegant friends and clients gather

THE END

Before and After: From 1968 to 2017. Almost fifty years later, still in love.

EPILOGUE

IN MY LAST book, *Red Blood, Yellow Skin*, I wrote, "I was born and grew up with nothing. At the age of six, I was alone, and my clothes were rags. My food was bugs, weeds, little raw fish, and shrimp. I grew up, through war and poverty, and became a dust of life on the street. Later, I was a club dancer and a black-market dealer. I fell in love and married an American officer and followed him to the United States."

In this book, *Endless Journey*, I am so grateful just to have a flushing toilet and not to have to defecate in the middle of a forest full of tigers ready to make a meal out of me. I know I am lucky, and that is why I want to share my life's story with you.

I turned seventy in March of 2017. I still own and operate Elegance by Linda B. Salon in Charleston, South Carolina. Friends call my salon *Steel Magnolias*, after the movie. I'm supposed to be Dolly, minus the boobs.

When I am at home, I write books, care for my animals, and work in my garden, where I grow exotic fruits, vegetables, flowers, and herbs. We make our own medicine from herbs and roots, which we take daily; I learned how to make herbal medicine from my stepfather. I grow them not just for my family but also for friends and neighbors who want or need them. I used to share fresh eggs, but I no longer raise chickens. My friends and neighbors nicknamed me Farmer Brown, and I loved it.

If I'm not at my salon or in my garden, I can be found at my Koi pond, feeding the fish or helping my brother clean it. Besides that, I care for the wild birds and even the insects in my backyard. I find all living creatures and growing things to be fascinating. I might be older, but some things about me will never change.

*Relaxing at home with my four-legged children.
Me and Orca, my parrot; Teena, the Yorkie; and Tow Tow, the cat.*

Orca is keeping an eye on my koi pond.

*My backyard and herb garden. Chives and
green onions grow inside the concrete blocks.*

Recently, I dropped out of the garden club and stopped going to the South Carolina Orchid Society (SCOS), after being a member for thirty years. At my age, I don't want to stop doing what I love. Although I've slowed down, I continue to work at my salon and try to finish my fourth book, *Dust of Life*, based on the true stories of homeless children on the streets of Saigon. I hope to continue working and writing until I am ninety-nine and a half, and then I will walk into the nursing home, dancing and singing. I hope you like this book as much as I liked writing it.

Don turned eighty in 2016 and has retired three times, first as a military officer, then from the Veteran's Administration, and most recently from Trident Technical College, where he taught computer engineering design graphics. Although Don's health is good, it could be better. He has been sober for a long time, but he still goes to AA meetings most mornings and sometimes to three meetings a day. He goes there not just for himself but also to help others who are suffering from alcohol and drug addictions. When I asked him why he has to go to so many meetings, he says he wants to give back. He also developed and is responsible for a twelve-step program designed to help veterans who suffer from drug and alcohol addictions at the VA Hospital's Substance Abuse Treatment Center. I am so proud and happy that Don has stayed clean and sober and is now helping others.

All of our children are grown and have their own families. Steve divorced and has one son. Eddie retired as a Japanese show chef. He is good with music and art and is married to Traci. They decided not to have kids. Teresa is a talented artist and an excellent hairdresser; she met and married Antonio, who came to America from Italy as a computer programmer. They have two smart and beautiful children, Gabriella and Sebastian. Nicky recently retired after twenty-two years in the army as a combat medic; he served tours in Korea, Iraq, Afghanistan, and Germany. He has four wonderful and sweet children, Dillan, Christian, Madison, and Sophia.

From left: Eddie, Nicky, Teresa, me, Don, and Steve

Nicky and his kids, Dillon, Madison, and Christian, minutes before his deployment to Iraq. He and his first wife divorced while he was overseas. He is now married to Jamie, and they all live in New Orleans, except for Sophia.

My niece, Alisson; my nephew, Joseph; and four of my six grandchildren, Madison, Christian, Gabriella, and Sebastian

My house guests on the fourth of July, 2015. In the crowd are three of my brothers, their wives and their children, my son and his wife, Don, and four of our grandkids. All stayed in our home; we had a great time. I never wanted them to leave.

My brothers Khai and Bay and my sister, Nho, live with their families in Texas. Kinh, who never remarried, has lived with us for thirty-four years. He is like a child who never wants to leave home. All of my siblings and I are very close. I love them very much; that has never changed. I also love their spouses, their children, and their grandkids too. Some of those kids, who came to America by boat and didn't speak English, are now business owners or doctors or married to one. Even though my siblings and I don't live close, we talk on the phone all the time, and we try to visit each other as often as we can. My house is often full of guests of all ages for a week or two. I love it, and I wish I could have them every day for the rest of my life.

Both of my parents and my stepbrother, Den, have passed away, as well as Don's mother, five of his six siblings, and all of his in-laws.

From the right: the oldest to the youngest, all of my brothers, with their wives, except for Kinh. I'm in dark clothes with our mother's picture above my head. My sister and her husband, Don and me.

My biological father, whom I wrote about in my last book, *Red Blood, Yellow Skin*, was killed in the Catholic Church of Tao Xa, Thai Binh, North Vietnam.

In 1995, I took Don back to my birthplace to visit; my relatives told me when we were there that my father's name had been submitted to the Vatican for sainthood but was not accepted, because no one could find his birth record.

The Tao Xa Church, where my father was shot and thrown to his death from this window, near the top of this steeple, in 1951. The window had still not been repaired when we took this picture in 1995.

However, when I visited our old church, in a corner I saw his shrine, to which people pray. Ironically, his parents helped build the church, and when he grew up, he helped take care of it, then was killed trying to defend it.

In the New Year of 2017, Don and I watched the ball drop in Times Square. "Happy! Happy New Year to you, baby," I said as I reached up and kissed him.

"Happy New Year to you too, sweetie," he said as he gave me a kiss on my forehead.

"I love you and will love you forever," I said.

He grabbed me and said, "I love you and will love you for eternity—even after death, if it's possible."

"Do you remember," I asked, "we will celebrate our forty-ninth anniversary this year, on September the fifth?"

Don loosened his grip and looked into my eyes. "How could I forget?" he said. "But do you know we will be celebrating our fiftieth anniversary next year?" He smiled.

"Oh my God! Where has the time gone?" I asked.

"Gone into our life's journey," Don said, grinning.

"You are right," I said. "You are so good about that. You never forget our anniversary. What a man you are!"

"That's because I count every day of every month and realize how lucky I am to grow old with you by my side." He continued, "You've kept me straight, healthy, and safe. Without you, I would have been dead a long time ago."

"Oh! I cannot ask for a better husband than you. You might not be a perfect man, but you are the perfect husband for me," I said sincerely.

Tears of happiness ran down our faces as we sat back on the couch and continued watching the New Year celebration on the TV.

There are no strangers; you are a friend that I haven't had the chance to meet. I hope one day I will. May God bless you all.

Best,
LINDA L.T. BAER

ABOUT THE AUTHOR

LINDA LOAN THI BAER was born Nguyen Thi Loan in 1947, in the small village of Tao Xa, Thai Binh Province, North Vietnam. Her father was killed during a Viet Minh attack in 1951. Her mother remarried to a wealthy practitioner of Chinese medicine, a war widower himself. Their family relocated to South Vietnam during the mass exodus of 1954, where they were forced to move constantly due to economic, political, and military conditions. They eventually settled near Vung Tau, south of Saigon.

Loan left home at the early age of thirteen to seek work at various menial jobs in Saigon to help her family and to escape the physical abuse of her stepfather. She became a dust of life on the street. At the age of sixteen, she became a club dancer and a black-market dealer. Later, she met and married an American Air Force officer in 1968 and followed him to the United States in 1971. She was naturalized and became an American citizen in 1973.

While raising two sons and a daughter, she obtained her GED and attended many college courses. Linda graduated first in her class at cosmetology school. Two years later, she owned and opened Linda B. Hair, Nail, and Skin Care Salon. In 2015, the salon was renamed Elegance by Linda B. Today, she is an author of three books, and she will soon finish her fourth.

She is the author of *Edge of Survival*; *Red Blood, Yellow Skin*; *Red Blood, Yellow Skin: Endless Journey*; and *Bui Doi: Dust of Life*, which is currently in progress.